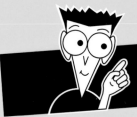

Canon® EOS Digital Rebel XTi/400D
FOR DUMMIES®

S0-AYH-596

Camera Road Map

Here's a handy map to the buttons, dials, and other external features on your Digital Rebel XTi/400D. Controls marked with an asterisk have multiple functions; for simplicity's sake, I refer to them in this book by the names you see here. See Chapter 1 for details.

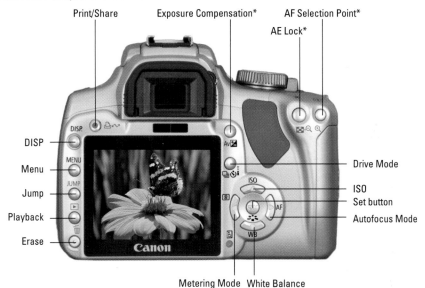

Print/Share — Exposure Compensation* — AF Selection Point*
AE Lock*

DISP
Menu
Jump
Playback
Erase

Drive Mode
ISO
Set button
Autofocus Mode

Metering Mode   White Balance

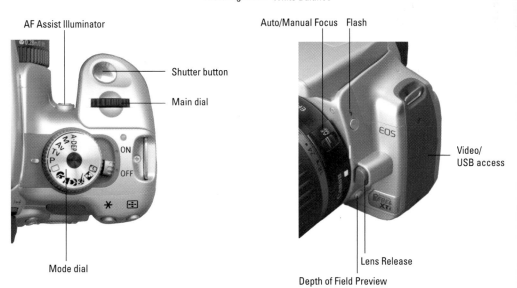

AF Assist Illuminator

Shutter button

Main dial

ON
OFF

Mode dial

Auto/Manual Focus   Flash

EOS

Video/
USB access

Rebel
XTi

Lens Release

Depth of Field Preview

For Dummies: Bestselling Book Series for Beginners

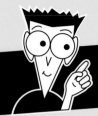

Automatic Exposure Mode Quick Reference

Refer to the table below for a quick explanation of your camera's fully automatic exposure modes. In these modes, you can choose between automatic or manual focusing, but you have little or no control over most other picture-taking settings. See Chapter 2 for details.

Symbol	Exposure Mode	Description
☐	Full Auto	Completely automatic photography; the camera analyzes the scene and tries to choose settings that produce the best results.
🙎	Portrait	Designed to produce softly focused backgrounds for flattering portraits.
🏞	Landscape	Designed to keep both near and distant subjects in sharp focus.
🌷	Close Up	Produces softly focused backgrounds especially suitable for close-ups of flowers and other nature subjects.
🏃	Sports	Selects a faster shutter speed to capture moving subjects without blur.
👤	Night Portrait	Same as Portrait, but combines flash with a slow shutter speed to produce softer lighting and brighter backgrounds. Use a tripod to avoid camera shake.
🚫	No Flash	Same as Full Auto, but with flash disabled.

Advanced Exposure Modes

These five modes, all covered in Chapter 5, give you more control over your camera settings. In P, Tv, Av, and M modes, you can adjust aperture (f-stop) to manipulate depth of field (the zone of sharp focus) and adjust shutter speed to determine whether moving objects appear sharply focused or blurry. In all five modes, you also can tweak color, ISO (light sensitivity), and exposure.

Symbol	Exposure Mode	Description
P	Programmed Autoexposure	Camera selects both the f-stop and shutter speed to ensure proper exposure, but the user can choose from multiple combinations of the two settings.
Tv	Shutter-Priority Autoexposure	The user sets shutter speed, and the camera selects the f-stop that will produce a good exposure.
Av	Aperture-Priority Autoexposure	The user selects the f-stop, and the camera selects the shutter speed that will produce a good exposure.
M	Manual Exposure	The user controls both the shutter speed and f-stop.
A-DEP	Automatic Depth of Field	Camera selects the f-stop needed to keep all objects in the frame in the zone of sharp focus and then selects the shutter speed that will produce a good exposure.

For Dummies: Bestselling Book Series for Beginners

Canon® EOS Digital Rebel XTi/400D

FOR

DUMMIES®

Canon® EOS
Digital Rebel XTi/400D

FOR

DUMMIES®

by Julie Adair King

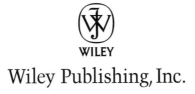

WILEY

Wiley Publishing, Inc.

Canon® EOS Digital Rebel XTi/400D For Dummies®

Published by
Wiley Publishing, Inc.
111 River Street
Hoboken, NJ 07030-5774

www.wiley.com

WILEY

About the Author

Julie Adair King is the author of many books about digital photography and imaging, including the best-selling *Digital Photography For Dummies.* Her most recent titles include *Digital Photography Before & After Makeovers, Digital Photo Projects For Dummies, Julie King's Everyday Photoshop For Photographers, Julie King's Everyday Photoshop Elements,* and *Shoot Like a Pro!: Digital Photography Techniques.* When not writing, King teaches digital photography at such locations as the Palm Beach Photographic Centre. A graduate of Purdue University, she resides in Indianapolis, Indiana.

Author's Acknowledgments

I am extremely grateful to the team of talented professionals at John Wiley & Sons for all their efforts in putting together this book. Special thanks go to my awesome project editor, Kim Darosett, who is the type of editor that all authors hope for but rarely experience: supportive, skilled, and amazingly calm in the face of any storm, including my not infrequent freakouts.

I also owe much to the rest of the folks in both the editorial and art departments, especially Heidi Unger, Rashell Smith, Shelley Lea, Steve Hayes, Andy Cummings, and Mary Bednarek. Thanks, too, to my friends at Canon U.S.A; to Jonathan Conrad for providing the awesome nighttime shot for Chapter 7, and to agent extraordinaire, Margot Maley Hutchison, for her continuing help and encouragement.

Last but oh, so not least, I am deeply indebted to technical editor Chuck Pace, whose keen eye and vast experience set me on the right track whenever I mistakenly thought I should go left. Thank you, thank you, for sharing your time and your expertise — the book would not have been the same without it.

Publisher's Acknowledgments

We're proud of this book; please send us your comments through our online registration form located at www.dummies.com/register/.

Some of the people who helped bring this book to market include the following:

Acquisitions and Editorial

Project Editor: Kim Darosett

Executive Editor: Steve Hayes

Copy Editor: Heidi Unger

Technical Editor: Chuck Pace

Editorial Manager: Leah Cameron

Editorial Assistant: Amanda Foxworth

Sr. Editorial Assistant: Cherie Case

Cartoons: Rich Tennant (www.the5thwave.com)

Composition Services

Project Coordinator: Katherine Key

Layout and Graphics: Alissa D. Ellet

Proofreaders: Caitie Kelly, Susan Moritz, Linda Seifert

Indexer: Sherry Masey

Publishing and Editorial for Technology Dummies

    Richard Swadley, Vice President and Executive Group Publisher

    Andy Cummings, Vice President and Publisher

    Mary Bednarek, Executive Acquisitions Director

    Mary C. Corder, Editorial Director

Publishing for Consumer Dummies

    Diane Graves Steele, Vice President and Publisher

    Joyce Pepple, Acquisitions Director

Composition Services

    Gerry Fahey, Vice President of Production Services

    Debbie Stailey, Director of Composition Services

Contents at a Glance

Table of Contents

Introduction

*I*n 2003, when Canon introduced the very first sub-$1000 digital SLR camera, the EOS Digital Rebel/300D, it revolutionized the camera scene. For the first time, photography enthusiasts could enjoy the benefits of digital SLR photography without breaking the bank. And even at the then-unheard-of price, the camera delivered exceptional performance and picture quality, earning it rave reviews and multiple industry awards. No wonder it quickly became a best seller.

That tradition of excellence and value lives on in the EOS Digital Rebel XTi/400D, known in most circles (and in this book) as simply the Rebel XTi/400D. For an even lower price than its older brother, this baby offers the range of advanced controls that experienced photographers demand plus an assortment of tools designed to help beginners to be successful as well.

If you count yourself among the latter camp, you may have a few questions about how to take advantage of all the features your camera offers, however. For starters, you may not even be sure what SLR means or how it affects your picture taking, let alone have a clue as to all the other techie terms you encounter in your camera manual — *resolution, aperture, white balance, file format,* and so on. And if you're like many people, you may be so overwhelmed by all the controls on your camera that you haven't yet ventured beyond fully automatic picture-taking mode. Which is a shame because it's sort of like buying a Porsche and never actually taking it on the road.

Therein lies the point of *Canon EOS Digital Rebel XTi/400D For Dummies:* Through this book, you can discover not just what each bell and whistle on your camera does, but also when, where, why, and how to put it to best use. Unlike many photography books, this one doesn't require any previous knowledge of photography or digital imaging to make sense of things, either. In classic *For Dummies* style, everything is explained in easy-to-understand language, with lots of illustrations to help clear up any confusion.

In short, what you have in your hands is the paperback version of an in-depth photography workshop tailored specifically to your Canon picture-taking powerhouse. Whether your interests lie in taking family photos, exploring nature and travel photography, or snapping product shots for your business, you'll get the information you need to capture the images you envision.

A Quick Look at What's Ahead

This book is organized into four parts, each devoted to a different aspect of using your camera. Although chapters flow in a sequence that's designed to take you from absolute beginner to experienced user, I've also tried to make each chapter as self-standing as possible so that you can explore the topics that interest you in any order you please.

The following sections offer brief previews of each part. If you're eager to find details on a specific topic, the index shows you exactly where to look.

Part I: Fast Track to Super Snaps

Part I contains four chapters that help you get up and running with your Rebel XTi/400D:

- ✔ Chapter 1, "Getting the Lay of the Land," offers a tour of the external controls on your camera, shows you how to navigate camera menus to access internal options, and walks you through initial camera setup and customization steps.

- ✔ Chapter 2, "Taking Great Pictures, Automatically," shows you how to get the best results when using the camera's fully automatic exposure modes, including Portrait, Sports, and Landscape modes.

- ✔ Chapter 3, "Controlling Picture Quality," introduces you to one setting that's critical whether you shoot in automatic or manual mode: the Quality setting, which affects resolution (pixel count), file format, file size, and picture quality.

- ✔ Chapter 4, "Reviewing Your Photos," explains how to view your pictures on the camera monitor and also how to display various types of picture information along with the image. In addition, this chapter discusses how to delete unwanted images and protect your favorites from accidental erasure.

Part II: Taking Creative Control

Chapters in this part help you unleash the full creative power of your camera by moving into semiautomatic or manual photography modes.

- ✔ Chapter 5, "Getting Creative with Exposure and Lighting," covers the all-important topic of exposure, starting with an explanation of three critical exposure controls: aperture, shutter speed, and ISO. This chapter also discusses your camera's advanced exposure modes (P, Tv, Av, M, and A-DEP), explains exposure options such as metering mode and exposure compensation, and offers tips for using the built-in flash.

- ✔ Chapter 6, "Manipulating Focus and Color," provides help with controlling those aspects of your pictures. Look here for information about your camera's manual and autofocusing features as well as details about color controls such as white balance and the Picture Style options.

- ✔ Chapter 7, "Putting It All Together," summarizes all the techniques explained in earlier chapters, providing a quick-reference guide to the camera settings and shooting strategies that produce the best results for specific types of pictures: portraits, action shots, landscape scenes, close-ups, and more.

Part III: Working with Picture Files

This part of the book, as its title implies, discusses the often-confusing aspect of moving your pictures from camera to computer and beyond.

- ✓ Chapter 8, "Downloading, Organizing, and Archiving Your Photos," guides you through the process of transferring pictures from your camera memory card to your computer's hard drive or other storage device. Just as important, this chapter explains how to organize and safeguard your photo files.

- ✓ Chapter 9, "Printing and Sharing Your Photos," helps you turn your digital files into "hard copies," covering both retail and do-it-yourself printing options. This chapter also explains how to prepare your pictures for online sharing and, for times when you have the neighbors over, how to display your pictures on a television screen.

Part IV: The Part of Tens

In famous For Dummies tradition, the book concludes with two "top ten" lists containing additional bits of information and advice.

- ✓ Chapter 10, "Ten Fast Photo-Editing Tricks," shows you how to fix less-than-perfect images using the free software provided with your camera. You can find out how to remove red-eye, adjust color and exposure, crop your photo, and more.

- ✓ Chapter 11, "Ten Special-Purpose Features to Explore on a Rainy Day," presents information about some camera features that, while not found on most "Top Ten Reasons I Bought My Rebel XTi/400D" lists, are nonetheless interesting, useful on occasion, or a bit of both.

Appendix: Firmware Facts and Menu Map

Wrapping up the book, the appendix explains how to find out what version of the Canon *firmware,* or internal software, is installed in your camera and how to find and download updates.

If the information you see on your camera menus and other displays isn't the same as what you see in this book, and you've explored other reasons for the discrepancy, a firmware update may be the issue. This book was written using version 1.1.1 of the firmware, which was the most current at the time of publication. Firmware updates typically don't carry major feature changes — they're mostly used to solve technical glitches in existing features — but if you do download an update, be sure to read the accompanying description of what it accomplishes so that you can adapt my instructions as necessary. (Again, changes that affect how you actually operate the camera should be minimal, if any.)

On a less technical note, the appendix also includes tables that provide brief descriptions of all commands found on the camera's five menus.

Icons and Other Stuff to Note

If this isn't your first For Dummies book, you may be familiar with the large, round icons that decorate its margins. If not, here's your very own icon-decoder ring:

A Tip icon flags information that will save you time, effort, money, or some other valuable resource, including your sanity.

When you see this icon, look alive. It indicates a potential danger zone that can result in much wailing and teeth-gnashing if ignored.

Lots of information in this book is of a technical nature — digital photography is a technical animal, after all. But if I present a detail that is useful mainly for impressing your technology-geek friends, I mark it with this icon.

I apply this icon either to introduce information that is especially worth storing in your brain's long-term memory or to remind you of a fact that may have been displaced from that memory by some other pressing fact.

Additionally, I need to point out two other details that will help you use this book:

- ✒ **Other margin art:** Replicas of some of your camera's buttons, dials, controls, and menu graphics also appear in the margins of some paragraphs. I include these to provide a quick reminder of the appearance of the button or option being discussed.

- ✒ **Software menu commands:** In sections that cover software, a series of words connected by an arrow indicates commands that you choose from the program menus. For example, if a step tells you to "Choose File➪Print, click the File menu to unfurl it and then click the Print command on the menu.

About the Software Shown in This Book

Providing specific instructions for performing photo organizing and editing tasks requires that I feature specific software. In sections that cover file downloading, organizing, printing, and e-mail sharing, I selected Canon

ZoomBrowser EX (for Windows users) and Canon ImageBrowser (for Mac users). These programs are part of the free software suite that ships with your camera.

Rest assured, though, that the tools used in ZoomBrowser EX and Image-Browser work very similarly in other programs, so you should be able to easily adapt the steps to whatever software you use. (I recommend that you read your software manual for details, of course.)

Practice, Be Patient, and Have Fun!

To wrap up this preamble, I want to stress that if you initially think that digital photography is too confusing or too technical for you, you're in very good company. *Everyone* finds this stuff a little mind-boggling at first. So take it slowly, experimenting with just one or two new camera settings or techniques at first. Then, each time you go on a photo outing, make it a point to add one or two more shooting skills to your repertoire.

I know that it's hard to believe when you're just starting out, but it really won't be long before everything starts to come together. With some time, patience, and practice, you'll soon wield your camera like a pro, dialing in the necessary settings to capture your creative vision almost instinctively.

So without further ado, I invite you to grab your camera, a cup of whatever it is you prefer to sip while you read, and start exploring the rest of this book. Your Rebel XTi/400D is the perfect partner for your photographic journey, and I thank you for allowing me, through this book, to serve as your tour guide.

Part I
Fast Track to Super Snaps

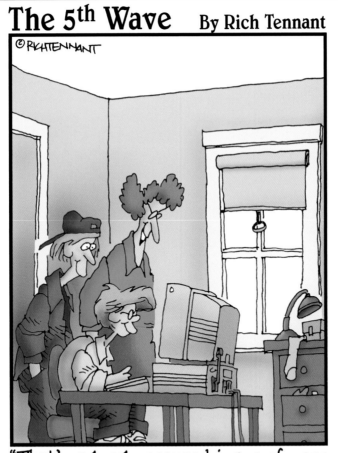

The 5th Wave   By Rich Tennant

©RICHTENNANT

"That's a lovely scanned image of your sister's portrait. Now take it off the body of that pit viper before she comes in the room."

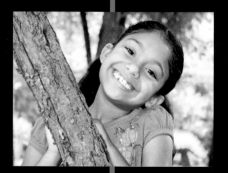

In this part . . .

Making sense of all the controls on your Rebel XTi/400D isn't something you can do in an afternoon — heck, in a week, or maybe even a month. But that doesn't mean that you can't take great pictures today. By using your camera's point-and-shoot automatic modes, you can capture terrific images with very little effort. All you do is compose the scene, and the camera takes care of almost everything else.

This part shows you how to take best advantage of your camera's automatic features and also addresses some basic setup steps, such as adjusting the viewfinder to your eyesight and getting familiar with the camera menus, buttons, and dials. In addition, chapters in this part explain how to obtain the very best picture quality, whether you shoot in an automatic or manual mode, and how to use your camera's picture-playback features.

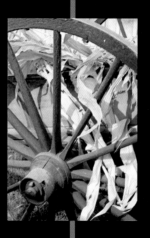

Getting the Lay of the Land

I still remember the day that I bought my first SLR film camera. I was excited to finally move up from my one-button point-and-shoot camera, but I was a little anxious, too. My new pride and joy sported several unfamiliar buttons and dials, and the explanations in the camera manual clearly were written for someone with an engineering degree. And then there was the whole business of attaching the lens to the camera, an entirely new task for me. I saved up my pennies a long time for that camera — what if my inexperience caused me to damage the thing before I even shot my first pictures?

You may be feeling similarly insecure if your Rebel XTi/400D is your first SLR, although some of the buttons on the camera back may look familiar if you've previously used a digital point-and-shoot camera. If your Canon is both your first SLR and first digital camera, you may be doubly intimidated.

Trust me, though, that your camera isn't nearly as complicated as its exterior makes it appear. With a little practice and the help of this chapter, which introduces you to each external control, you'll quickly become as comfortable with your camera's buttons and dials as you are with the ones on your car's dashboard.

This chapter also guides you through the process of mounting and using an SLR lens, working with digital memory cards, and navigating your camera's internal menus. Finally, the end of the chapter walks you through options that enable you to customize many aspects of your camera's basic operation.

Getting Comfortable with Your Lens

One of the biggest differences between a point-and-shoot camera and an SLR *(single-lens reflex)* camera is the lens. With an SLR, you can swap out lenses to suit different photographic needs, going from an extreme close-up lens to a super-long telephoto, for example. In addition, an SLR lens has a movable focusing ring that gives you the option of focusing manually instead of relying on the camera's autofocus mechanism.

Of course, those added capabilities mean that you need a little background information to take full advantage of your lens. To that end, the next three sections explain the process of attaching, removing, and using this critical part of your camera.

Attaching a lens

Your camera can accept two categories of Canon lenses: those with a so-called EF-S design and those with a plain old EF design.

The EF stands for *electro focus;* the S, for *short back focus.* And no, you don't really need to remember that little detail — but you do need to make sure that if you buy a Canon lens other than the one sold with the camera, it carries either the EF or EF-S specification. (If you want to buy a non-Canon lens, check the lens manufacturer's Web site to find out which lenses work with the Rebel XTi/400D.)

Whatever lens you choose, follow these steps to attach it to the camera body:

1. **Remove the cap that covers the lens mount on the front of the camera.**

2. **Remove the cap that covers the back of the lens.**

3. **Locate the proper lens mounting index on the camera body.**

   A *mounting index* is simply a marker that tells you where to align the lens with the camera body when connecting the two. Your camera has two of these markers, one red and one white, as shown in Figure 1-1.

   Which marker you use to align your lens depends on the lens type:

   • *Canon EF-S lens:* Align the lens mounting index with the white square on the camera body.

   • *Canon EF lens:* Align the lens mounting index with the red dot instead.

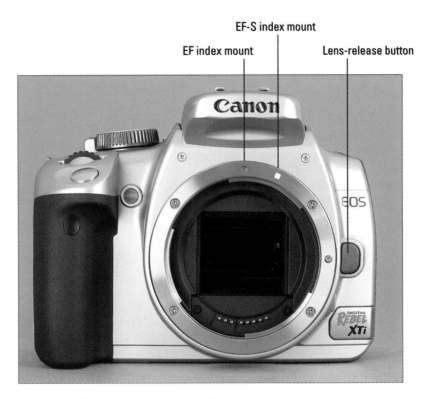

Figure 1-1: Which index marker you should use depends on the lens type.

If you buy a non-Canon lens, check the lens manual for help with this step.

4. **Align the mounting index on the lens with the correct one on the camera body.**

   The lens also has a mounting index; Figure 1-2 shows the one that appears on the so-called "kit lens" — the 18–55mm zoom lens that Canon sells as a unit with the Rebel XTi/400D. If you buy a different lens, the index marker on the lens may be red or some other color, so again, check the lens instruction manual.

5. **Keeping the mounting indexes aligned, position the lens on the camera's lens mount.**

   When you do so, grip the lens by its back collar as shown in the figure.

6. **Turn the lens in a clockwise direction until the lens clicks into place.**

   In other words, turn the lens toward the lens release button (see Figure 1-1), as indicated by the red arrow in Figure 1-2.

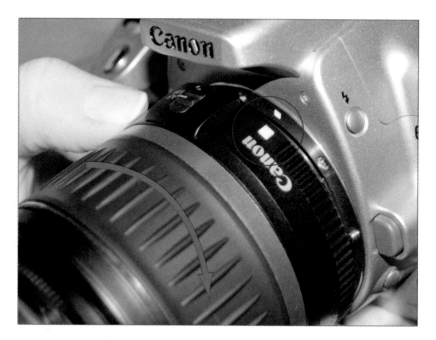

Figure 1-2: Place the lens in the lens mount with the mounting indexes aligned.

7. On a lens that has an aperture ring, set and lock the ring so the aperture is set at the highest f-number.

Check your lens manual to find out whether your lens sports an aperture ring and how to adjust it. (The Rebel XTi/400D kit lens doesn't.) To find out more about apertures and f-stops, see Chapter 5.

Always attach (or switch) lenses in a clean environment to reduce the risk of getting dust, dirt, and other contaminants inside the camera or lens. Changing lenses on a sandy beach, for example, isn't a good idea. For added safety, point the camera body slightly down when performing this maneuver, as shown in the figure; doing so helps prevent any flotsam in the air from being drawn into the camera by gravity. See Chapter 3 for tips on cleaning your lens.

Removing a lens

To detach a lens from the camera body, take these steps:

1. Locate the lens-release button on the front of the camera.

I labeled the button in Figure 1-1.

2. Grip the rear collar of the lens.

In other words, hold onto the stationary part of the lens that's closest to the camera body.

3. **Press the lens-release button while turning the lens away from the lens-release button.**

   You should feel the lens release from the mount at this point. Just lift the lens off the mount to remove it.

4. **Place the rear protective cap onto the back of the lens.**

   If you aren't putting another lens on the camera, cover the lens mount with the protective cap that came with your camera, too.

Focusing and zooming the lens

Like any modern camera, digital or film, yours offers autofocusing capabilities, which you can explore in detail in Chapters 2 and 6. But with some subjects, autofocusing can be slow or impossible, which is why your camera also offers manual focusing. The process is quick and easy: You just turn the focusing ring on the lens until your subject comes into focus.
To try it out, take these steps:

1. **Locate the AF/MF switch on the side of the lens.**

   Figure 1-3 shows you the switch as it appears on the Rebel XTi/400D kit lens. The switch should be in a similar location on other Canon lenses; if you use a lens from another manufacturer, check the lens instruction manual.

2. **Set the switch to the MF position, as shown in the figure.**

   Don't try to move the focusing ring with the switch set to the AF (autofocus) position; with some lenses, doing so can damage the lens.

3. **While looking through the viewfinder, twist the focusing ring to adjust focus.**

   The focusing ring is at the far end of the lens barrel, as indicated in Figure 1-3.

   If you have trouble focusing, you may be too close to your subject; every lens has a minimum focusing distance. (See Chapter 6 for more tips on focus issues.) You may also need to adjust the viewfinder to accommodate your eyesight; see the next section for details.

If you bought a zoom lens, a movable zoom barrel lies behind the focusing ring, as shown in Figure 1-3. To zoom in or out, just move that zoom barrel forward and backward.

The numbers on the zoom barrel, by the way, represent *focal lengths*. I explain focal lengths in Chapter 6. In the meantime, just note that when the lens is mounted on the camera, the number that's aligned with the white focal-length indicator, labeled in Figure 1-3, represents the current focal length. In Figure 1-3, for example, the focal length is 55mm.

Zoom barrel   Focal length indicator

Focusing ring   AF/MF switch

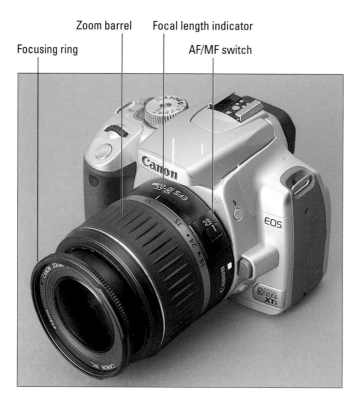

Figure 1-3: Set the focusing switch to MF before turning the manual focus ring.

Adjusting the Viewfinder Focus

Perched on the top right edge of the viewfinder is a tiny black knob, officially called the *dioptric adjustment control.* I labeled the knob in Figure 1-4. With this control, you can adjust the magnification of the viewfinder to mesh with your eyesight. If you don't take this step, scenes that appear out-of-focus through the viewfinder may actually be sharply focused through the lens, and vice versa.

Here's how to make the necessary adjustment:

1. **Remove the lens cap from the front of the lens.**

2. **Look through the viewfinder and concentrate on the focusing screen shown on the right side of Figure 1-4.**

   The *focusing screen* is the collective name assigned to the group of nine autofocus points that appear in the center of the viewfinder — the little squares with the dots inside. I labeled one of the little guys in Figure 1-4.

Dioptric adjustment control   Autofocus point

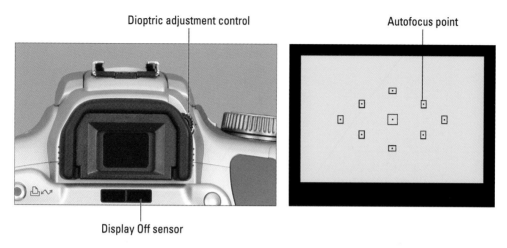

Display Off sensor

Figure 1-4: Use the dioptric adjustment control to set the viewfinder focus for your eyesight.

Don't worry about focusing the actual picture now; just pay attention to the autofocus points.

3. **Rotate the dioptric adjustment knob until the autofocus points appear to be in focus.**

If your eyesight is such that you can't get the autofocus points to appear sharp by using the dioptric adjustment control, you can buy an additional eyepiece adapter. This accessory, which you pop onto the eyepiece, just enables further adjustment of the viewfinder display. Prices range from about $15–30 depending on the magnification you need. Look for an adapter called an *E-series dioptric adjustment lens.*

One other note about the viewfinder: See that little black window underneath the viewfinder — the one labeled Display Off sensor in Figure 1-4? When you put your eye up to the viewfinder, the sensor tells the camera to turn off the monitor display, saving you the trouble of doing the job yourself. If the monitor doesn't turn off automatically, the upcoming section "Setup Menu 1" tells you how to fix things; see the information related to the LCD Auto Off feature.

Working with Memory Cards

Instead of recording images on film, digital cameras store pictures on *memory cards.* Some people, in fact, refer to memory cards as *digital film,* but I hate that term because film and memory cards actually have little in common. Film must be developed before you can view your pictures, a process that involves time and some not-so-nice chemicals. Film can be damaged when exposed to some airport security scanners; memory cards are immune to those devices. The cost per picture is also much higher for film: You have to develop and print each negative, whether the shot is a keeper or a clunker. With digital, you print only the pictures you like — and you can reuse your memory cards over and over and over, saving even more money.

Whatever term you prefer, your Canon can use the following two types of memory cards:

✔ **CompactFlash, or CF, cards:** You can use CompactFlash cards that carry either the Type I or Type II specification. The only difference between the two card types is thickness; Type II cards are a little thicker than Type I cards. Type I is the most commonly sold version of the cards today. In Figure 1-5, you can see one such card in the foreground and another partially inserted into the camera's card slot.

✔ **Microdrives:** These devices are actually tiny hard drives that are encased in Type II CompactFlash-style housings. Microdrives are more susceptible to damage if dropped or exposed to vibration, however, so I don't really recommend them. However, if you already own one, feel free to use it, albeit carefully.

Memory card access light   Card-eject button

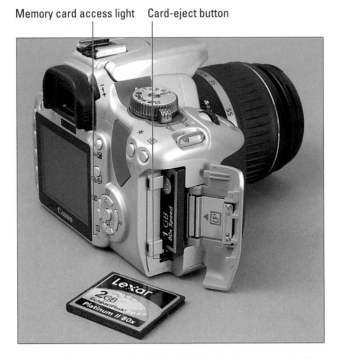

Figure 1-5: Insert the card with the label facing the camera back.

Do you need high-speed memory cards?

Memory cards are categorized not just by their storage capacity, but also by their data-transfer speed. The speed specs you see on memory cards — 10x, 40x, 80x, 133x, and the like — reflect the transfer rate compared to a single-speed CD-ROM, which can move about 156K (kilobytes) of data per second. So a 10x card, for example, is 10 times faster than that, offering a transfer speed of 1.5MB (megabytes) per second.

Faster data-transfer speeds reduce the time your camera needs to write a picture file onto the card and the time required to download files from the card to your computer. Of course, card prices rise along with card speed. And whether you will really notice much difference depends on a couple of factors.

On the picture-taking end, users who want to capture fast-paced action benefit the most from high-speed cards. Bumping up your card speed can enable you to fire off a continuous series of shots at a slightly faster pace than with a slower

card. Users who shoot at the highest resolution or prefer the Raw file format (CR2 files, on Canon cameras) also gain the most from high-speed cards; both options increase file size and, thus, the time needed to store the picture on the card. (See Chapter 3 for details.)

When it comes to picture downloading, you may or may not enjoy much of a speed increase because transfer time isn't just dependent on the card. How long it takes for files to shuffle from card to computer also depends on the capabilities of your computer and, if you use a memory-card reader to download files, on the speed of that device. (Chapter 8 covers the file-downloading process.)

To sum up, if you want to push your camera to its speed limit — and money is no object — go for a high-speed card. Otherwise, you probably don't need to make the extra investment; even a "slow" card is usually more than fast enough to satisfy all but the most demanding users.

Safeguarding your memory cards — and the images you store on them — requires just a few precautions:

- ✔ **Inserting a card:** First, be sure that the camera is turned off. Then put the card in the card slot with the label facing the back of the camera, as shown in Figure 1-5. Push the card into the slot until it clicks into place. The card-eject button — the tiny black push button labeled in the figure — should pop up. When you close the card-access door, the memory-card access light, also labeled in Figure 1-5, blinks for a second to let you know the card is inserted properly. (You probably can't make it out in the figure, but the letters *CF* appear next to the light to remind you of its purpose.)

- ✔ **Formatting a card:** The first time you use a new memory card, take a few seconds to *format* it by choosing the Format command from the camera's Setup Menu 1. This step simply ensures that the card is properly prepared to record your pictures. See the upcoming section "Setup Menu 1" for details.

- ✔ **Removing a card:** After making sure that the memory-card access light is off, indicating that the camera has finished recording your most recent photo, turn the camera off. Open the memory-card door, as shown in

Figure 1-5. Push in the card-eject button. The card should pop halfway out of the slot, enabling you to grab it by the tail and remove it.

- **Handling cards:** When cards aren't in use, store them in the protective cases they came in or in a memory card wallet. Keep cards away from extreme heat and cold as well.

Exploring External Camera Controls

Scattered across your camera's exterior are a number of buttons, dials, and switches that you use to change picture-taking settings, review and edit your photos, and perform various other operations.

In later chapters, I discuss all your camera's functions in detail and provide the exact steps to follow to access those functions. This section provides just a basic road map to the external controls plus a quick introduction to each. You may want to put a sticky note or other bookmark on this page so that you can find it for easier reference later. (The cheat sheet at the front of the book offers a similar guide, albeit with less detail.)

With that preamble out of the way, the next three sections break down the external controls found on the top, back, and front-left side of the camera.

Topside controls

Your virtual tour begins on the top right side of the camera, shown in Figure 1-6. There are five items of note here, as follows:

- **On/Off switch:** Okay, I'm pretty sure you already figured this one out, but just move the switch to On to fire up the camera and then back to Off to shut it down.

By default, the camera automatically shuts itself off after 30 seconds of inactivity to save battery power. To wake up the camera, just press the shutter button halfway; you don't need to use the On/Off switch. You can adjust the auto shutdown timing via Setup Menu 1, covered later in this chapter.

- **Mode dial:** Rotate this dial to select an *exposure mode,* which determines whether the camera operates in fully automatic, semi-automatic, or manual photography mode. The little pictographs, or icons, on the dial represent *Image Zone modes,* which are automatic settings geared to specific types of photos: action shots, portraits, landscapes, and so on.

Canon uses the term *Basic Zone* to refer to collectively to the Image Zone modes and Full Auto mode (that's the one represented by the green rectangle on the Mode dial). The more advanced modes (P, Tv, Av, M, and A-DEP) get the label *Creative Zone.* I think that having all those zones can be a little confusing, especially because the modes in the Image Zone category are often referred to generically in photography discussions as *creative scene mode* or *creative modes.* So, just to help keep things a little simpler in this book, I use the generic terms *fully automatic exposure modes* to refer to all the Basic Zone modes and *advanced exposure modes* to refer to the Creative Zone modes.

✔ **Main dial:** Just forward of the Mode dial, you see a black dial that has the official name *Main dial.* This dial plays such an important role in choosing camera settings that you'd think it might have a more auspicious name, but Main dial it is.

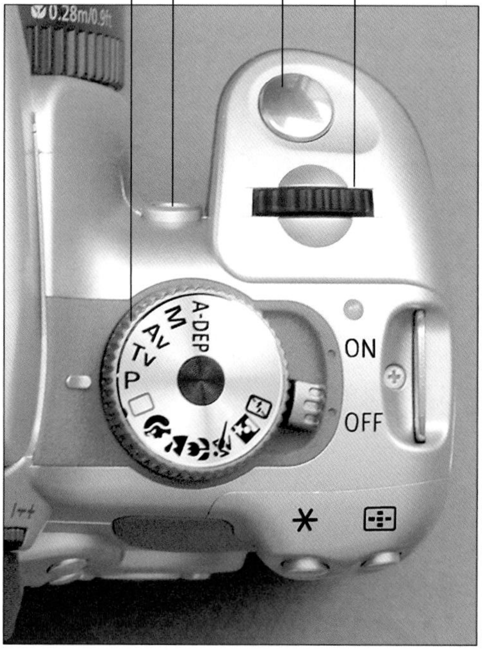

✔ **Shutter button:** You probably already understand the function of this button, too.

Red-eye Reduction/Self-timer Lamp   Main dial

Mode dial   Shutter button

Figure 1-6: The tiny pictures on the Mode dial represent special automatic shooting modes.

But check out Chapter 2 to discover the proper shutter-button-pressing technique — you'd be surprised how many people mess up their pictures because they press that button incorrectly.

✔ **Red-eye Reduction/Self-timer Lamp:** When you set your flash to Red-eye Reduction mode, this little lamp emits a brief beam of light prior to the real flash — the idea being that your subjects' pupils will constrict in response to the light, thus lessening the chances of red-eye. If you use the camera's self-timer feature, the lamp blinks to provide you with a visual countdown to the moment at which the picture will be recorded. See Chapter 2 for more details about Red-eye Reduction flash mode and the self-timer function.

Back-of-the-body controls

Traveling over the top of the camera to its back side, you encounter a smorgasbord of buttons — 15, in fact, not including the viewfinder's dioptric adjustment control, discussed earlier in this chapter. Figure 1-7 gives you a look at the entire layout of backside controls.

Don't let the abundance of buttons intimidate you. Having all those external controls actually makes operating your camera easier. On cameras that have only a few external buttons, you have to dig through menus to access the camera features, which is a big pain in the keister. But on your camera, you can access almost every critical shooting setting via the external buttons. That's a convenience you'll come to appreciate after you familiarize yourself with all the camera options.

Also, as you look through this book, you may notice that the margins contain little representations of the buttons to help you locate the one being discussed. So even though I provide the official control names in the following list, don't worry about getting all those straight right now. The list I provide here is just to get you acquainted with the *possibility* of what you can accomplish with all these features.

Do note, however, that many of the buttons have multiple names because they serve multiple purposes depending on whether you're taking pictures, reviewing images, or performing some other function. In this book, I refer to these buttons by the first label you see in the following list just to simplify things. For example, I refer to the AF Point Selection/Enlarge button as the AF Point Selection button. Again, though, the margin icons help you know exactly which button I'm describing.

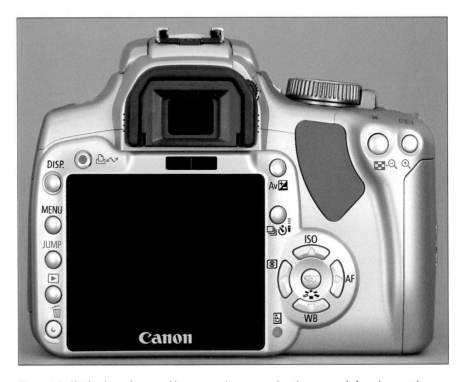

Figure 1-7: Having lots of external buttons makes accessing the camera's functions easier.

And here's another tip: If the label or icon for a button is blue, it indicates that the button has a function related to viewing, printing, or downloading images. Black labels indicate a shooting-related function.

With that preamble out of the way, journey with me now over the camera back, starting at the top right corner and working westward (well, assuming that your lens is pointing north, anyway):

✐ **AF Point Selection/Enlarge button:** When you use certain advanced shooting modes, you use this button to specify which of the nine autofocus points you want the camera to use when establishing focus. Chapter 6 tells you more about this feature. But in playback mode, you use the button to magnify the image display (thus the plus sign in the button's magnifying glass icon). See Chapter 4 for help with that one.

✐ **AE Lock/FE Lock/Index/Reduce button:** As you can guess from the official name of this button, it serves many purposes. The first two are related to image capture functions: You use the button to lock in the autoexposure (AE) setting and to lock flash exposure (FE). Chapter 5 details both issues. The button also serves two playback functions: It switches the display to index mode, enabling you to view multiple image thumbnails at once, and it also reduces the magnification of images when viewed in single-picture mode. Again, Chapter 4 explains all the playback features.

✐ **Aperture/Exposure Compensation button:** When you work in M (manual) exposure mode, you press this button and rotate the Main dial to choose the aperture setting, better known as the *f-stop*. In the other advanced exposure modes, you instead use the button and dial to adjust *exposure compensation,* a feature that enables you to adjust the exposure selected by the camera's autoexposure mechanism. Chapter 5 discusses both issues.

✐ **Drive mode button:** You press this button to access the Drive mode setting, which enables you to switch the camera from single-frame shooting to continuous capture or self-timer/remote-control shooting. See Chapter 2 for details.

✐ **Set/Picture Style button and cross keys:** The Set button and the four surrounding buttons, known as *cross keys,* team up to perform several functions, including choosing options from the camera menus. You use the cross keys to navigate through menus and then press the Set key to select a specific menu setting. (The later section, "Ordering from Camera Menus," has details.)

In this book, the instruction "Press the left cross key" just means to press the one that sports the left-pointing arrowhead. "Press the up cross key" means to press the one with the up-pointing arrowhead, and so on. Also, the official name for the Set button is Setting button, but I go with just what's on the button itself.

The cross keys and the Set button also have individual responsibilities, as follows:

- *Press the Set button to access Picture Style settings.* If you press the button without first displaying any camera menu, you're taken to the Picture Style settings screen. Chapter 6 discusses this feature.

- *Press the up cross key to adjust ISO.* You can read about this exposure-related setting in Chapter 5.

- *Press the right cross key to adjust the AF mode.* This option controls the camera's autofocus behavior, as outlined in Chapter 6.

- *Press the down cross key to adjust white balance.* Chapter 6 also explains white balance, which is a feature that you can use to tweak image colors.

- *Press the left cross key to change the metering mode.* The metering mode determines which area of the frame the camera uses when determining the correct exposure settings. Chapter 5 has details.

You can customize the functions of these buttons; Chapter 11 explains how. But while you're working with this book, stick with the default setup, just described. Otherwise, the instructions I give in the book won't work.

✔ **Erase button:** Sporting a trash can icon, the universal symbol for delete, this button lets you erase pictures from your memory card. Chapter 4 has specifics.

✔ **Playback button:** Press this button to switch the camera into picture review mode. Chapter 4 details the camera's playback features.

✔ **Jump button:** If your memory card contains boatloads of images, you can press this button to "jump" the display forward by 10 or 100 images. You can even jump through images based on the date pictures were taken. This button also enables you to toggle between the five camera menus. Chapter 4 details playback jumping; see the next section for details on menu jumping.

✔ **Menu button:** Press this button to access the camera menus. See the next section for details on navigating menus; see the appendix for a complete listing of all menus and menu options.

✔ **DISP button:** The camera monitor turns on automatically when you press the shutter button halfway, press the Menu button, or press the Playback button. When you put your eye up to the viewfinder, the display automatically turns off. If the monitor doesn't turn off or on as expected, press this button to kick it into or out of gear.

But that's just the start of the DISP button's tricks. If the camera menus are displayed, pressing the button takes you to the Camera Functions display, explained in the upcoming section "Monitoring Camera Settings." In playback mode, pressing the button changes the picture-display style, as outlined in Chapter 4.

✔ **Print/Share button:** This button and its accompanying tiny light get involved in the action when you transfer images to your computer or print pictures directly from the camera. See Chapter 8 for details on the transfer process; check out Chapter 9 for help with printing.

Front-left buttons

On the front-left side of the camera body, you find three more buttons, all labeled in Figure 1-8. One, the lens-release button, is key to taking the lens off the camera body, as discussed earlier in the chapter. The other two buttons work as follows:

✔ **Flash button:** Press this button to bring the camera's built-in flash out of hiding when you use the advanced shooting modes. (In fully automatic modes, the camera pops up the flash without your help if it decides the flash light is needed.) Chapters 5 and 7 provide tips on flash photography.

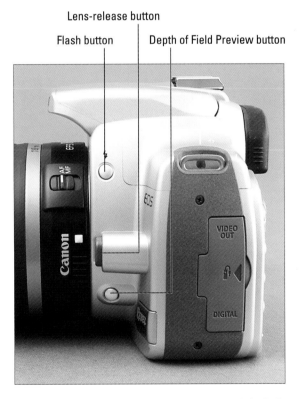

Figure 1-8: Press the Flash button to bring the built-in flash out of hiding.

✔ **Depth-of-Field Preview button:** When you press this button, the image in the viewfinder offers an approximation of the depth of field that will result from your selected aperture setting, or f-stop. *Depth of field* refers to how much of the scene will be in sharp focus. Chapter 6 provides details on depth of field, which is an important aspect of your picture composition. Chapter 5 explains aperture and other exposure settings.

Ordering from Camera Menus

 You access many of your camera's features via internal menus, which, conveniently enough, appear when you press the Menu button. Features are grouped into five main menus, described briefly in Table 1-1.

Table 1-1	Rebel XTi/400D Menus	
Symbol	*Open This Menu . . .*	*to Access These Functions*
⏺1	Shooting Menu 1	Picture Quality settings, red-eye reduction flash mode, and a few other basic camera settings.
⏺2	Shooting Menu 2	Advanced photography options such as flash exposure compensation and automatic exposure bracketing. Menu appears only when you use advanced exposure modes (P, Tv, Av, M, and A-DEP).
▶	Playback	Viewing, deleting, and marking pictures for printing.
ⵟ1	Setup Menu 1	Basic camera-customization options, such as monitor brightness and the file-numbering system.
ⵟ2	Setup Menu 2	More customization options and camera maintenance functions, such as sensor cleaning.

After you press the Menu button, a screen similar to the one shown in Figure 1-9 appears. Along the top of the screen, you see the icons shown in Table 1-1, each representing one of the five available menus. The icon that is highlighted is the active menu; options on that menu automatically appear on the main part of the screen. In the figure, Shooting Menu 1 is active, for example.

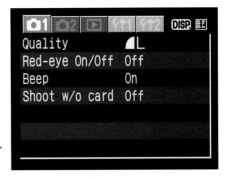

Shooting Menu 2 does not appear in the menu display when you set the camera Mode dial to Full Auto or any of the other fully automatic exposure modes (Portrait, Landscape, Sports, and so on). You see this menu only when you use the advanced exposure modes (P, Tv, Av, M, and A-DEP). And some menu items on Setup Menu 2 are hidden in the fully automatic exposure modes.

Figure 1-9: Highlight a menu icon to display its contents.

I explain all the important menu options elsewhere in the book; for now, just familiarize yourself with the process of navigating menus and selecting options. Here's the drill:

✔ **To select a different menu:** Press the Jump button to cycle through the available menus.

✔ **To select and adjust a function on the current menu:** Press the up or down cross key to highlight the feature you want to adjust. On the left side of Figure 1-10, the Quality option is highlighted, for example. Next, press the Set button. Settings available for the selected item then appear either right next to the menu item or on a separate screen, as shown on the right side of the figure. Either way, use the up and down cross keys to highlight your preferred setting and then press Set again to lock in your choice.

In this book, the instruction "Press the left cross key" simply means to press the cross key to the left of the Set button — the one marked with the left-pointing arrowhead. "Press the up cross key" means to press the cross key on the top side of the Set button, and so on.

As an alternative to pressing the cross keys, you can rotate the Main dial to scroll through menu options.

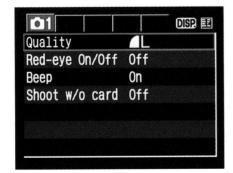

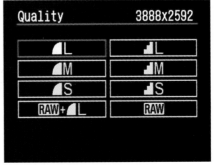

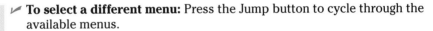

Figure 1-10: Use the up and down cross keys to highlight an option; press Set to select it.

Again, I present this information just as a general introduction, so don't worry about memorizing it. I tell you exactly which button combos to use whenever I explain a function that you activate via the menus.

Monitoring Critical Camera Settings

As you advance in your photography and begin to move beyond the automatic exposure modes, you need a way to keep track of what camera settings are currently active. To that end, your camera offers the Camera Settings display, shown in Figure 1-11. The display appears automatically when you turn on the camera and also when you depress the shutter button halfway — unless your eye is up to the viewfinder. In that case, the display is automatically turned off, but you can monitor some settings in the viewfinder, as explained in the next section.

If what you see in the figure looks like a big confusing mess, don't worry. Most of it won't mean anything to you until you make your way through later chapters. The figure does label two key points of data that are helpful even in fully automatic mode, though: how many more pictures can fit on your memory card at the current settings and the status of the battery. A "full" battery icon like the one in the figure shows that the battery is fully charged; if the icon appears empty, go look for your battery charger.

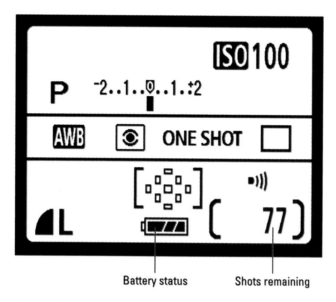

Figure 1-11: Press the shutter button halfway to activate the Camera Settings display.

In addition to the Camera Settings display, you get the Camera Function Setting display, shown in Figure 1-12. To display this screen, first display the camera menus by pressing the Menu button. Then press the DISP button.

This screen shows you the current status of the following camera options, listed from top to bottom in the order they appear:

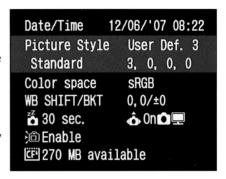

Date/Time	12/06/'07 08:22
Picture Style	User Def. 3
Standard	3, 0, 0, 0
Color space	sRGB
WB SHIFT/BKT	0, 0/±0
30 sec.	On
Enable	
270 MB available	

Figure 1-12: Press the DISP button when the menus are active to view this screen.

- **Date/Time:** To find out how to adjust the date and time, jump to the upcoming section "Setup Menu 1."

- **Picture Style:** You can use Picture Style options to tweak color, sharpness, and contrast when you shoot in the advanced exposure modes. Chapter 6 has the lowdown.

- **Color Space:** Here's another advanced color option, also explained in Chapter 6.

- **White Balance Shift/Bracketing:** Add this to the list of color options covered in Chapter 6.

- **Auto Power Off and Auto Rotate Display:** For information on these two settings, represented in the display by groups of little icons, see the upcoming section "Setup Menu 1."

- **LCD Monitor Auto Off:** This setting, also covered in the section "Setup Menu 1," controls whether the monitor turns off automatically when you put your eye to the viewfinder.

- **Memory Card Space Available:** The number shown here indicates how much space remains on your camera memory card. How many pictures you can fit into that space depends on the Quality setting you select. Chapter 3 explains this issue.

Of course, with the exception of the last item, you also can simply go to the menu that contains the option in question to check its current status. The two displays featured here just give you a quick way to monitor some of the critical functions.

Decoding Viewfinder Data

When the camera is turned on, you can view critical exposure settings and a few other pieces of information in the viewfinder as well as on the Camera

Settings display. The viewfinder data changes depending on what action you're currently undertaking. For example, when you press the shutter button halfway, you see the current f-stop (aperture setting), shutter speed, and exposure meter, as shown in Figure 1-13.

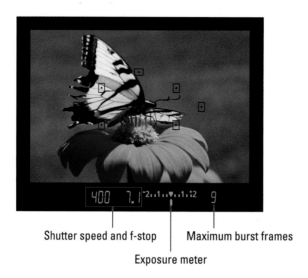

Shutter speed and f-stop | Maximum burst frames

Exposure meter

Figure 1-13: You also can view some camera information at the bottom of the viewfinder.

The final value (9, in the figure) shows you the number of *maximum burst frames.* This number relates to shooting in the continuous-capture mode, where the camera fires off multiple shots in rapid-fire succession as long as you hold down the shutter button. (Chapter 2 has details on this mode.) Note that although the highest number that the viewfinder can display is 9, the actual number of maximum burst frames may be higher. At any rate, you don't really need to pay attention to the number until it starts dropping toward 0, which indicates that the camera's memory buffer (its temporary internal data-storage tank) is filling up. If that happens, just give the camera a moment to catch up with your shutter-button finger.

Rather than give you a full guide to all the possible viewfinder readouts here, which would only boggle your mind and cause lots of unnecessary page-flipping, I detail the relevant viewfinder data as I cover the various photo-graphic topics later in the book.

Reviewing Basic Setup Options

You know how sometimes you visit someone's house and their kitchen cabinets are arranged in a way that doesn't make sense to you? Why are the mugs above the microwave instead of above the coffeepot? And wouldn't it be better if the serving spoons were next to the stove instead of by the dishwasher? That's how I feel about the way that settings that relate to basic camera setup are organized on the camera menus. They surely make sense to *somebody* — namely, I'm guessing, the important somebodies at Canon. But to me, a couple of the basic setup options are out of place, found on menus other than Setup Menu 1 or Setup Menu 2, where you might expect to find them. And Setup Menu 2 offers some options that are related more to advanced exposure controls than basic camera operation.

Well, I can't rearrange the menus for you any more than I can put those mugs near the coffeemaker, so instead, the following sections describe the basic customization options found on the aforementioned Setup Menu 1 and 2, plus two additional options found on Shooting Menu 1.

If you don't yet know how to select options from the menus, see the earlier section, "Ordering from Camera Menus" for help.

Setup Menu 1

At the risk of being labeled conventional, I suggest that you start your camera customization by opening this menu, shown in Figure 1-14.

Here's a quick rundown of each menu item:

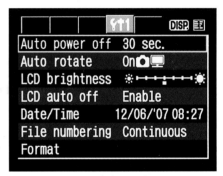

Figure 1-14: Options on Setup Menu 1 deal mainly with basic camera behavior.

✓ **Auto Power Off:** To help save battery power, your camera automatically powers down after a certain period of inactivity. By default, the shutdown happens after 30 seconds, but you can change the shutdown delay to 1, 2, 4, 8, or 15 minutes. Or you can disable auto shutdown altogether by selecting the Off setting.

✔ **Auto Rotate:** If you enable this feature, your picture files include a piece of data that indicates whether the camera was oriented in the vertical or horizontal position when you shot the frame. Then, when you view the picture on the camera monitor or on your computer, the image is automatically rotated to the correct orientation.

To automatically rotate images both in the camera monitor and on your computer monitor, stick with the default setting. In the menu, this setting is represented by On followed by a camera icon and a monitor icon, as shown in Figure 1-14. If you want the rotation to occur just on your computer and not on the camera, select the second On setting, which is marked with the computer monitor symbol but not the camera symbol. To disable rotation for both devices, choose the Off setting.

Note, though, that the camera may record the wrong orientation data for pictures that you take with the camera pointing directly up or down. Also, whether your computer can read the rotation data in the picture file depends on the software you use; the programs bundled with the camera can perform the auto rotation.

✔ **LCD Brightness:** This option enables you to make the camera monitor brighter or darker, as shown in Figure 1-15. After highlighting the option on the menu, press Set to display a screen similar to what you see on the right screen in the figure. (The camera displays a picture from your memory card in the main preview area; if the card is empty, you see a black box instead.) Press the right and left cross keys to adjust the brightness setting. Press Set again to return to the menu.

If you take this step, keep in mind that what you see on the display may not be an accurate rendition of the actual exposure of your image. Crank up the monitor brightness, for example, and an underexposed photo may look just fine. So I recommend that you keep the brightness at the default setting, which places the brightness marker at dead center on the little brightness scale, as shown in Figure 1-15. As an alternative, you can display the *histogram,* an exposure guide that I explain in Chapter 4, when reviewing your images.

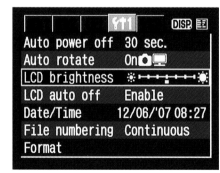
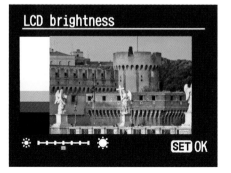

Figure 1-15: You can adjust the brightness of the camera monitor.

✏ **LCD Auto Off:** When the Enable setting is selected, as it is by default, the camera automatically turns off the camera monitor when you put your eye up to the camera viewfinder. (The little sensor underneath the viewfinder notes the presence of your eye and signals the camera to turn off the monitor.) You can deactivate this feature by choosing the Disable setting if you prefer. The monitor is one of the biggest battery drains on the camera, however, so in my opinion, the auto shutoff feature is a good thing.

✏ **Date/Time:** When you turn on your camera for the very first time, it automatically displays this option and asks you to set the current date and time.

Keeping the date/time accurate is important because that information is recorded as part of the image file. In your photo browser, you can then see when you shot an image and, equally handy, search for images by the date they were taken. Chapter 8 shows you where to locate the date/time data when browsing your picture files.

✏ **File Numbering:** This option controls how the camera names your picture files. When the option is set to Continuous, as it is by default, the camera numbers your files sequentially, from 0001 to 9999, and places all images in the same folder. The initial folder name is 100Canon; when you reach image 9999, the camera creates a new folder, named 101Canon, for your next 9999 photos. This numbering sequence is retained even if you change memory cards, which helps to ensure that you don't wind up with multiple images that have the same file name.

By contrast, the Auto Reset option automatically starts file numbering at 0001 each time you put in a different memory card. I discourage the use of this option, for the reason already stated.

Whichever of these two options you choose, beware one gotcha: If you swap out memory cards and the new card already contains images, the camera may pick up numbering from the last image on the new card, which throws a monkey wrench into things. To avoid this problem, just format the new card before putting it into the camera. (See the next bullet point for details.)

Finally, if you choose Manual Reset, the camera begins a new numbering sequence, starting at 0001, for your next shot. The Continuous mode is then automatically selected for you again.

✏ **Format:** The first time you insert a new memory card, you should use this option to *format* the card, a maintenance function that wipes out any existing data on the card and prepares it for use by the camera.

If you previously used your card in another device, such as a digital music player, be sure to copy those files to your computer before you format the card.

Setup Menu 2

Setup Menu 2, shown in Figure 1-16, offers an additional batch of customization options. But you can adjust and take advantage of only the following three options in all exposure modes (Full Auto, Manual, Portrait, and so on):

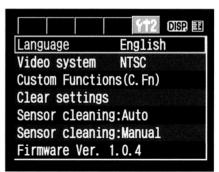

Figure 1-16: Most options on Setup Menu 2 can be used only in advanced exposure modes.

- ✓ **Language:** This option determines the language of any text displayed on the camera monitor. Screens in this book display the English language, but I find it entertaining on occasion to hand my camera to a friend after changing the language to, say, Swedish. I'm a real yokester, yah?

- ✓ **Video System:** This option is related to viewing your images on a television, a topic I cover in Chapter 9. Select NTSC if you live in North America or other countries that adhere to the NTSC video standard; select PAL for playback in areas that follow that code of video conduct.

- ✓ **Sensor Cleaning:Auto:** By default, the camera's sensor-cleaning mechanism activates each time you turn the camera on and off. This process helps keep the image sensor — which is the part of the camera that captures the image — free of dust and other particles that can mar your photos. You have the option of turning the feature off, but I can't imagine why you would choose to do so.

That leaves the following four options which, again, you cannot access in the fully automatic exposure modes:

- ✓ **Custom Functions:** Selecting this option opens the door to customizing 11 camera functions, which are labeled on the menu as C.Fn-1, C.Fn-2, and so on. These functions either relate to advanced exposure options or are otherwise designed for people with some photography experience. I cover functions 2, 3, 6, 8, and 9 in Chapter 5, which explains the advanced exposure modes; I detail the remaining Custom Functions in Chapter 11.

- ✓ **Clear Settings:** You can restore the default settings that are used for the advanced exposure modes via this menu option. You also can reset all the Custom Functions settings to their defaults through this option.

- ✓ **Sensor Cleaning:Manual:** This feature enables you to clean the image sensor manually, by opening up the camera and using special tools to do the job. My advice on this procedure can be summed up in one word: *Don't.* The sensor is extremely delicate, and this is a task best left to professional camera technicians. Expect to pay about $30 to $50 for the service. (Some stores, however, provide sensor cleaning free if you purchased your camera from them.)

✔ **Firmware Ver.:** This screen tells you the current version of the camera *firmware* (internal operating software). The appendix in this book explains how to check which version is installed in your camera and how to update it via the Canon Web site if needed.

Keeping your camera firmware up-to-date is pretty important, and I suggest that you skip to the appendix and do a firmware check now even if you're not ready to actually use the advanced exposure modes. That way, you can be confident that you're taking advantage of the most recent internal software.

Two more customization options

Shooting Menu 1, shown in Figure 1-17, offers two more basic setup options — at least, these options fall into that category if you share my logic, which some may consider a frightening prospect. At any rate, these two options work as follows:

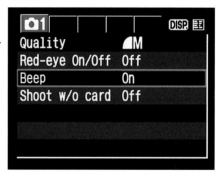

Figure 1-17: You can silence the camera via Shooting Menu 1.

✔ **Beep:** By default, your camera beeps at you after certain operations, such as after it sets focus when you shoot in autofocus mode. If you're doing top-secret surveillance work and need the camera to hush up, set this option to Off.

✔ **Shoot w/o Card:** Setting this option to Off prevents shutter-button release when no memory card is in the camera. If you turn the option on, you can take a picture and then review the results for a few seconds in the camera monitor. The image isn't stored anywhere, however; it's temporary.

If you're wondering about the point of this option, it's designed for use in camera stores, enabling salespeople to demonstrate cameras without having to keep a memory card in every model. Unless that feature somehow suits your purposes, keep this option set to Off.

Why does this camera have two names?

As is the case with some other Canon cameras, yours goes by different names — EOS Digital Rebel XTi or EOS 400D — depending on the part of the world where it's sold.

The *EOS* part, by the way, stands for Electro Optical System, the core technology used in Canon's autofocus SLR (single-lens reflex) cameras. According to Canon, the proper pronunciation is *ee-ohs,* which is also how you pronounce the name *Eos,* the goddess of dawn in Greek mythology.

With apologies to the goddess, I save a little room in this book by shortening the camera name to simply Rebel XTi/400D, which is already long enough.

2

Taking Great Pictures, Automatically

Are you old enough to remember the Certs television commercials from the 1960s and '70s? "It's a candy mint!" declared one actor. "It's a breath mint!" argued another. Then a narrator declared the debate a tie and spoke the famous catchphrase: "It's two, two, two mints in one!"

Well, that's sort of how I see the Rebel XTi/400D. On one hand, it provides a full range of powerful controls, offering just about every feature a serious photographer could want. On the other, it also offers fully automated exposure modes that enable people with absolutely no experience to capture beautiful images. "It's a sophisticated photographic tool!" "It's as easy as 'point and shoot!'" "It's two, two, two cameras in one!"

Now, my guess is that you bought this book for help with your camera's advanced side, so that's what other chapters cover. This chapter, however, is devoted to your camera's simpler side, because even when you shoot in the fully automatic modes, following a few basic guidelines can help you get better results. For example, your camera offers a variety of fully automatic exposure modes, some of which may be new to you. The mode affects the look of your pictures, so this chapter explains those options. I also cover techniques that enable you to get the best performance from your camera's autofocus and autoexposure systems and review the flash options available to you in automatic modes.

Getting Good Point-and-Shoot Results

Your camera offers several fully automatic exposure modes, all of which I explain later in this chapter. But in any of those modes, the key to good photos is to follow a specific picture-taking technique.

To try it out, set the Mode dial on top of the camera to Full Auto, as shown in the left image in Figure 2-1. Then set the focusing switch on the lens to the AF (autofocus) position, as shown in the right image in Figure 2-1. (The figure features the lens that is bundled with the Rebel XTi/400D. If you own a different lens, the switch may look and operate differently; check your lens manual for details.)

AF/MF switch

Full Auto mode

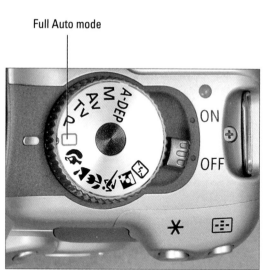
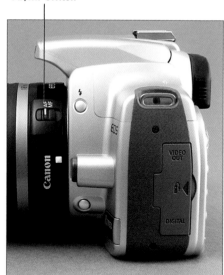

Figure 2-1: Choose these settings for fully automatic exposure and focus.

Your camera is now set up to work in the most automatic of automatic modes. Follow these steps to take the picture:

   1. Looking through the viewfinder, frame the image so that your subject appears under an autofocus point.

   The *autofocus points* are those nine tiny rectangles clustered in the center of the viewfinder, as shown in Figure 2-2.

2. **Press and hold the shutter button halfway down.**

The camera's autofocus and autoexposure meters begin to do their thing. In dim light, the flash may pop up if the camera thinks additional light is needed. Additionally, the flash may shoot out an *af-assist beam,* emitting a few rapid pulses of light designed to help the autofocusing mechanism find its target. (The *af* stands for autofocus.)

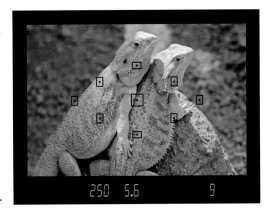

Figure 2-2: The tiny rectangles in the viewfinder indicate autofocus points.

When focus is established, the camera beeps at you, assuming that you didn't silence its voice via Shooting Menu 1, as discussed at the end of Chapter 1. Additionally, the focus indicator in the viewfinder lights, as shown in Figure 2-3, and the dot inside one autofocus point starts to blink red. That blinking dot indicates which autofocus point the camera used to establish focus. Sometimes multiple dots blink, which simply tells you that all the objects within those autofocus areas are now in focus.

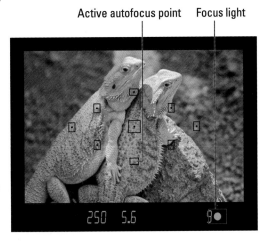

Active autofocus point   Focus light

Figure 2-3: The green light indicates that the camera has locked focus.

3. **Press the shutter button the rest of the way down to record the image.**

While the camera sends the image data to the camera memory card, the memory card access lamp lights, as shown in Figure 2-4. Don't turn off the camera or remove the memory card while the lamp is lit, or you may damage both camera and card.

When the recording process is finished, the picture appears briefly on the camera monitor. See Chapter 4 to find out how to switch to playback mode and take a longer look at your image.

I need to add a couple important notes about this process, especially related to Step 2:

Memory card access lamp

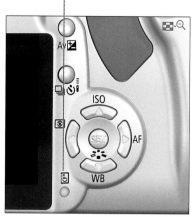

✔ **Solving autofocus problems:** When you shoot in the fully automatic modes, the camera typically focuses on the closest object. If the camera insists on selecting an autofocus point that isn't appropriate for your subject, the easiest solution is to switch to manual focusing and be done with it. Chapter 1 shows you how. Or you can use the advanced exposure modes, which enable you to select a specific autofocus point. Chapter 6 explains that option plus a few other tips for getting good autofocus results.

Figure 2-4: The card access lamp lights while the camera sends the picture data to the card.

✔ **Shooting moving subjects:** If the focus indicator doesn't light but you hear a continuous series of beeps, the camera's telling you that it detected motion in the scene. To accommodate that motion, it shifts to an autofocusing mode called AI Servo (the AI stands for *artificial intelligence*). In this mode, the camera focuses continually after you press the shutter button halfway. As long as you keep the subject within one of the autofocus points, focus should be correct. See Chapter 6 for more tips about this and other autofocus modes.

✔ **Locking exposure:** By default, pressing the shutter button halfway does not lock exposure along with focus. Your camera instead continues metering and adjusting exposure until you fully depress the shutter button. If you want to lock exposure, you must use an advanced exposure mode and rely on the AE (autoexposure) Lock button. Again, see Chapter 5 for how-to's. Alternatively, you can set up the shutter button to lock exposure instead of focus; Chapter 11 explains this option, available through one of the Custom Functions. (While working with this book, however, stick with the default arrangement.)

✔ **Changing the Drive mode setting:** In most of the automatic exposure modes, your camera automatically sets the Drive mode to Single, which records a single image with each press of the shutter button. But in Portrait and Sports mode, the camera instead selects Continuous mode, which records pictures as long as you hold down the shutter button. You can change the Drive mode to the Self-Timer/Remote Control setting for any exposure mode, however. See the end of this chapter for details.

Using Flash in Automatic Exposure Modes

Your options for using flash depend on which of the fully automatic exposure modes you choose, as follows:

- **Sports, Landscape, and Flash Off:** Flash is disabled for these modes. For the Flash Off mode, that behavior makes sense, of course. But why no flash in the other two modes? Well, Sports mode is designed to enable you to capture moving subjects, and the flash can make that more difficult because it needs time to recycle between shots. Additionally, action photos usually aren't taken at a range close enough for the flash to reach the subject, which is also the reason why flash is disabled for Landscape mode.

- **Full Auto, Portrait, Close Up, and Night Portrait:** In these modes, the camera automatically pops up the built-in flash when needed. You do have the option of setting the flash to either normal or Red-eye Reduction mode, however. You can do this via the Red-Eye On/Off setting on Shooting Menu 1, shown on the left in Figure 2-5.

TIP

More focus factors to consider

When you focus the lens, either in autofocus or manual focus mode, you determine only the point of sharpest focus. The distance to which that sharp-focus zone extends — what photographers call the *depth of field* — depends in part on the *aperture setting,* which is an exposure control. And the aperture setting varies depending on the automated photography mode you select.

The Portrait setting, for example, uses an aperture setting that shortens the depth of field so that background objects are softly focused — an artistic choice that most people prefer for portraits. On the flip side of the coin, the Landscape setting selects an aperture that produces a large depth of field so that both foreground and background objects appear sharp.

Another exposure-related control, *shutter speed,* plays a focus role when you photograph moving objects. Moving objects appear blurry at slow shutter speeds; at fast shutter speeds, they appear sharply focused. On your camera, the Sports shooting mode automatically selects a high shutter speed to help you "stop" action, producing blur-free shots of the subject.

A fast shutter speed can also help safeguard against allover blurring that results when the camera is moved during the exposure. The faster the shutter speed, the shorter the exposure time, which reduces the time that you need to keep the camera absolutely still. Using a tripod is the best way to avoid the problem when you use a slow shutter speed.

If you want to manipulate focus and depth of field to a greater extent than the automated exposure modes produce, visit Chapter 6. For an explanation of the role of shutter speed and aperture in exposure, check out Chapter 5.

Red-eye Reduction flash symbol

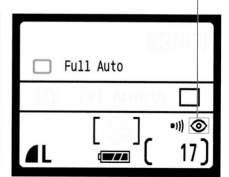

Figure 2-5: Turn Red-eye Reduction flash mode on and off via Shooting Menu 1.

 WARNING!

In Red-eye Reduction mode, the camera fires a brief preflash when you press the shutter button halfway. The purpose of this light is to attempt to shrink the subject's pupils, which helps reduce the chances of red-eye. So be sure to warn your subjects to keep posing until the second, real flash light fires. See Chapters 5 and 7 for more tips about using your flash.

When the flash is set to red-eye reduction mode, you see the universal "red-eye" icon in the Camera Settings display, as shown on the right in Figure 2-5. Additionally, the viewfinder displays the following symbols to alert you to the flash status:

✔ **Flash on:** A little lightning bolt like the one you see in the margin here and in the highlighted area of Figure 2-6 tells you that the flash is enabled.

✔ **Flash recycling:** If you see the word *Busy* along with the lightning bolt, as shown in Figure 2-6, the flash needs a few moments to recharge. When the flash is ready to go, the *Busy* message disappears.

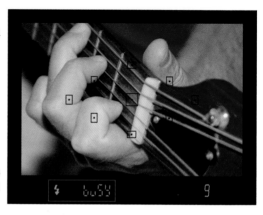

Figure 2-6: A *Busy* signal means that the flash is recharging.

 TIP

✔ **Red-eye signal:** After you press the shutter button halfway in Red-eye Reduction flash mode, a row of vertical bars appears in the lower right half of the viewfinder display. A few instants later, the bars turn off one by one. For best results, wait until all the bars are off to take the picture. (The delay gives the subject's pupils time to constrict.)

Exploring Your Automatic Options

You can choose from seven fully automatic exposure modes, all of which you access via the Mode dial on the top of the camera, shown in Figure 2-7.

The next sections provide details on each of these options. For information about the five other settings on the Mode dial — P (Programmed Auto), Tv (shutter-priority autoexposure), Av (aperture-priority autoexposure), M (manual exposure), and A-DEP (automatic depth-of-field autoexposure), see Chapter 5.

Fully automatic exposure modes

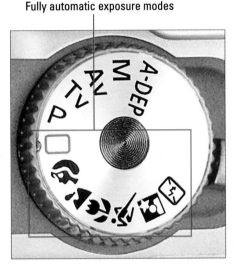

Figure 2-7: You can select from seven fully automatic exposure modes.

Full Auto mode

In this mode, represented on the Mode dial by the green rectangle you see in the margin here, the camera selects all settings based on the scene that it detects in front of the lens. Your only job is to lock in focus, using the two-stage autofocus technique I outline at the beginning of the chapter, or by setting the lens to manual mode and using the focus ring on the lens, as explained in Chapter 1.

Full Auto mode is great for casual, quick snapshooting. But keep these limitations in mind:

- ✔ **Picture Style:** Full Auto mode records your photo using the Standard Picture Style setting. The aim of this mode is to produce a crisp, vivid image. You can get more details about how Picture Styles affect your photos in Chapter 6.

- ✔ **Drive mode:** The camera selects the Single setting automatically, so you record one image for every press of the shutter button. For information on how to change the setting to Self-Timer/Remote Control, see the last section in this chapter.

- ✔ **Flash:** The camera takes control over whether you can use flash. You can't enable the flash if the camera's autoexposure meter doesn't sense that additional light is needed. Nor can you disable the flash or adjust its intensity, a feature I cover in Chapter 5. You can, however, choose to use Red-eye Reduction flash mode; see the preceding section for details.

- ✔ **Autofocus control:** In most cases, the camera focuses on the object closest to it. To focus on a different area, the easiest option is to switch to manual focusing.

If you do stick with autofocus, note that the camera adjusts its auto-focusing behavior depending on whether it thinks you're shooting a still or moving subject. For still subjects, the camera locks focus when you depress the shutter halfway. But if the camera senses motion, it continually adjusts focus from the time you depress the shutter button halfway. You must reframe your shot as necessary to keep the subject within one of the nine autofocus points to ensure sharp focus.

See Chapter 6 for additional information on getting good autofocus results.

✔ **Color:** You can't adjust color. If the image displays a color cast, you must switch to a mode that enables you to adjust the White Balance setting, covered in Chapter 6.

✔ **Exposure:** You also give up total control over exposure to the camera. Chapter 5 shows you what you're missing.

✔ **Quality:** For the Quality setting, which determines both the image resolution, or pixel count, and the file format, you are limited to settings that use the JPEG file format. Chapter 3 discusses this issue.

I purposely didn't include an example of a photo taken in Full Auto mode because, frankly, the results that this setting create vary widely depending on how well the camera detects whether you're trying to shoot a portrait, landscape, action shot, or whatever. But the bottom line is that Full Auto is a one-size-fits-all approach that may not take best advantage of your camera's capabilities. So if you want to more consistently take great pictures instead of good ones, I encourage you to explore the exposure, focus, and color information found in Part II so that you can abandon this exposure mode in favor of ones that put more photographic decisions in your hands.

Automatic scene modes (a.k.a. Image Zone modes)

In Full Auto mode, the camera tries to figure out what type of picture you want to take by assessing what it sees through the lens. If you don't want to rely on the camera to make that judgment, your camera offers six other fully automatic modes that are specifically designed for taking popular categories of pictures. For example, most people prefer portraits that have softly focused backgrounds. So in Portrait mode, the camera selects settings that can produce that type of background.

These six automatic modes — the ones represented by the little pictographs on the Mode dial — are officially known as _Image Zone_ modes in Canon lingo and in your camera manual. For reasons I state in Chapter 1, I avoid using the whole "zone" moniker system in this book and instead refer to the six Image Zone modes as _automatic scene modes_. But if you should seek information about these modes elsewhere, whether online or in your manual, be sure to search for the topic under its official name.

Whatever you call them, all six modes share a few limitations — or benefits, depending on how you look at things:

- ✔ **Color:** As with Full Auto mode, you can't tweak color. Some modes manipulate colors in ways that you may or may not appreciate, and you're stuck if you have a color cast problem.

- ✔ **Exposure:** The camera takes complete control of exposure, too.

- ✔ **Quality:** You can't take advantage of the Raw file format (CR2, on your Canon); you must use the JPEG format. See Chapter 3 to find out which of the JPEG settings is most appropriate for the way you plan to use your pictures.

In the next sections, you can read about the unique features of each of the six automatic scene modes. To see whether you approve of how your camera approaches the different scenes, take some test shots. If you aren't happy with the results, you can switch to one of the advanced exposure modes and then check out Chapters 5–7 to find out how to manipulate whatever aspect of the picture isn't to your liking.

Portrait mode

Portrait mode attempts to select exposure settings that produce a blurry background, which puts the visual emphasis on your subject. Figure 2-8 offers an example. Keep in mind, though, that in certain lighting conditions, the camera may not be able to choose the exposure settings that best produce the soft background. Additionally, the background blurring requires that your subject be at least a few feet from the background. The extent to which the background blurs also depends on the other depth-of-field factors that I discuss in Chapter 6.

In addition, Portrait mode selects these camera settings:

- ✔ **Picture Style:** Logically enough, the camera automatically sets the Picture Style option to Portrait. As detailed in Chapter 6, this Picture Style results in a slightly less sharp image, the main idea being to keep skin texture nice and soft. Colors are also adjusted subtly to enhance skin tones.

- ✔ **Drive mode:** Contrary to what you may expect, the Drive mode is set to Continuous, which means that the camera records a series of images in rapid succession as long as you hold down the shutter button. This technique can come in especially handy if your portrait subject can't be counted on to remain still for very long — a toddler or pet, for example.

  Should you want to include yourself in the shot, you can switch the Drive mode setting to the Self-Timer/Remote Control mode. See the end of this chapter for details.

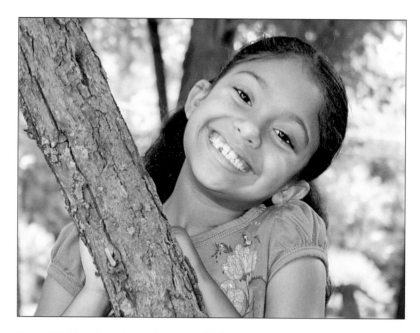

Figure 2-8: Portrait setting produces a softly focused background.

- **Flash:** You have the option of using regular or Red-Eye Reduction mode — but only if the camera decides that you need a flash to properly light the scene.

  For outdoor portraits, this can pose a problem: A flash generally improves outdoor portraits, and if the ambient light is very bright, the camera doesn't give you access to the flash. For an illustration of the difference a flash can make, see Chapter 7. That chapter also contains tips on using flash in nighttime and indoor portraits.

- **Autofocusing:** Portrait mode employs the One-Shot AF (autofocus) mode. This is one of three AF modes available on your camera, all detailed in Chapter 6. In One-Shot mode, the camera locks focus when you press the shutter button halfway. Typically, the camera locks focus on the object that's closest to the camera. If your subject moves out of the selected autofocus point, the camera doesn't adjust focus to compensate.

Keep in mind that you can use Portrait mode any time you want a slightly blurry background, not just for people pictures. Try this mode when shooting statues, still-life arrangements (such as a vase of flowers on a kitchen table), and the like. And one more tip: If you're not sure that your subject will remain motionless, Sports mode, which is designed to capture moving subjects without blur, may deliver better results. I often suggest this mode for shooting children and pets, for example.

Landscape mode

 Whereas Portrait mode aims for a very shallow depth of field (small zone of sharp focus), Landscape mode, which is designed for capturing scenic vistas, city skylines, and other large-scale subjects, produces a large depth of field. As a result, objects both close to the camera and at a distance appear sharply focused. Figure 2-9 offers an example. Notice that everything from the foreground saplings to the architectural ruins to the background trees appear about the same in terms of sharpness.

Like Portrait mode, Landscape mode achieves the greater depth of field by manipulating the exposure settings — specifically, the aperture, or f-stop setting. So the extent to which the camera can succeed in keeping everything in sharp focus depends on the available light. To fully understand this issue, see Chapter 6. And in the meantime, know that you also can extend depth of field by zooming out, if your camera offers a zoom lens.

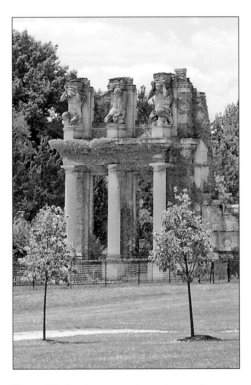

Figure 2-9: Landscape mode produces a large zone of sharp focus and also boosts color intensity slightly.

As for other camera settings, Landscape mode results in the following options:

- ✏ **Picture Style:** The camera automatically sets the Picture Style option to Landscape, which produces a sharper image, with well-defined "edges" — the borders between areas of contrast or color change. The Picture Style setting also produces more vivid blues and greens, which is what most people prefer from their landscape photos. You can read more about Picture Styles in Chapter 6.

- ✏ **Drive mode:** The camera selects the Single option, which records one image for each press of the shutter button. As with the other scene modes, you can switch to self-timer or remote-control shooting by following the steps laid out at the end of this chapter.

- ✏ **Flash:** The built-in flash is disabled, which is typically no big deal: Because of its limited range, a built-in flash is of little use when shooting most landscapes anyway.

- ✏ **Autofocusing:** The AF mode is set to One-Shot, which means that focus is locked when you depress the shutter button halfway. (See Chapter 6 for details.) Focus usually is set on the nearest object, but remember that because of the large depth of field that the Landscape mode produces, both far and near objects may appear equally sharp, depending on their distance from the lens.

Again, think beyond the Landscape moniker when you look for good ways to put this mode to use: Try it when shooting long-range pictures of animals at the zoo, for example, so that critters both near and far appear sharp.

Close-Up mode

Switching to Close-Up mode doesn't enable you to focus at a closer distance to your subject than normal as it does on some non-SLR cameras. The close-focusing capabilities of your camera depend entirely on the lens you bought.

But choosing Close-Up mode does result in exposure settings that are designed to blur background objects so that they don't compete for attention with your main subject. As with Portrait mode, though, how much the background blurs varies depending on the distance between your subject and the background as well as on the lighting conditions.

For example, the amount of background blurring in the Close-Up mode example shown in Figure 2-10 isn't as great as in the earlier Portrait example because not as much distance exists between subject and background. Still, you can see a slight shift in focus from the front of the wagon wheel to the blue wagon bed behind it. Should you prefer a greater or shorter depth of field, see Chapter 6 for other ways to adjust this aspect of your pictures.

Other settings selected for you in Close-Up mode are as follows:

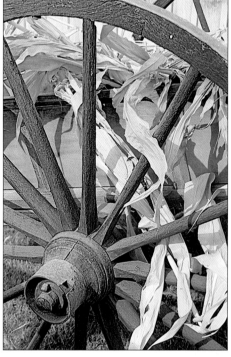

- ✔ **Picture Style:** Close-Up mode uses the Standard picture style, just like Full Auto. The resulting image features crisp edges and vivid colors.

- ✔ **Drive mode:** The Drive mode is set to Single, so you record one photo each time you fully depress the shutter button. You can, however, select Self-Timer/Remote Control mode if needed.

- ✔ **Flash:** Flash is enabled when the camera thinks additional light is needed and disabled if not. You can set the flash to Red-Eye Reduction mode, but frankly, you shouldn't be firing the flash at close range to either human or animal subjects — you can hurt their eyes.

- ✔ **Autofocusing:** The AF mode is set to One-Shot mode; again, that simply means that when you depress the shutter button halfway, the camera locks focus, usually on the nearest object.

Figure 2-10: Close-Up mode also produces short depth of field.

See Chapter 6 for more details about AF modes and other focusing issues. Chapter 7 offers additional tips on close-up photography.

Sports mode

Sports mode results in a number of settings that can help you photograph moving objects such as the swinging girl in Figure 2-11. First, the camera selects a fast shutter speed, which is needed to "stop motion." *Shutter speed* is an exposure control that you can explore in Chapter 5.

Also keep these Sports mode settings in mind:

- ✔ **Picture Style:** The camera automatically sets the Picture Style option to Standard, the same one used for Full Auto and Close-Up mode. This picture style is designed to produce sharp images with bold colors.

✓ **Drive mode:** To enable rapid-fire image capture, the Drive mode is set to Continuous. This mode enables you to record multiple frames with a single press of the shutter button. You also have the option of switching to the Self-Timer/Remote Control mode. Check out the end of this chapter for details on both Drive mode settings.

✓ **Flash:** Flash is disabled, which can be a problem in low-light situations, but it also enables you to shoot successive images more quickly because the flash needs a brief period to recycle between shots.

✓ **Autofocusing:** The AF mode is set to AI Servo. In this mode, the camera establishes focus initially when you depress the shutter button halfway. But if the subject moves, the camera attempts to refocus.

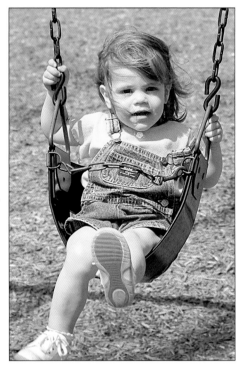

Figure 2-11: To capture moving subjects without blur, try Sports mode.

For this feature to work correctly, you must adjust framing so that your subject remains within one of the autofocus points. You may find it easier to simply switch to manual focusing and twist the focusing ring as needed to track the subject's movement yourself.

The other critical thing to understand about Sports mode is that whether the camera can select a shutter speed fast enough to stop motion depends on the available light and the speed of the subject itself. In Figure 2-11, the camera selected a shutter speed that did, in fact, catch my subject in midswing, although if you look very closely, you can see some slight blurring of the foot near the bottom of the frame.

To fully understand shutter speed, visit Chapter 6. And for more tips on action photography, check out Chapter 7.

Night Portrait mode

 As its name implies, Night Portrait mode is designed to deliver a better-looking portrait at night (or in any dimly lit environment). It does so by combining flash with a slow shutter speed. That slow shutter speed produces a longer exposure time, which enables the camera to rely more on ambient light and less on the flash to expose the picture. The result is a brighter background and softer, more even lighting.

 I cover the issue of using a slow shutter speed in detail in Chapter 5; Chapter 7 has some additional nighttime photography tips. For now, the critical thing to know is that the slower shutter speed means that you probably need a tripod; if you try to handhold the camera, you run the risk of moving the camera during the long exposure, resulting in a blurry image. Your subjects also must stay perfectly still during the exposure, which can also be a challenge.

If you do try Night Portrait mode, be aware of these other settings that are automatically selected by the camera:

- **Picture Style:** The Standard setting, designed to deliver sharp, bold photos, is selected. See Chapter 6 for more about Picture Style options and how they affect your images.

- **Drive mode:** The default setting is Single, but you also can choose the Self-Timer/Remote Control mode. Check out the end of this chapter for details on both Drive mode settings.

- **Flash:** Flash is enabled when the camera thinks ambient light is needed — which, assuming that you're actually shooting at night, should be most of the time. You can set the flash to Red-Eye Reduction mode if you prefer. See the section "Using Flash in Automatic Exposure Modes," earlier in this chapter, for details.

- **Autofocusing:** The AF mode is set to One-Shot, which locks focus when you depress the shutter button halfway. Focus isn't adjusted if your subject moves out of the selected autofocusing point before you record the image.

Flash Off mode

 The Flash Off mode delivers the same results as Full Auto mode but ensures that the flash doesn't fire, even in dim lighting. This mode provides an easy way to ensure that you don't break the rules when shooting in locations that don't permit flash: museums, churches, and so on. But it can also come in handy any time you prefer not to use flash. See Chapters 5 and 7 for information about flash photography.

Changing the Drive Mode

Your camera offers three Drive mode settings, which work as follows:

- ✐ **Single:** This setting, which is the default for all of the fully automatic modes except Portrait and Sports, records a single image each time you press the shutter button. In other words, this is normal-photography mode.

- ✐ **Continuous:** Sometimes known as *burst mode,* this setting records a continuous series of images as long as you hold down the shutter button. On the Rebel XTi/400D, you can capture as many as three shots per second. Obviously, this mode is great for capturing fast-paced subjects, which is why it's the default setting for Sports mode. It's also the selected option for Portrait mode, which is a great benefit if your subject is the fidgety type. (See Chapter 7 for more action-photography tips.)

- ✐ **Self-Timer/Remote Control:** Want to put yourself in the picture? Select this mode and then press the shutter button and run into the frame. You have about 10 seconds to get yourself in place and pose before the image is recorded.

  To help you gauge the timing of the image capture, a tiny lamp on the front of the camera, just beneath the Mode dial, begins to blink as soon as you press the shutter button. (The lamp is officially known as the Red-eye Reduction/Self-Timer lamp.) Additionally, the camera emits a series of beeps, assuming that you didn't disable its voice, a setting I cover in Chapter 1. When the beeps speed up and the light becomes a solid beam instead of blinking, the image capture is imminent.

I also often use the self-timer function when I want to avoid any possibility of camera shake. The mere motion of pressing the shutter button can cause slight camera movement, which can blur an image. So I put the camera on a tripod and then activate the self-timer function. This enables "hands-free" — and therefore motion-free — picture-taking.

As another way to enable hands-free shooting, you can purchase the optional, wireless remote-control unit sold by Canon. Choose the Self-Timer/Remote Control mode to use that gadget to trigger the shutter release button.

To select a Drive mode, press the Self-Timer button, found near the top right corner of your camera monitor and shown in the margin here. You then see a screen similar to the one in Figure 2-12. However, you see all three Drive mode options *only* in the advanced exposure modes (P, Tv, Av, M, and A-DEP). In the fully automatic modes, you see only the default Drive mode option plus the Self-Timer/Remote Control option.

Either way, press the right or left cross key to highlight your Drive mode of choice. Then press the Set button to select it.

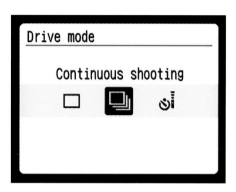

 Your selected Drive mode remains in force until you change it. And the selected setting applies to all exposure modes that offer that particular Drive mode. For example, if you turn on self-timer shooting while the Mode dial is set to Portrait, the setting carries over if you change the dial to the Landscape mode. And if you choose the Continuous mode while working in Manual exposure

Figure 2-12: You can access all three Drive options only in advanced exposure modes.

mode, it applies also to all the other advanced exposure modes *as well as* to Sports and Portrait modes. However, the Drive mode changes to Single if you switch to any other fully automatic exposure mode except Portrait — because those other modes offer only Single and Self-Timer/Remote Control as the Drive mode options.

3

Controlling Picture Quality

*A*lmost every review of the Rebel XTi/400D contains glowing reports about the camera's top-notch picture quality. As you've no doubt discovered for yourself, those claims are true, too: This baby can create large, beautiful images.

Getting the maximum output from your camera, however, depends on choosing the right capture settings. Chief among them, and the topic of this chapter, is the appropriately named Quality setting. Found on Shooting Menu 1, this critical control determines two important aspects of your pictures: *resolution,* or pixel count; and *file format,* which refers to the type of computer file the camera uses to store your picture data.

Resolution and file format work together to determine the quality of your photos, so selecting from the eight Quality settings on your camera is an important decision. Why not just dial in the setting that produces the maximum quality level and be done with it, you ask? Well, that's the right choice for some photographers. But because choosing that maximum setting has some disadvantages, you may find that stepping down a notch or two on the quality scale is a better option every now and then.

To help you figure out which Quality setting meets your needs, this chapter explains exactly how resolution and file format affect your pictures. Just in case you're having quality problems related to other issues, though, the first section of the chapter provides a handy quality-defect diagnosis guide.

Diagnosing Quality Problems

When I use the term *picture quality,* I'm not talking about the composition, exposure, or other traditional characteristics of a photograph. Instead, I'm referring to how finely the image is rendered in the digital sense.

Figure 3-1 illustrates the concept: The first example is a high-quality image, with clear details and smooth color transitions. The other examples show five common digital-image defects.

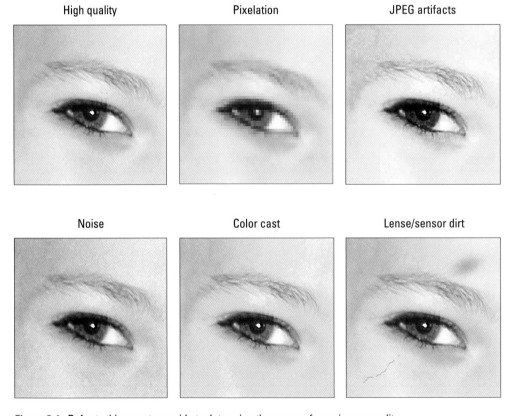

Figure 3-1: Refer to this symptom guide to determine the cause of poor image quality.

Each of these defects is related to a different issue, and only two are affected by the Quality setting on Shooting Menu 1. So if you aren't happy with your image quality, first compare your photos to those in the figure to properly diagnose the problem. Then try these remedies:

- ✓ **Pixelation:** When an image doesn't have enough *pixels* (the colored tiles used to create digital images), details aren't clear, and curved and diagonal lines appear jagged. The fix is to increase image resolution, which you do via the Quality control. See the upcoming section, "Considering Resolution: Large, Medium, or Small?" for details.

- ✓ **JPEG artifacts:** The "parquet tile" texture and random color defects that mar the third image in Figure 3-1 can occur in photos captured in the JPEG *(jay-peg)* file format, which is why these flaws are referred to as *JPEG artifacts.* This defect is also related to the Quality setting; see "Understanding File Type (JPEG or Raw)" to find out more.

- ✓ **Noise:** This defect gives your image a speckled look, as shown in the lower-left example in Figure 3-1. Noise is most often related to a very long exposure time (that is, a very slow shutter speed) or to an exposure control called ISO, which you can explore in Chapter 5. To adjust shutter speed or ISO, you must switch to one of the advanced exposure modes (P, Tv, Av, M, or A-DEP).

- ✓ **Color cast:** If your colors are seriously out of whack, as shown in the lower-middle example in the figure, try adjusting the camera's white balance setting. Chapter 6 covers this control and other color issues. Note, though, that you also must use an advanced exposure mode to adjust white balance.

- ✓ **Lens/sensor dirt:** A dirty lens is the first possible cause of the kind of defects you see in the last example in the figure. If cleaning your lens doesn't solve the problem, dust or dirt may have made its way onto the camera's image sensor. See the sidebar "Maintaining a pristine view," elsewhere in this chapter, for information on safe lens and sensor cleaning.

When diagnosing image problems, you may want to open the photos in your photo software and zoom in for a close-up inspection. Some defects, especially pixelation and JPEG artifacts, have a similar appearance until you see them at a magnified view.

I should also tell you that I used a little digital enhancement to exaggerate the flaws in my example images to make the symptoms easier to see. With the exception of an unwanted color cast or a big blob of lens or sensor dirt, these defects may not even be noticeable unless you print or view your image at a very large size. And the subject matter of your image may camouflage some flaws; most people probably wouldn't detect a little JPEG artifacting in a photograph of a densely wooded forest, for example.

In other words, don't consider Figure 3-1 as an indication that your Canon is suspect in the image quality department. First, *any* digital camera can produce these defects under the right circumstances. Second, by following the guidelines in this chapter and the others mentioned in the preceding list, you can resolve any quality issues that you may encounter.

Decoding the Quality Options

As I mentioned in the introduction to this chapter, the Quality control determines both the image resolution and file format of the pictures you shoot. To access the control, press the Menu button and then display Shooting Menu 1, shown on the left in Figure 3-2. Highlight Quality and press the Set button to display the screen you see on the right in the figure.

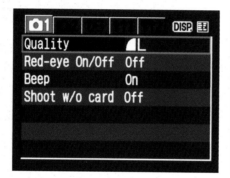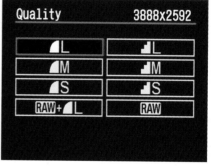

Figure 3-2: You set resolution and file format together via the Quality menu.

If you're new to digital photography, the Quality settings won't make much sense to you until you read the rest of this chapter, which explains format and resolution in detail. But even if you are schooled in those topics, you may need some help deciphering the way that the settings are represented on your camera. As you can see from the right side of Figure 3-2, the options are presented in rather cryptic fashion, so here's your decoder ring:

✓ The first three rows of settings produce files in the JPEG file format.

✓ The little arc-like icons represent the level of JPEG *compression,* which affects picture quality and file size. You get two JPEG options, which carry the labels *Fine* and *Normal.* The Fine setting is represented by the smooth arcs you see in the left column of options. The Normal setting is represented by the stairstepped icon, shown in the right column. Check out the section "JPEG: The imaging (and Web) standard" for details on this issue.

✔ Within the JPEG category, you can choose from three resolution settings, represented by L, M, and S *(large, medium,* and *small).* See the next section for information that will help you select the right resolution.

✔ The Quality settings on the fourth row, which enable you to capture images in the Raw file format, appear only if you set the camera Mode dial to one of the advanced exposure modes (P, Tv, Av, M, or A-DEP). All Raw files are created at the Large resolution setting, giving you the maximum pixel count. One of the two Raw settings also records a JPEG Fine version of the image, also at the maximum resolution. The section "Raw (CR2): The purist's choice" explains the benefits and downsides to using the Raw format.

To select a Quality option, just highlight it and press the Set button. The selected setting then appears next to the Quality item in Shooting Menu 1 and also in the lower-left corner of the Camera Settings display, as shown in Figure 3-3.

Note that changing the Quality setting also changes the number of pictures that you can store on your memory card. That number appears in the lower-right corner of the display, as labeled in Figure 3-3. See the upcoming sidebar "How many pictures fit on my memory card?" for details on this issue.

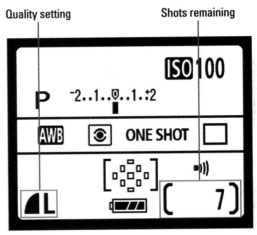

Quality setting | Shots remaining

Figure 3-3: The Quality setting affects the number of pictures remaining.

So, which Quality option is best? The answer depends on several factors, including how you plan to use your pictures and how much time you care to spend in the digital darkroom, processing your images on your computer. The rest of this chapter explains these and other issues related to the Quality settings.

Considering Resolution: Large, Medium, or Small?

To decide upon a Quality setting, the first decision you need to make is how many *pixels* you want your image to contain. Pixels are the little square tiles from which all digital images are made; the word *pixel* is short for *picture element.* You can see some pixels close up in the right image in Figure 3-4, which shows a greatly magnified view of the eye area of the left image.

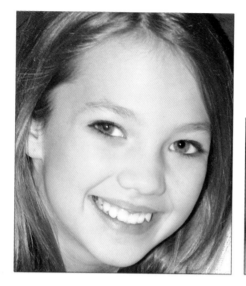
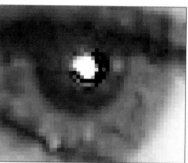

Figure 3-4: Pixels are the building blocks of digital photos.

The number of pixels in an image is referred to as *resolution*. Your Canon offers you three resolution levels, which are assigned the generic labels Large, Medium, and Small and are represented on the list of Quality settings by the initials L, M, and S. Table 3-1 shows you the pixel count that results from each option. (If you select Raw as your Quality setting, images are always captured at the Large resolution value.)

Table 3-1	The Resolution Side of the Quality Settings	
Symbol	*Setting*	*Pixel Count*
L	Large	3888 x 2592 (10 MP)
M	Medium	2816 x 1880 (5.3 MP)
S	Small	1936 x 1288 (2.5 MP)

In the table, the first pair of numbers shown for each setting represents the image *pixel dimensions* — that is, the number of horizontal pixels and the number of vertical pixels. The values in parentheses indicate the total resolution, which you get by multiplying the horizontal and vertical pixel values. This number is usually stated in *megapixels,* abbreviated MP for short. One megapixel equals 1 million pixels. (I rounded off the megapixel values in the table.)

To figure out how many pixels are enough, you need to understand how resolution affects print quality, display size, and file size. The next sections explain these issues, as well as a few other resolution factoids.

Pixels and print quality

When mulling over resolution options, your first consideration is how large you want to print your photos, because pixel count determines the size at which you can produce a high-quality print. If you don't have enough pixels, your prints may exhibit the defects you see in the pixelation example in Figure 3-1, or worse, you may be able to see the individual pixels, as in the right example in Figure 3-4.

Depending on your photo printer, you typically need anywhere from 200 to 300 pixels per linear inch, or *ppi,* of the print. To produce an 8-by-10-inch print at 200 ppi, for example, you need 1600 horizontal pixels and 2000 vertical pixels.

Table 3-2 lists the pixel counts needed to produce traditional print sizes at 200 ppi and 300 ppi. But again, the optimum ppi varies depending on the printer — some printers prefer even more than 300 ppi — so check your manual or ask the photo technician at the lab that makes your prints. (And note that ppi is *not* the same thing as *dpi,* which is a measurement of printer resolution. *Dpi* refers to how many dots of color the printer can lay down per inch; most printers use multiple dots to reproduce one pixel.)

Table 3-2	Pixel Requirements for Traditional Print Sizes	
Print Size	*Pixels for 200 ppi*	*Pixels for 300 ppi*
4 x 6 inches	800 x 1200	1200 x 1800
5 x 7 inches	1000 x 1400	1500 x 2100
8 x 10 inches	1600 x 2000	2400 x 3000
11 x 14 inches	2200 x 2800	3300 x 4200

Even though many photo-editing programs enable you to add pixels to an existing image, doing so isn't a good idea. For reasons I won't bore you with, adding pixels — known as *resampling* — doesn't enable you to successfully enlarge your photo. In fact, resampling typically makes matters worse. The printing discussion at the start of Chapter 9 includes some example images that illustrate this issue.

Pixels and screen display size

Resolution doesn't affect the quality of images viewed on a monitor, television, or other screen device as it does printed photos. What resolution *does* do is determine the *size* at which the image appears.

This issue is one of the most misunderstood aspects of digital photography, so I explain it thoroughly in Chapter 9. For now, just know that you need *way* fewer pixels for onscreen photos than you do for printed photos. For example, Figure 3-5 shows a 450-x-300-pixel image that I attached to an e-mail message.

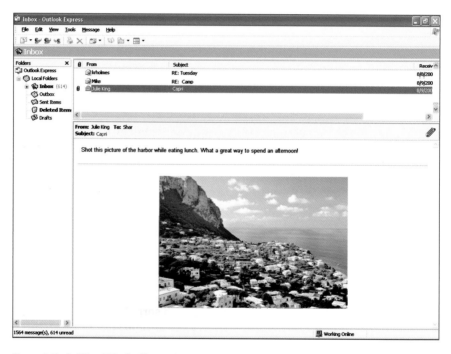

Figure 3-5: A 450-x-300-pixel image is plenty large for sharing via e-mail.

For e-mail images, I usually stick with a maximum horizontal pixel count of 450 and a maximum vertical size of 400 pixels, depending on whether the picture is oriented horizontally, as in the figure, or vertically. If your image is much larger, the recipient can't view the entire picture without scrolling the display.

In short, even if you use one of the Small Quality settings on your Canon, which produce images that contain 1936 x 1288 pixels, you'll have more than enough pixels for most onscreen uses. The only exception might be an image that you want to display via a digital projector that has a very large screen resolution. Again, Chapter 9 details this issue and also shows you how to prepare your pictures for online sharing.

Pixels and file size

Every additional pixel increases the amount of data required to create a digital picture file. So a higher-resolution image has a larger file size than a low-resolution image.

Large files present several problems:

- ✔ You can store fewer images on your memory card, on your computer's hard drive, and on removable storage media such as a CD-ROM.

- ✔ The camera needs more time to process and store the image data on the memory card after you press the shutter button. This extra time can hamper fast-action shooting.

- ✔ When you share photos online, larger files take longer to upload and download.

- ✔ When you edit your photos in your photo software, your computer needs more resources and time to process large files.

To sum up, the tradeoff for a high-resolution image is a large file size. But note that file format, which is the other half of the Quality equation on your Canon, also affects file size. See the section "Understanding File Type (JPEG or Raw)" for more on that topic. The upcoming sidebar "How many pictures fit on my memory card?" provides details on the file-storage issue.

Resolution recommendations

As you can see, resolution is a bit of a sticky wicket. What if you aren't sure how large you want to print your images? What if you want to print your photos *and* share them online?

Personally, I take the "better safe than sorry" route, which leads to the following recommendations about whether to choose Large, Medium, or Small when you select a Quality setting:

- ✔ **Always shoot at a resolution suitable for print.** You then can create a low-resolution copy of the image in your photo editor for use online. Chapter 9 shows you how.

  Again, you *can't* go in the opposite direction, adding pixels to a low-resolution original in your photo editor to create a good, large print. Even with the very best software, adding pixels doesn't improve the print quality of a low-resolution image.

- ✔ **For everyday snapshots, the Medium setting (5.3 MP) is probably sufficient.** I find that 10 MP, which is what you get from the Large setting, to be overkill for most casual snapshots, which means that you're creating huge files for no good reason. So I stick with Medium unless I'm shooting critical images.

✓ **Jump up to Large (10 MP) if you plan to crop your photos or make huge prints.** Always use the maximum resolution if you think you may want to crop your photo and enlarge the remaining image. For example, when I shot the left photo in Figure 3-6, I wanted to fill the frame with the butterfly, but I couldn't do so without getting so close that I risked scaring it away. So I kept my distance and took the picture at the Large setting, which enabled me to crop the photo and still have enough pixels left to produce a great print, as you see in the right image.

✓ **Reduce resolution if shooting speed is paramount.** If you're shooting action and the shot-to-shot capture time is slower than you'd like — that is, the camera takes too long after you take one shot before it lets you take another — dialing down the resolution may help. Lower resolution produces smaller files, and the smaller the file, the less time the camera needs to record the image to your memory card. Also see Chapter 7 for other tips on action photography.

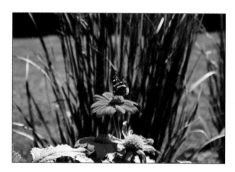 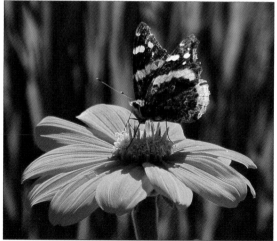

Figure 3-6: Capture images that you plan to crop and enlarge at the highest possible resolution (Large).

Understanding File Type (JPEG or Raw)

In addition to establishing the resolution of your photos, the Quality setting determines the *file format.* The file format simply refers to the type of image file that the camera produces.

Your Canon offers two file formats, JPEG and Raw, with a couple variations of each. The next sections explain the pros and cons of each setting.

Don't confuse *file format* with the Format option on Setup Menu 1. That option erases all data on your memory card; see Chapter 1 for details.

How many pictures fit on my memory card?

That question is one of the first asked by new camera owners — and it's an important one because you don't want to run out of space on your memory card just as the perfect photographic subject presents itself.

As explained in the discussions in this chapter, image resolution (pixel count) and file format (JPEG or Raw) together determine the size of the picture file which, in turn, determines how many photos fit in a given amount of camera memory.

The table below shows you the approximate size of the files, in megabytes (MB) that are generated at each of the possible resolution/format combinations on your Rebel XTi/400D. Following that number, you see approximately how many pictures you can store at the setting on a 1GB (gigabyte) memory card. If you have a 2GB card, double the picture counts; for a 526MB (megabyte) card, expect to fit half the number of pictures.

	Picture Capacity of a 1GB Memory Card		
Symbol	*Quality Setting*	*File Size*	*Image Capacity*
◢ L	Large/Fine	3.8MB	256
◢ L	Large/Normal	2.0MB	496
◢ M	Medium/Fine	2.3MB	430
◢ M	Medium/Normal	1.2MB	818
◢ S	Small/Fine	1.3MB	748
◢ S	Small/Normal	0.7MB	1416
◢ L RAW	Raw+Large/Fine	13.6MB*	52
RAW	Raw	9.8MB	96

*Combined size of the two files produced at this setting.

JPEG: The imaging (and Web) standard

Pronounced *jay-peg,* this format is the default setting on your Canon, as it is for most digital cameras. JPEG is popular for two main reasons:

- ✔ **Web compatibility:** All Web browsers and e-mail programs can display JPEG files, so you can share them online immediately after you shoot them.

- ✔ **Small files:** JPEG files are smaller than those produced by the other common format offered by today's digital cameras, known as Camera Raw, or just Raw. And smaller files means that your pictures consume less room on your camera memory card and in your computer's storage tank.

The downside — you knew there had to be one — is that JPEG creates smaller files by applying *lossy compression.* This process actually throws away some image data. Too much compression leads to the defects you see in the JPEG Artifacts example in Figure 3-1, near the start of this chapter.

On your camera, the amount of compression that is applied depends on whether you choose a Quality setting that carries the label *Fine* or *Normal.* The difference between the two breaks down as follows:

- ✔ **Fine:** At this setting, represented by the symbol you see in the margin here, the compression ratio is 4:1 — that is, the file is four times smaller than it would otherwise be. In plain English, that means that very little compression is applied, so you shouldn't see many compression artifacts, if any.

- ✔ **Normal:** Switch to Norm (for Normal), and the compression ratio rises to 9:1. The chance of seeing some artifacting increases as well. Notice the jaggedy-ness of the Normal icon, shown in the margin here? That's your reminder that all may not be "smooth" sailing when you choose a Normal setting.

For comparison, Figures 3-7 and 3-8 show you the same subject shot at the Large/Fine and Large/Normal settings, along with the respective file sizes that each option produces. (I captured each image at the same resolution so that file type is the only variable.)

When you view the left examples in the comparison figures, you may not see much difference between the images, although the type on the lighter cases looks a little sharper in the Large/Fine example. For most printed photos, in fact, compression defects aren't terribly distinct when the print size is small. But when you enlarge your photos, as I did for the right examples in the figures, the exact nature of the quality loss that occurs with JPEG compression become clearer.

Large/Fine, 3.8MB

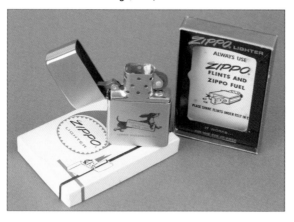 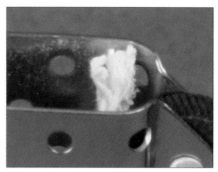

Figure 3-7: The Fine setting produces very good image quality and reasonable file sizes.

Large/Normal, 2MB

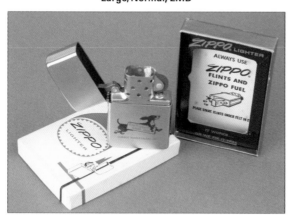 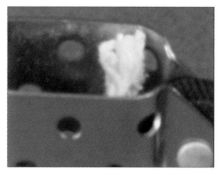

Figure 3-8: Enlarging an image captured at the Normal setting reveals some quality loss.

Know, too, that compression artifacts usually are significantly easier to spot when you view digital images on a computer monitor. (The print process itself softens some of the compression defects.) Artifacting is also usually more visible in areas of flat color than it is in detailed or textured areas.

For my money, the file size benefit you gain when going from Fine to Normal isn't worth the risk of artifacts, especially with the price of camera memory cards getting lower every day. And of all the defects that you can correct in a photo editor, artifacting is perhaps the hardest to accomplish. So if I shoot in the JPEG format, I stick with Fine.

I suggest that you do your own test shots, however, carefully inspect the results in your photo editor, and make your own judgment about what level of artifacting you can accept. Again, artifacting is often much easier to spot when you view images onscreen than I can reproduce here in print.

If you don't want *any* risk of artifacting, bypass JPEG altogether and change the file type to Raw, explained next.

Raw (CR2): The purist's choice

The other picture-file type that you can create on your Canon is called *Camera Raw,* or just *Raw* (as in uncooked) for short.

Each manufacturer has its own flavor of Raw files; Canon's are called CR2 files. If you use a Windows computer, you see that three-letter designation at the end of your picture filenames.

Raw is popular with advanced, very demanding photographers, for two reasons:

- **Greater creative control:** With JPEG, internal camera software tweaks your images, making adjustments to color, exposure, and sharpness as needed to produce the results that Canon believes its customers prefer. With Raw, the camera simply records the original, unprocessed image data. The photographer then copies the image file to the computer and uses special software known as a *raw converter* to produce the actual image, making decisions about color, exposure, and so on at that point. The upshot is that "shooting Raw" enables you, not the camera, to have the final say on the visual characteristics of your image.

- **Best picture quality:** Because Raw doesn't apply the destructive compression associated with JPEG, you don't run the risk of the artifacting that can occur with JPEG.

But of course, as with most things in life, Raw isn't without its disadvantages. To wit:

- **You can't do anything with your pictures until you process them with a Raw converter.** You can't share them online, print them, put them in a document — nada. So when you shoot Raw, you add to the time you must spend in front of the computer instead of behind the camera lens. Chapter 8 shows you how to process your Raw files using the converter found in the Canon software that was included in your camera box.

Note, too, that technology that will enable retail printers to print Raw files is on the horizon, so you may not have to process the images to get prints made in the near future. Of course, that means that the printer would do the processing, making all those color, exposure, and other judgments for you, but only for the prints you order. You could still process the images for your own use on your computer.

✔ **Raw files are larger than JPEGs.** The type of file compression that Raw applies doesn't degrade image quality, but the tradeoff is larger files. In addition, Raw files are always captured at the maximum resolution available on your camera, even if you don't really need all those pixels. For both reasons, Raw files are significantly larger than JPEGs, so they take up more room on your memory card and on your computer's hard drive or other picture-storage device.

Are the disadvantages worth the gain? Only you can decide. But before you make up your mind, compare the Large/Fine JPEG image in Figure 3-7 with its Raw counterpart, shown in Figure 3-9. You may be able to detect some subtle quality differences in the enlarged view, but most people would be hard pressed to distinguish between the two otherwise. And JPEG certainly wins out in terms of convenience, time savings, and smaller file size. (Note that during the Raw conversion process, I tried to use settings that kept the Raw image as close as possible to its JPEG cousin in all aspects but quality. But any variations in exposure, color, and contrast are a result of the conversion process, not of the format per se.)

Raw, 9.8MB

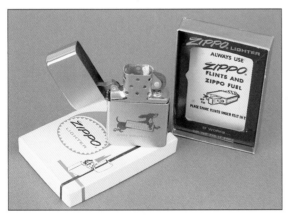

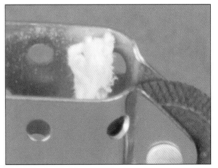

Figure 3-9: The difference between Raw and Large/Fine images typically is noticeable only when images are greatly enlarged.

That said, I *do* shoot in the Raw format when I'm dealing with tricky lighting because doing so gives you more control over the final image exposure. For example, if you use a capable Raw converter, you can specify how bright you want the brightest areas of your photo to appear and how dark you prefer your deepest shadows. With JPEG, the camera makes those decisions, which can potentially limit your flexibility if you try to adjust exposure in your photo editor later.

I also go Raw if I know that I'm going to want huge prints of a subject. But keep in mind: I'm a photography geek, I have all the requisite software, and I don't really have much else to do with my time than process scads of Raw images. Oh, and I'm a bit of a perfectionist, too. (Although I'm more bothered by imperfections than I am motivated to remove them. A lazy perfectionist, if you will.)

If you do decide to try Raw shooting, you can select from the following two Quality options:

- ✔ **RAW:** This setting produces a single Raw file at the maximum resolution (10 megapixels).

- ✔ **RAW+Large/Fine:** This setting produces two files: the standard Raw file plus a JPEG file captured at the Large/Fine setting. At first glance, this option sounds great: You can share the JPEG online or get prints made and then process your Raw files when you have time.

The problem is that, like the Raw file, the JPEG image is captured at the maximum pixel count — which is *too* large for onscreen viewing. That means that you have to edit the JPEG file anyway to trim down the pixel count before online sharing, although you can produce great prints right away. In addition, creating two files for every image eats up substantially more memory card space. I leave it up to you to decide whether the pluses are worth the minuses.

My take: Choose Fine or Raw

At this point, you may be finding all this technical goop a bit much — I recognize that panicked look in your eyes — so allow me to simplify things for you. Until you have time or energy to completely digest all the ramifications of JPEG versus Raw, here's a quick summary of my thoughts on the matter:

- ✔ If you require the absolute best image quality and have the time and interest to do the Raw conversion process, shoot Raw. See Chapter 8 for more information the conversion process.

- ✔ If great photo quality is good enough for you, you don't have wads of spare time, or you aren't that comfortable with the computer, stick with one of the Fine settings (Large/Fine, Medium/Fine, or Small/Fine).

Maintaining a pristine view

Often lost in discussions of digital photo defects — compression artifacts, pixelation, and the like — is the impact of plain-old dust and dirt on picture quality. But no matter what camera settings you use, you aren't going to achieve great picture quality with a dirty lens. So make it a practice to clean your lens on a regular basis, using one of the specialized cloths and cleaning solutions made expressly for that purpose.

If you continue to notice random blobs or hair-like defects in your images (refer to the last example in Figure 3-1), you probably have a dirty *image sensor.* That's the part of your camera that does the actual image capture — the digital equivalent of a film negative, if you will.

Especially if you frequently change lenses in a dirty environment, regular sensor cleaning

may be necessary. You can do this job yourself, but . . . I don't recommend it. Image sensors are pretty delicate beings, and you can easily damage it or other parts of your camera if you aren't careful. Instead, find a local camera store that offers this service. In my area (central Indiana), sensor cleaning costs about $30 to $50. If you bought your camera at a traditional camera store, the store may even provide free sensor cleaning as a way to keep your business.

One more cleaning tip: Never — and I mean *never* — try to clean any part of your camera using a can of compressed air. Doing so can not only damage the interior of your camera, blowing dust or dirt into areas where it can't be removed, but also crack the external monitor.

▸ Stay away from JPEG Normal. The tradeoff for smaller files isn't, in my opinion, worth the risk of compression artifacts. As with my recommendations on resolution, this fits the "better safe than sorry" formula: You never know when you may capture a spectacular, enlargement-worthy subject, and it would be a shame to have the photo spoiled by compression defects.

▸ Finally, remember that the format and resolution together determine the ultimate picture quality. So be sure that you select the Quality setting that offers both the appropriate number of pixels and format for how you plan to use your image. If you capture an image at the Small/Normal setting, for example, and then print the photo at a large size, the combination of a lower pixel count and a higher level of JPEG compression may produce disappointing picture quality.

Reviewing Your Photos

*W*ithout question, my favorite thing about digital photography is being able to view my pictures on the camera monitor the instant after I shoot them. No more guessing whether I captured the image I wanted or need to try again; no more wasting money on developing and printing pictures that stink. In fact, this feature alone was reason enough for me to turn my back forever on my closetful of film photography hardware and all the unexposed film remaining from my predigital days.

But simply seeing your pictures is just the start of the things you can do when you switch your camera to playback mode. You also can review many of the camera settings you used to take the picture, display graphics that alert you to serious exposure problems, delete crummy photos, and add file markers that protect the picture from accidental erasure. This chapter tells you how to use all these playback features and more.

After you explore these playback functions, be sure to also visit Chapter 9, which covers some additional ways to view your images, including how to create in-camera slide shows and display your photos on a television screen.

Adjusting the Instant Review Time

After you take a picture, it automatically appears briefly on the camera monitor. By default, the instant-review period lasts just two seconds. But you can customize this behavior via the Review Time option on the Playback menu, as shown in Figure 4-1.

Your choices are as follows:

✓ Select one of three specific review periods: 2, 4, or 8 seconds.

✓ Select Off to disable the automatic instant review altogether.

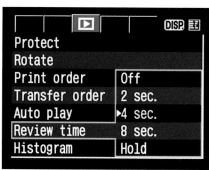

Figure 4-1: You can extend or disable automatic picture review.

Why would you do so? Because you can't take any new pictures until the review period ends, which can hamper your ability to capture action. (You can still view your pictures by pressing the Playback button. See the next section for details.)

✓ Select Hold to display the current image indefinitely — or, at least until the camera automatically shuts itself off to save power or you put your eye up to the viewfinder, which automatically turns off the monitor. (See the Chapter 1 section about Setup Menu 1 to find out about the auto-shutdown and auto-display-off features.)

Viewing Images in Playback Mode

To switch your camera to playback mode and view the images currently on your memory card, take these steps:

1. **Press the Playback button, labeled in Figure 4-2 and shown in the margin here.**

   The monitor displays the last picture you took. You may see just the image itself or the image plus some shooting data.

   To find out how to interpret the picture data and specify what data you want to see, see the upcoming section "Viewing Picture Data." If you're curious now, though, or if the picture data is hampering your ability to see the picture itself, press the DISP button to cycle through the three data-display formats. (Figure 4-2 shows the image in the one mode that does not include any shooting data.)

Playback button

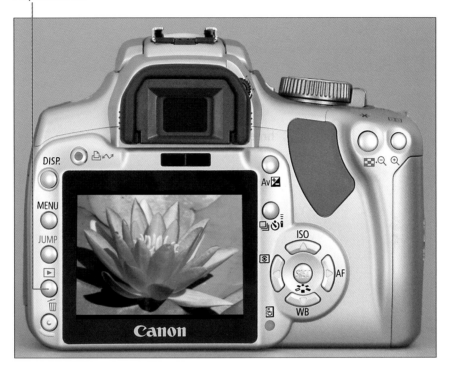

Figure 4-2: Press the Playback button to inspect your photos.

2. **Press the right or left cross key to scroll through your pictures.**

   • Press the right cross key to view images starting with the oldest one on the card.

   • Press the left cross key to view images in reverse order, starting with the most current picture.

   Just keep pressing either key to browse through all of your images. Or, if you prefer, you also can rotate the Main dial to scroll through your photos.

3. **To return to picture-taking mode, press the Playback button or press the shutter button halfway.**

   The camera exits playback mode, and the Camera Settings display appears on the monitor. Chapter 1 introduces you to that display.

These steps assume that the camera is currently set to display a single photo at a time, as shown in Figure 4-2. You can also display multiple images at a time; the next section tells all.

Jumping through images

If your memory card contains scads of images, here's a trick you'll love: By using the Jump button, you can leapfrog through them instead of pressing the right or left cross key a bazillion times to get to the picture you want to see. You also can search for the last image shot on a specific date.

This feature works like so:

1. **Press the Playback button to put the camera into play-back mode.**

2. **Press the Jump button.**

   As soon as you press the button, the *jump bar* appears at the bottom of the moni-tor, as shown in Figure 4-3.

3. **Select a Jump mode by pressing the up or down cross key.**

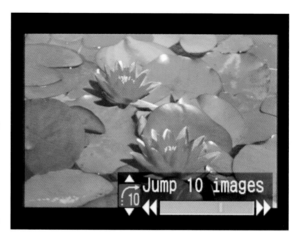

Figure 4-3: The current Jump mode appears on the jump bar.

   The current Jump mode appears on the jump bar. You have three Jump mode options:

   • *Jump 10 Images:* Select this option to advance 10 images at a time.

   • *Jump 100 Images:* Select this option to advance 100 images at a time.

   • *Jump Shot Date:* This option enables you to jump to the last image that you shot on the same day as the currently displayed image. For example, if you shot the current photo on May 1, you can jump to the last photo you shot on that day.

4. **Press the right or left cross key to browse images using the selected Jump mode.**

   How many images you advance with each press of a cross key depends upon the Jump mode you selected. Again, you can also rotate the Main dial to browse images instead of pressing the cross keys if you like that method better.

5. **To exit Jump mode, press the Jump button again.**

You can use this method of browsing your images only in regular, single-image playback mode. The Jump button performs a different function in *index display* mode, in which you view nine image thumbnails at a time. The next section explains this viewing mode.

Viewing multiple images at a time

If you want to quickly review and compare several photos, you can set the camera to *index display* and view thumbnails of nine images at a time, as shown in Figure 4-4. Just press the AE Lock button, found on the upper-right corner of the camera back and shown in the margin here.

Note the little blue checkerboard and magnifying glass icons next to the button — they're reminders of the function the button serves in playback mode. The checkerboard indicates the index function, and the minus sign in the magnifying glass tells you that pressing the button reduces the size of the image display. (Remember, the black labels near these buttons indicate a function related to picture-taking.)

Remember these factoids about navigating and viewing your photo collection in index display mode:

✓ **The green border indicates the currently selected image.** For example, in Figure 4-4, the top-right photo is selected.

✓ **Press the AF Point Selection button to view the selected image at full size.** This button lives right next door to the AE Lock button. It, too, has a blue magnifying glass icon, this time with a plus sign in the center to indicate that pressing the button enlarges the view. To return to index display mode, press the AE Lock button again.

✓ **Use the cross keys or Main dial to select a different image.** Press the up cross key to shift the selection box up, the right cross key to move it right, and so on.

Selected image

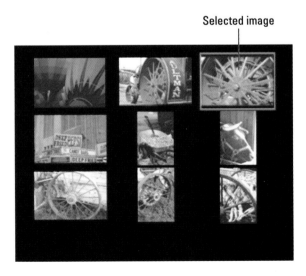

Figure 4-4: You can view nine thumbnails at once.

✔ **Press the Jump button to switch to "fast-forward" mode.** When you press the button, all nine thumbnails become selected. Now you can press the right cross key or rotate the Main dial to the right to advance to the next nine images. Press the left cross key or rotate the Main dial to the left to view the previous nine images. To exit this mode, press Jump again.

Rotating vertical pictures

When you take a picture, the camera can record the image *orientation* — that is, whether you held the camera normally, creating a horizontally oriented image, or turned the camera on its side to shoot a vertically oriented photo. This bit of data is simply added into the picture file. Then when you view the picture, either during the instant-review period or after you set the camera to playback mode, the camera reads the data and automatically rotates the image so that it appears in the upright position in the monitor, as shown on the left in Figure 4-5. The image is also rotated automatically when you view it in the photo software that shipped with your camera.

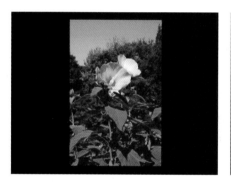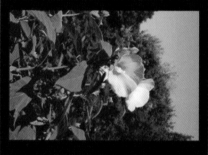

Figure 4-5: You can display vertically oriented pictures in their upright position (left) or sideways (right).

Official photo lingo uses the term *portrait orientation* to refer to vertically oriented pictures and *landscape orientation* to refer to horizontally oriented pictures.

By default, automatic picture rotation is enabled for you. If for some reason you want to turn it off, you can do so through the Auto Rotate option on Setup Menu 1, shown in Figure 4-6. You also can specify that you want the picture to be rotated just on your computer monitor by choosing the second of the two On settings (the one that doesn't sport the little camera icon).

If you do turn off automatic rotation, you can rotate one or more images on your memory card by taking these steps:

1. **Display the Playback menu and highlight Rotate, as shown in Figure 4-7.**

2. **Press the Set button.**

   An image appears on the monitor.

3. **Navigate to the photo that you want to rotate.**

   Just press the right and left cross keys or rotate the Main dial to do so.

4. **Press Set to rotate the image 90 degrees clockwise.**

   Each time you press Set, you rotate the image another 90 degrees.

5. **Repeat Steps 3 and 4 to rotate additional photos.**

6. **Press Menu to exit Rotate mode and return to the Playback menu.**

You can also rotate images in index display mode; just use the cross keys or Main dial to select and rotate each photo as desired. Remember, the green box indicates the selected photo.

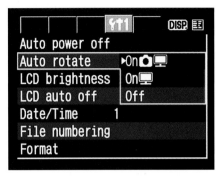

Figure 4-6: Go to Setup Menu 1 to disable or adjust automatic image rotation.

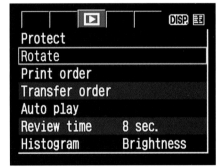

Figure 4-7: You also can rotate individual images from the Playback menu.

Zooming in for a closer view

By pressing the AF Point Selection button, posing here in the margin, you can more closely inspect a portion of the onscreen image. This feature comes in especially handy for checking small details, such as whether anyone's eyes are closed in a group portrait, for example, and for determining whether the subject of your picture is sharply focused.

Here's the scoop on this feature:

- **Zoom in.** You can enlarge an image display to a maximum of 10 times its original size. Just keep pressing the AF Point Selection button until you reach the magnification you want.

✔ **View another part of the picture.** Whenever the image is magnified, a little thumbnail representing the entire image appears briefly in the lower-right corner of the monitor, as shown in Figure 4-8. The white box indicates the portion of the image that's currently consuming the rest of the monitor space.

Use the cross keys to scroll the display to view a different portion of the image. Press the up cross key to scroll up, the left cross key to scroll left, and so on.

✔ **View more images at the same magnification.** Here's an especially neat trick: While the display is zoomed, you can rotate the Main dial to display the same area of the next photo at the same magnification. So, for example, if you shot that group portrait several times, you can easily check each one for shut-eye problems.

You also even maintain the same magnification while jumping ahead 10 images at a time. To do so, press the Jump button and then press the right or left cross key or rotate the Main dial. Press Jump again to go back to regular, one-by-one browsing mode.

✔ **View magnified images in index display mode.** You can get close-up views of the currently selected thumbnail (the one surrounded by the green border) by pressing the AF Point Selection button. But you must press the button twice: Press once to view the selected image at full frame view; then press again to switch to zoom-in mode.

✔ **Zoom out.** To zoom out to a reduced magnification, press the AE Lock button. Continue holding the button down until you reach the magnification you want.

Magnified image area

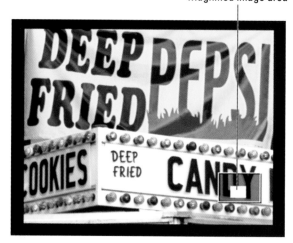

Figure 4-8: Press the cross keys to scroll the display of the magnified image.

✔ **Return to full-frame view.** When you're ready to return to the normal magnification level, you don't need to keep pressing the AE Lock button until you're all the way zoomed out. Instead, just press the Playback button, which quickly returns you to the standard view.

For one more magnification trick, available only when you shoot in the advanced exposure modes, see Chapter 11. (*Hint:* By using a Custom Function setting, you can magnify images even during the instant review period.)

Viewing Picture Data

In playback mode, you can choose from three information-display styles, which determine whether any shooting data appears along with the image in the monitor. Your options are as follows:

✔ **Image Only:** You see just the image in the monitor, without shooting data.

✔ **Basic Information:** In this mode, the picture folder number and the last four digits of the filename appear in the upper-right corner of the frame, as shown in Figure 4-9. In the lower-left corner, you see the shutter speed and aperture setting (f-stop) used to record the image, along with the current image number and the total number of images on the card.

✔ **Shooting Information:** This mode presents you with a more complete report of the camera settings that were in force when you took the picture. The next two sections help you sort out all the bits and pieces of onscreen data.

Frame number/total images

Shutter speed and f-stop   Folder and file number

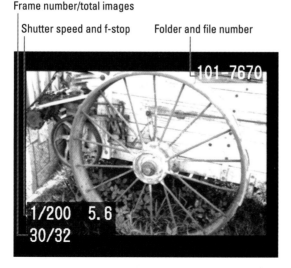

Figure 4-9: In Basic Information mode, you see just a few pieces of shooting data.

To cycle through the display styles, just press the DISP button. In single-image playback mode, you can access all three display styles. When you switch to index mode (viewing nine thumbnails at a time) or magnify an image, you can choose from just the first two display modes (no information or basic information).

You can view even more shooting data, officially referred to as *metadata,* when you open your images in your photo software. Chapter 8 shows you how.

Decoding Shooting Information data

In the Shooting Information display mode, the camera presents a thumbnail of your image along with scads of shooting data, as shown in Figure 4-10. (*Remember:* Just press the DISP button to cycle from this mode to view only basic information or no information with your image.)

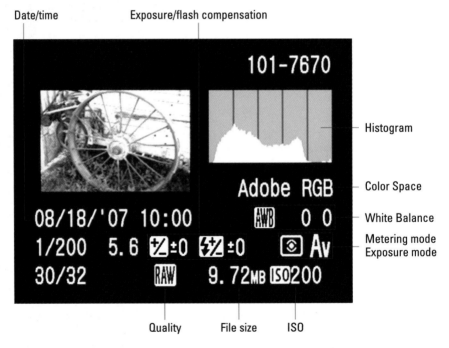

Date/time Exposure/flash compensation

101-7670

Histogram

Adobe RGB — Color Space

08/18/'07 10:00 AWB 0 0 — White Balance

1/200 5.6 ±0 ±0 Av — Metering mode / Exposure mode

30/32 RAW 9.72MB ISO200

Quality File size ISO

Figure 4-10: You can view more data in Shooting Information playback mode.

Here's a brief description of what you can glean from the different areas of the screen:

- **Basic Information data:** The file number, folder number, aperture, shutter speed, frame number, and total number of images appear in the same locations as in Basic Information mode.

✔ **Histogram:** That little graph to the right of the image thumbnail is the *histogram,* which is an exposure evaluation tool. Check out the next sections for details on interpreting the histogram and changing the histogram style.

✔ **Blinking highlights:** Are any areas of the image thumbnail blinking? The blinking spots indicate areas that are completely white — known in the photography business as *blown highlights*. Depending on where in the image those areas occur, you may or may not have an exposure problem. For example, if someone's face contains the blinking spots, that someone is overexposed, and you should take steps to correct the problem. But if the blinking occurs in, say, a bright window behind the subject, and the subject itself looks fine, you may choose to just ignore the alert.

✔ **Date and Time:** Just below the image thumbnail, you see the date and time that you took the picture. Of course, the accuracy of this data depends on whether you set the camera's date and time values correctly, which you do via Setup Menu 1. Chapter 1 has details.

✔ **Exposure and Flash Compensation values:** To the right of the aperture readout, you see the exposure compensation and flash compensation settings that were used to take the picture. Chapter 5 explains these features, which are available only in the advanced exposure modes. (The flash compensation data does not appear if you didn't use flash when taking the picture, however.)

✔ **Metering mode:** This icon represents the exposure metering mode, another advanced exposure control that you can explore in Chapter 5.

✔ **Exposure mode:** Just to the right of the metering mode icon, you see a symbol or letter that indicates which of the camera's exposure modes you used (Full Auto, Portrait, Tv, and so on). Chapter 2 explains the fully automatic modes; Chapter 5 introduces you to the advanced modes.

✔ **White Balance setting:** Just above the metering mode and exposure mode data, you see an icon representing the White Balance setting and any custom adjustment you made to that setting. Chapter 6 has details on white balance.

✔ **Color Space:** Your camera can capture images in two *color spaces,* sRGB and Adobe RGB. A *color space* is just a definition of the spectrum of colors that an image can contain. The color space that you used for the current picture appears just beneath the histogram in the display. You can change color spaces only in advanced exposure modes; Chapter 6 has details about how and why to do so.

✔ **Quality and File Size:** These two bits of information appear on the bottom row of the display. For details on the Quality setting and how it affects file size and picture quality, see Chapter 3.

✔ **ISO:** This setting controls your camera's sensitivity to light. You can adjust ISO only in the advanced exposure modes; Chapter 5 has the scoop.

Although not shown in Figure 4-10, the following two pieces of data may also show up:

- ✔ **Image Protect:** Using a feature described later in this chapter, you can "lock" an image to prevent it from being accidentally deleted. If you do so, a little key icon appears to the left of the Quality icon, on the bottom row of the display.

- ✔ **B/W:** If you capture an image using the Monochrome Picture Style, the letters B/W appear next to the metering mode icon. You can capture monochrome images only in the advanced exposure modes; Chapter 6 has details.

Interpreting the histogram

One of the most difficult photo problems to correct in a photo-editing program is known as *blown highlights* in some circles and *clipped highlights* in others. In plain English, both terms mean that *highlights* — the brightest areas of the image — are so overexposed that areas that should include a variety of light shades are instead totally white. For example, in a cloud image, pixels that should be light to very light gray become white due to overexposure, resulting in a loss of detail in those clouds.

In Shooting Information display mode, areas that fall into this category blink in the image thumbnail. This warning is a great feature because simply viewing the image isn't always a reliable way to gauge exposure; the relative brightness of the monitor and the ambient light in which you view it affect the appearance of the image onscreen. Again, though, blinking highlights doesn't necessarily indicate that your exposure is off. If you have a dark subject against a very bright background, for example, you may not be able to properly expose the subject without creating at least some blown highlights in the background.

For a detailed analysis of the image exposure, check the *histogram,* the graph that appears to the right of the image thumbnail in Shooting Info display mode. By default, the histogram is set to Brightness Display mode and appears similar to what you see in Figure 4-11. In this mode, the histogram indicates the distributions of shadows, highlights, and midtones (areas of medium brightness) in your image. Photographers use the term *tonal range* to describe this aspect of their pictures.

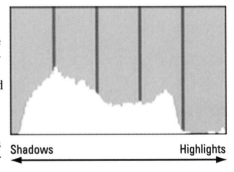

Shadows   Highlights

Figure 4-11: The standard histogram indicates the tonal range of your image.

The horizontal axis of the graph represents the possible picture brightness values, from the darkest shadows on the left to the brightest highlights on the right. And the vertical axis shows you how many pixels fall at a particular brightness value. A spike indicates a heavy concentration of pixels.

For example, in Figure 4-11, which shows the histogram for the wagon wheel image shown in Figure 4-10, the histogram shows that the picture doesn't contain a lot of highlight pixels or any pixels at the darkest end of the spectrum. To put it in photography terms, the image is a little lacking in *contrast* — most of the image is relatively similar in brightness, without strong highlights or shadows.

As with the highlight alerts, the Brightness Display mode of the histogram is provided to give you a way to gauge exposure that's a little more reliable than simply eyeballing the image on the monitor. Remember, if you adjust the brightness of the monitor or the ambient light affects the display brightness, you may not get the real story on exposure.

For information about the other histogram mode, check out the next section. For help with adjusting exposure, see Chapter 5.

Viewing the RGB histogram

By visiting the Playback menu and selecting the Histogram option, as shown in Figure 4-12, you can change the histogram from its default mode, Brightness Display, to RGB Display. In this mode, the histogram appears similar to the one you see in Figure 4-13.

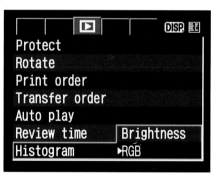

Figure 4-12: Change the histogram mode via the Playback menu.

To make sense of the RGB histogram, you first need to know that digital images are called *RGB images* because they are created out of three primary colors of light: red, green, and blue. The RGB histogram shows you the brightness values for each of those primary colors.

What's the point? Well, by checking the brightness levels of the individual color components, sometimes referred to as color *channels,* you can assess the picture's color saturation levels. If most of the image pixels are clustered toward the right end of the histogram, colors may be oversaturated, which destroys detail. On the flip side, a heavy concentration of pixels at the left end of the histogram indicates an image that may be undersaturated.

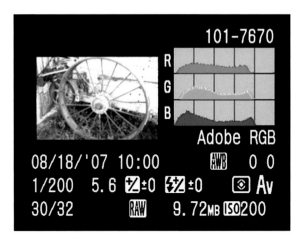

Figure 4-13: The RGB histogram shows the red, green, and blue brightness values.

A savvy RGB histogram reader can also spot color balance issues by looking at the pixel values. But frankly, color-balance problems are fairly easy to notice just by looking at the image itself. And understanding how to translate the histogram data for this purpose requires more knowledge about RGB color theory than I have room to present in this book.

In fact, unless you are really interested in the subject, I suggest that you leave the histogram in the Brightness Display mode and leave RGB Display mode for a day when you've mastered all the other controls on your camera. (I do find, however, that reviewing my pictures in RGB mode seems to impress the heck out of nosy airplane seatmates, especially those of the engineer and mathematician variety.)

For more information about manipulating color, see Chapter 6.

Deleting Photos

When you spot a clunker image during your picture review, you can erase it from your memory card as follows:

1. **Select the image that you want to delete.**

   If you are viewing images in single-frame mode, just display the image on the monitor. In index display mode, use the cross keys to move the green selection box over the image thumbnail.

2. **Press the Erase button.**

   It's the one with the little trash can icon, as shown in the margin here.

Three options — Cancel, Erase, and All — appear at the bottom of the screen, as shown in Figure 4-14.

3. **Highlight Erase and then press the Set button.**

Your picture is zapped into digital oblivion.

To erase all pictures on the memory card, just select All instead of Erase in Step 3. After you press Set, you see a confirmation screen asking whether you really want to delete all your pictures. Select OK and press Set to go ahead and dump the photos. (Note, though, that pictures that you have protected, a step discussed in the next section, are left intact.)

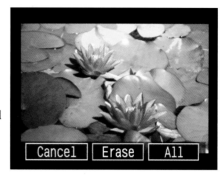

Figure 4-14: You can erase the current image or all images.

You can use the Protect feature to prevent a group of pictures from being deleted when you choose the Erase All option. First, protect the pictures that you want to keep. Then press the Erase button and select the All option to get rid of all the unprotected photos. If you are getting rid of lots of images, this technique is usually faster than deleting them one by one.

If you accidentally erase a picture, don't panic — you *may* be able to restore it by using data-restoration software. One memory-card manufacturer, SanDisk, even provides this type of software free on some of its memory cards. You also can buy stand-alone programs such as MediaRecover ($30, www.mediarecover.com) or Lexar Image Rescue (also $30, www.lexar.com). But in order to have a chance at recovering deleted data, you must not take any more pictures or perform any other operations on your camera while the current memory card is in it. If you do, you may overwrite the erased picture data for good and eliminate the possibility of recovering the image.

Protecting Photos

You can protect pictures from accidental erasure by giving them *protected status*. After you take this step, the camera doesn't allow you to delete a picture.

Formatting your memory card, however, *does* erase even protected pictures. See the sidebar elsewhere in this chapter for more about formatting.

The picture protection feature comes in especially handy if you share a camera with other people. You can protect pictures so that those other people know that they shouldn't delete your super-great images to make

---

Deleting versus formatting: What's the diff?

In Chapter 1, I introduce you to the Format command, which lives on Setup Menu 1 and erases everything on your memory card. What's the difference between erasing photos by formatting and by using the Erase button and then selecting the All option?

Well, in terms of pictures taken with your Canon, none. But if you happen to have stored other data on the card, such as, say, a music file or a picture taken on another type of camera, you need to format the card to erase everything on it. You can't view those files on the monitor, so you can't use the Erase button to get rid of them.

One final — and important — note: Although using the Protect feature (explained elsewhere in this chapter) prevents the Erase function from erasing a picture, formatting erases all pictures, protected or not. Formatting also ensures that the card is properly prepared to store any new images you may take.

---

room on the memory card for their stupid, badly photographed ones. (This step isn't foolproof, though, because anyone can remove the protected status from an image.)

Perhaps more importantly, when you protect a picture, it shows up as a "read only" file when you transfer it to a Windows-based computer. Files that have that read-only status can't be altered. Again, anyone with some computer savvy can remove the status in Windows, but this feature can keep casual users from messing around with your images after you've downloaded them to your system. Of course, *you* have to know how to remove the read-only status yourself if you plan on editing your photo in your photo software. (*Hint:* In Canon ZoomBrowser EX, the free Windows-based software that ships with your camera, you can do this by choosing File➪Protect. That command toggles image protection on and off.)

Anyway, protecting a picture is easy. Just take these steps:

1. **Display the Playback menu and highlight Protect, as shown in Figure 4-15.**

2. **Press Set.**

   An image appears on the monitor, along with a little key icon in the upper-left corner, as shown on the right in Figure 4-15.

3. **Navigate to the picture that you want to protect.**

   Just press the right or left cross key or rotate the Main dial to scroll through your pictures.

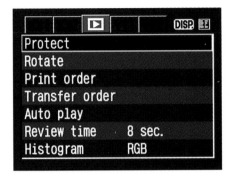 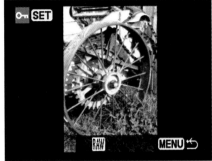

Figure 4-15: Apply Protect status to prevent accidental erasure of important images.

4. Press Set to lock the picture.

Now a second key icon appears with the data at the bottom of the screen, as shown in Figure 4-16.

5. To lock more pictures, repeat Steps 3 and 4.

6. Press the Menu button to exit the protection process.

To remove picture protection, follow these same steps. When you display the locked picture, just press Set to turn the protection off.

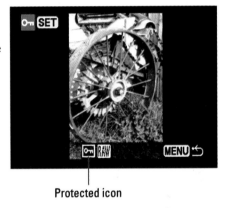

Protected icon

Figure 4-16: The key icon indicates that the picture is protected.

Part II
Taking Creative Control

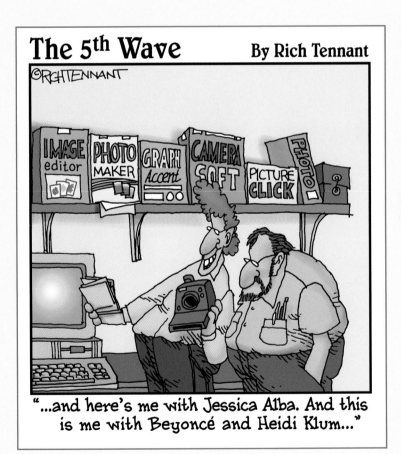

The 5th Wave   By Rich Tennant

"...and here's me with Jessica Alba. And this is me with Beyoncé and Heidi Klum..."

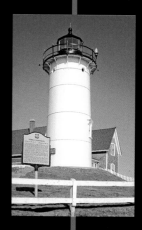

In this part . . .

As nice as it is to be able to set your camera to automatic mode and let it handle most of the photographic décisions, I encourage you to also explore the advanced exposure modes (P, Tv, Av, M, and A-DEP). In these modes, you can make your own decisions about the exposure, focus, and color characteristics of your photo, which is key to capturing an image as you see it in your mind's eye. And don't think that you have to be a genius or spend years to be successful — adding just a few simple techniques to your photographic repertoire can make a huge difference in how happy you are with the pictures you take.

The first two chapters in this part explain everything you need to know to do just that, providing some necessary photography fundamentals and details about using the advanced exposure modes. Following that, Chapter 7 helps you draw together all the information presented earlier in the book, summarizing the best camera settings and other tactics to use when capturing portraits, action shots, landscapes, and close-up shots.

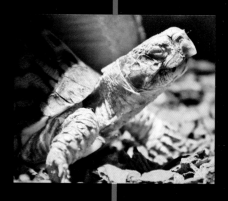

5

Getting Creative with Exposure and Lighting

*B*y using the fully automatic modes covered in Chapter 2, you can take great pictures with your Rebel XTi/400D. But to really exploit your camera's capabilities — and, more important, to exploit *your* creative capabilities — you need to explore your camera's five advanced exposure modes, represented on the Mode dial by the letters P, Tv, Av, M, and A-DEP.

This chapter explains everything you need to know to start taking advantage of these five modes. First, you get an introduction to the critical exposure controls known as *aperture, shutter speed,* and *ISO.* Adjusting these settings enables you to not only fine-tune image exposure but also affect other aspects of your image, such as *depth of field* (the zone of sharp focus) and motion blur. In addition, this chapter explains other advanced exposure features, such as exposure compensation and metering modes, and discusses the flash options available to you in the advanced exposure modes.

If you're worried that this stuff is too complicated for you, by the way, don't be. Even in these advanced exposure modes, the camera provides you with enough feedback that you're never truly flying without a net. Between the in-camera support and the information in this chapter, you can easily master aperture, shutter speed, and all the other exposure features — an important step in making the shift from picture-taker to photographer.

Kicking Your Camera into Advanced Gear

The first step to taking the exposure reins is to set your camera's Mode dial to one of the five shooting modes highlighted in Figure 5-1: P, Tv, Av, M, or A-DEP. You also need to shoot in one of these modes to use certain other camera features, such as manual white balancing, a color feature that you can explore in Chapter 6.

Each of the five modes offers a different level of control over two critical exposure settings, *aperture* and *shutter speed.* Later in this chapter, I explain these controls fully, but here's a quick introduction:

- ✔ **P (programmed auto):** In this mode, the camera selects both the aperture and shutter speed for you. But you can choose from different combinations of the two, which gives you creative flexibility not possible in the fully automatic modes discussed in Chapter 2.

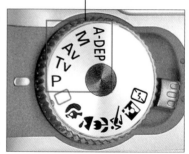

Advanced exposure modes

Figure 5-1: You can control exposure and other picture properties only in P, Tv, Av, M, and A-DEP modes.

- ✔ **Tv (shutter-priority autoexposure):** In this mode, you select a shutter speed, and the camera chooses the aperture setting that produces a good exposure. Why *Tv?* Well, shutter speed controls exposure time; *Tv* stands for *time value.*

- ✔ **Av (aperture-priority autoexposure):** The opposite of shutter-priority autoexposure, this mode asks you to select the aperture setting — thus *Av,* for *aperture value.* The camera then selects the appropriate shutter speed to properly expose the picture.

- ✔ **A-DEP (auto depth-of-field):** *Depth of field* refers to the extent to which objects at a distance from your subject appear sharply focused. One way to control depth of field is to adjust the aperture setting. In this exposure mode, the camera assesses the distance between the lens and major objects in the frame and tries to choose an aperture setting that keeps all those objects within the zone of sharp focus. Then the camera sets the shutter speed appropriate for the aperture it selected.

The length of time that the shutter is open is called the *shutter speed* and is measured in seconds: 1/60 second, 1/250 second, 2 seconds, and so on. Shutter speeds on the Rebel XTi/D400 range from 30 seconds to 1/4000 second when you shoot without flash. Should you want a shutter speed longer than 30 seconds, manual (M) exposure mode also provides a feature called *bulb* exposure. At this setting, the shutter stays open indefinitely as long as you press the shutter button down.

If you do use a flash, the fastest available shutter speed is 1/200 second; the slowest ranges from 1/60 second to 30 seconds, depending on the exposure mode. See the section "Understanding your camera's approach to flash," later in this chapter, for details.

✓ **ISO (controls light sensitivity):** ISO, which is a digital function rather than a mechanical structure on the camera, enables you to adjust how responsive the image sensor is to light. The term ISO is a holdover from film days, when an international standards organization rated each film stock according to light sensitivity: ISO 200, ISO 400, ISO 800, and so on. Film or digital, a higher ISO rating means greater light sensitivity, which means that less light is needed to produce the image, enabling you to use a smaller aperture, faster shutter speed, or both.

On your camera, you can select ISO settings ranging from 100 to 1600, but only when you shoot in the advanced exposure modes. For the fully automatic modes, you're limited to ISO speeds from 100 to 400, and the camera chooses the setting for you automatically.

Distilled down to its essence, the image-exposure formula is just this simple:

✓ Aperture and shutter speed together determine the quantity of light that strikes the image sensor.

✓ ISO determines how much the sensor reacts to that light.

The tricky part of the equation is that aperture, shutter speed, and ISO settings affect your pictures in ways that go *beyond* exposure. You need to be aware of these side effects, explained in the next section, to determine which combination of the three exposure settings will work best for your picture.

Understanding exposure-setting side effects

As illustrated by the images in Figure 5-4, you can create the same exposure with different combinations of aperture, shutter speed, and ISO. And although the figure shows you only two variations of settings, your choices are pretty much endless — you're limited only by the aperture range allowed by the lens and the shutter speeds and ISO settings offered by the camera.

f/13, 1/25 second, ISO 200   f/5.6, 1/125 second, ISO 200

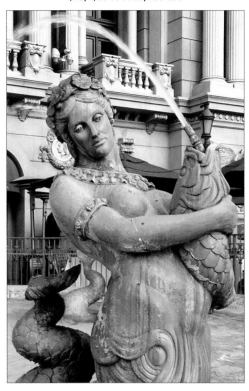
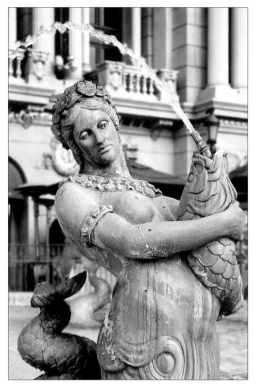

Figure 5-4: Aperture and shutter speed affect depth of field and motion blur.

But the settings you select impact your image beyond mere exposure, as follows:

✔ **Aperture affects depth of field.** The aperture setting, or f-stop, affects *depth of field,* which is the range of sharp focus in your image. I introduce this concept in Chapter 2, but here's a quick recap: With a shallow depth of field, your subject appears more sharply focused than faraway objects; with a large depth of field, the sharp-focus zone spreads over a greater distance.

As you reduce the aperture size — or *stop down the aperture,* in photo lingo — by choosing a higher f-stop number, you increase depth of field. As an example, notice that the background in the first image in Figure 5-4, which I shot using an aperture setting of f/13, appears noticeably sharper than in the right example, which was taken at f/5.6. Aperture is just one contributor to depth of field, however; see Chapter 6 for the complete story.

✔ **Shutter speed affects motion blur.** At a slow shutter speed, moving objects appear blurry, whereas a fast shutter speed captures motion cleanly. Compare the fountain water in the photos in Figure 5-4, for example. At a shutter speed of 1/125 second, the water droplets appear much more sharply focused than at 1/25 second. At the slower shutter speed, the water blurs, giving it a misty look. How high a shutter speed you need to freeze action depends on the speed of your subject, of course.

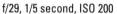
f/29, 1/5 second, ISO 200

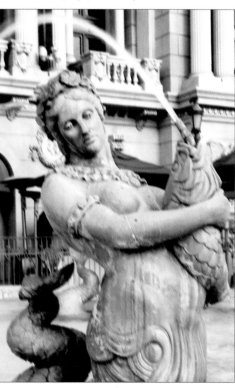

If your picture suffers from overall image blur like you see in Figure 5-5, where even stationary objects appear out of focus, the camera itself moved during the exposure. As you increase the exposure time (by selecting a slower shutter speed), you increase the risk of this problem because you have to keep the camera still for a longer period of time. Most people enter the camera-shake zone at speeds slower than about 1/50 second, although some people have steadier hands than others.

Figure 5-5: Slow shutter speeds increase the risk of all-over blur caused by camera shake.

My abilities vary depending on the day and my caffeine intake; I was able to snap the first example in Figure 5-4 at 1/25 second, but frankly, that was a lucky accident as I usually can't handhold at speeds that slow. At the 1/5 second used in Figure 5-5, camera shake was almost inevitable.

To avoid this issue, use a tripod or otherwise steady the camera. And see Chapter 6 for tips on solving other focus problems and Chapter 7 for more help with action photography.

✔ **ISO affects image noise.** As ISO increases, making the image sensor more reactive to light, you increase the risk of producing a defect called *noise.* This defect looks like sprinkles of sand and is similar in appearance to film *grain,* a defect that often mars pictures taken with high ISO film.

Ideally, then, you should always use the lowest ISO setting on your camera — 100 — to ensure top image quality. But sometimes, the lighting conditions simply don't permit you to do so and still use the aperture and shutter speeds you need. As an example, I shot the rose images in Figure 5-6 on a windy day. Even after I opened the aperture to f/5.6, the maximum possible for the lens I was using, I needed a shutter speed of 1/50 second to expose the image at ISO 100. Because the flower was moving quite a bit in the wind, 1/50 second was too slow to capture it without blur, as shown in the left image.

Fortunately, you usually don't encounter serious noise with the Rebel XTi/400D until you really crank up the ISO. You'd be hard pressed to find noise in the ISO 200 example in Figure 5-6, for example. But take a look at the examples in Figure 5-7, taken at ISO 800 and 1600. You may be able to get away with ISO 800 if you keep the print or display size of the picture small — as with other image defects, noise becomes more apparent as you enlarge the photo. Noise also is more problematic in areas of flat

f/5.6, 1/50 second, ISO 100   f/5.6, 1/80 second, ISO 200

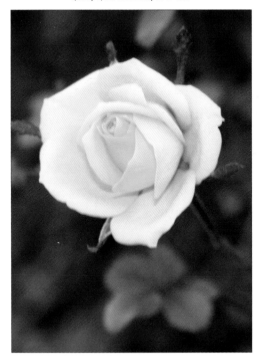 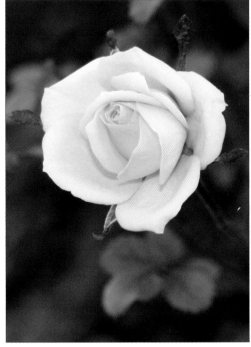

Figure 5-6: Raising the ISO enabled me to increase the shutter speed and avoid blur.

f/5.6, 1/320 second, ISO 800 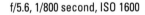   f/5.6, 1/800 second, ISO 1600

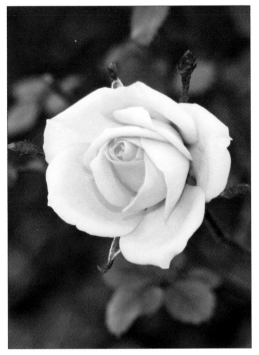 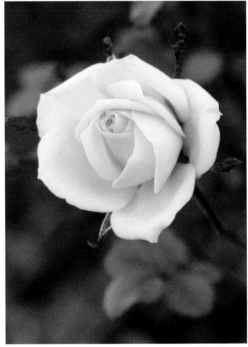

Figure 5-7: Very high ISO settings usually produce "noisy" images, which appear speckled.

color. When you bump ISO all the way up to 1600, however, expect to see noise throughout the image, as in the right photo in the figure.

Just to give you a better look at how ISO affects noise, Figure 5-8 offers magnified views of an area of my ISO 100, 200, 800, and 1600 images, plus an additional shot captured at ISO 400.

One more important note about noise: A long exposure time — say, 1 second or more — also can produce this defect. Your camera has a built-in noise-reduction filter that aims to compensate for long-exposure noise; see the sidebar "Dampening long-exposure noise" elsewhere in this chapter for details.

Long story short, understanding how aperture, shutter speed, and ISO affect your image enables you to have much more creative input over the look of your photographs — and, in the case of ISO, to also control the quality of your images. (Chapter 3 discusses other factors that affect image quality.)

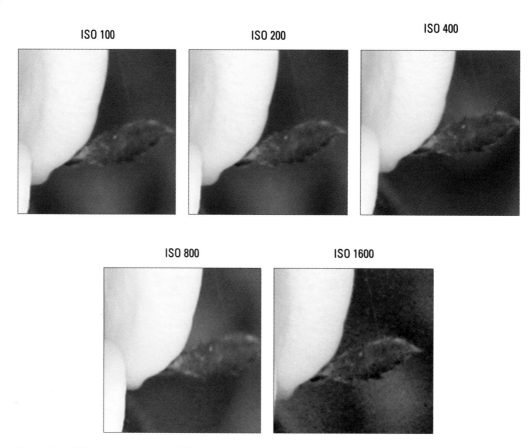

Figure 5-8: Noise becomes more visible as you enlarge your images.

Doing the exposure balancing act

As you change any of the three exposure settings — aperture, shutter speed, and ISO — one or both of the others must also shift in order to maintain the same image brightness. If you want a faster shutter speed, for example, you have to compensate with either a larger aperture, to allow in more light during the shorter exposure, or a higher ISO setting, to make the camera more sensitive to the light, or both. And as the preceding section explains, changing these settings impacts your image in ways beyond exposure. So when you boost that shutter speed, you have to decide whether you prefer the shorter depth of field that comes with a larger aperture or the increased risk of noise that accompanies a higher ISO. Figure 5-9 offers an illustration to help you envision this balancing act.

All photographers have their own approaches to finding the right combination of aperture, shutter speed, and ISO, and you'll no doubt develop your own system as you become more practiced at using the advanced exposure modes. In the meantime, here's how I handle things:

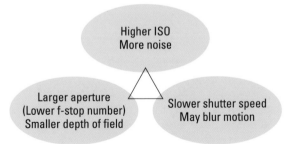

For a brighter exposure

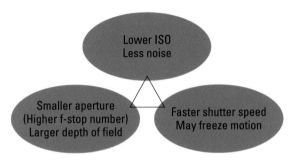

For a darker exposure

Figure 5-9: When adjusting exposure, remember the side effects produced by different aperture, shutter speed, and ISO settings.

✔ I always use the lowest possible ISO setting unless the lighting conditions are so poor that I can't use the aperture and shutter speed I want without raising the ISO.

✔ If my subject is moving (or might move, as with a squiggly toddler or antsy pet), I give shutter speed the next highest priority in my exposure decision. I might choose a fast shutter speed to ensure a blur-free photo or, on the flip side, select a slow shutter to intentionally blur that moving object, an effect that can create a heightened sense of motion. When shooting waterfalls, for example, I use a slow shutter to give the water a blurry, misty look.

✔ For images of non-moving subjects, I make aperture a priority over shutter speed, setting the aperture according to the depth of field I have in mind. For portraits, for example, I use a wide-open aperture (low f-stop number) so that I get a short depth of field, creating a nice, soft background for my subject. For landscapes, I go the opposite direction, stopping down the aperture as much as possible to capture the subject at the greatest depth of field.

Putting the f (stop) in focus

One way to remember the relationship between f-stop and depth of field, or the range of distance over which objects remain in sharp focus, is simply to think of the *f* as standing for *focus*. A higher f-stop number produces a longer depth of field, so if you want to extend the zone of sharp focus to cover a larger distance from your subject, you set the aperture to a higher f-stop. Higher f-stop number, greater zone of sharp focus.

Please *don't* share this tip with photography elites, who will roll their eyes and inform you that the *f* in *f-stop* most certainly does *not* stand for focus but for the ratio between the aperture size and lens focal length — as if *that's* helpful to know if you aren't an optical engineer. (Chapter 6 explains focal length, which *is* helpful to know.)

As for the fact that you open the aperture to a *larger* size by choosing a *smaller* f-stop number, well, I'm still working on the ideal mnemonic tip for that one. But try this in the meantime: A **s**maller f-**s**top **s**oaks the **s**ensor with more light. Or maybe this: A **s**maller f-stop produces a more **s**ubstantial aperture opening. (As I said, I'm working on it.)

I know that keeping all this straight is a little overwhelming at first, but the more you work with your camera, the more the whole exposure equation will make sense to you. You can find tips for choosing exposure settings for specific types of pictures in Chapter 7; keep moving through this chapter for details on how to actually monitor and adjust aperture, shutter speed, and ISO settings. And for specifics on selecting exposure settings in each of the four advanced exposure mode, jump ahead to the section "Setting ISO, f-stop, and Shutter Speed."

Monitoring Exposure Settings

When you press the shutter button halfway, the current f-stop and shutter speed appear in both the viewfinder display, as shown in Figure 5-10, and in the Camera Settings display, as shown in Figure 5-11. For the ISO setting, you must look to the Camera Settings display, as labeled in Figure 5-11.

In the viewfinder, shutter speeds are presented as whole numbers, even if the shutter speed is set to a fraction of a second. For example, for a shutter speed of 1/500 second, you see just the number 500 in the display. When the shutter speed slows to 1 second or more, you see quote marks after the number in both displays — 1" indicates a shutter speed of 1 second, 4" means 4 seconds, and so on.

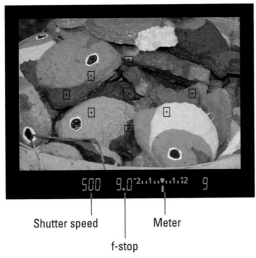

Shutter speed   Meter

f-stop

Figure 5-10: The shutter speed and f-stop appear in the viewfinder display.

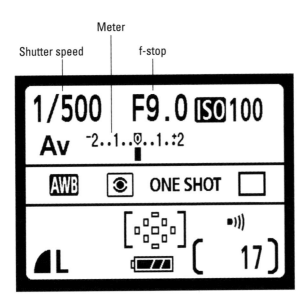

Figure 5-11: You also can view the settings in the Camera Settings display.

In addition to showing you the current shutter speed and f-stop, the viewfinder and Camera Settings display also offer an *exposure meter,* labeled in Figures 5-10 and 5-11. This little graphic serves two different purposes, depending on which of the advanced exposure modes you're using:

✓ In manual mode, the meter acts in its traditional role, which is to indicate whether your current settings will properly expose the image. Figure 5-12 gives you three examples. When the exposure indicator aligns with the center point, as in the middle example, the current settings will produce a proper exposure. If the indicator moves to the left of center, toward the minus side of the scale, as in the left example in the figure, the camera is alerting you that the image will be underexposed. If the indicator moves to the right of center, as in the right example, the image will be overexposed. The farther the indicator moves toward the plus or minus sign, the greater the potential exposure problem.

✓ In the other modes (P, Tv, Av, and A-DEP), the meter displays the current *exposure compensation* setting. Exposure compensation is a feature that enables you to tell the camera to produce a brighter or darker exposure than its autoexposure brain thinks is correct. When the exposure indicator is at 0, no compensation is being applied. See the upcoming section "Overriding Autoexposure Results with Exposure Compensation" for details.

Underexposed   Correct exposure   Overexposed

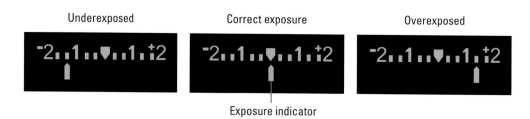

Exposure indicator

Figure 5-12: In Manual mode, the meter indicates whether exposure settings are on target.

Because the meter is designated as an exposure compensation guide when you shoot in the P, Tv, Av, and A-DEP modes, the camera alerts you to exposure problems in those modes as follows:

✓ **Av mode (aperture-priority autoexposure):** The shutter speed value blinks to let you know that the camera can't select a shutter speed that will produce a good exposure at the aperture you selected. You need to choose a different f-stop or adjust ISO.

✓ **Tv mode (shutter-priority autoexposure):** The aperture value blinks instead of the shutter speed. That's your notification that the camera can't open or stop down the aperture enough to expose the image at your selected shutter speed. Your options are to change the shutter speed or ISO.

✓ **P mode (programmed autoexposure):** In P mode, both the aperture and shutter speed values blink if the light is such that the camera can't select a combination of the two that will properly expose the image. Your only recourse is to either adjust the lighting or change the ISO setting.

✓ **A-DEP mode (auto depth-of-field):** Either the aperture or shutter speed value may blink. If the shutter speed value blinks 30" or 4000, the light is too dark or too bright, respectively, for the camera to expose the image properly at any combination of aperture and shutter speed. To compensate for dim lighting, you can raise the ISO or add flash or another light source. In too-bright light, lower the ISO if possible — otherwise, find a way to shade the subject or relocate it.

If the aperture setting blinks, the camera's telling you that the exposure will be okay, but the f-stop won't produce the depth of field needed to keep everything in the frame in sharp focus. (See Chapter 6 for complete details on depth of field and the A-DEP mode.)

One more word of advice: Keep in mind that the camera's take on exposure may not always be the one you want to follow. First, the camera's exposure decisions are based on the current *exposure metering mode*. As covered next, you can choose three different metering modes, and each one calculates exposure on a different area of the frame. Second, you may want to purposely choose exposure settings that leave parts of the image very dark or parts very light for creative reasons. For example, in a sunset scene, you may want to choose exposure settings that leave the foreground very dark but capture the fading colors of the sky properly. Again, depending on the metering mode, the camera may not understand your creative intent and report an exposure problem. In other words, the meter and the blinking alerts are guides, not dictators.

Choosing an Exposure Metering Mode

The *metering mode* determines which part of the frame the camera analyzes to calculate the proper exposure. Your Canon offers three metering modes, described in the following list and represented in the Camera Settings display by the icons you see in the margins:

 ✓ **Evaluative metering:** The camera analyzes the entire frame and then selects an exposure that's designed to produce a balanced exposure.

 ✓ **Partial metering:** The camera bases exposure only on the light that falls in the center portion of the frame.

 ✓ **Center-Weighted Average metering:** The camera bases exposure on the entire frame but with puts extra emphasis — or *weight* — on the center.

In most cases, Evaluative metering does a good job of calculating exposure. But it can get thrown off when a dark subject is set against a bright background or vice versa. As an example, Figure 5-13 shows the same image captured in P (programmed auto) mode, with no changes to exposure settings between shots except to the metering mode. In the Evaluative example, the amount of bright background caused the camera to select an exposure that left the statue too dark. Partial metering, in which the camera based exposure just on the center of the frame, did a good job exposing the statue, but the background then became a little overexposed for my taste. Center-Weighted Average metering produced a better background but left the statue just a tad underexposed.

Sadly, there is no way to get both background and subject properly exposed in situations like this, so you just have to decide which part of the image is most important.

Evaluative　　　　　　　　Partial　　　　　　Center-Weighted Average

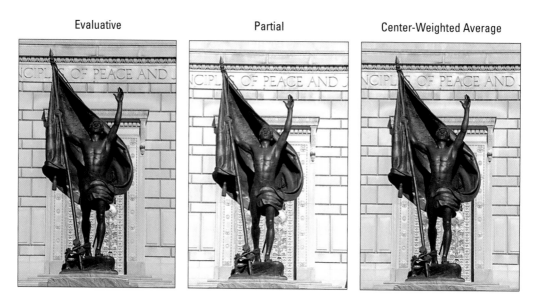

Figure 5-13: The metering mode determines which area of the frame the camera considers when calculating exposure.

You don't have a choice of metering modes in any of the fully automatic exposure modes; the camera uses Evaluative mode for all shots. But in the advanced exposure modes, you can specify which metering mode you prefer, as follows:

1. Press the left cross key.

The key is marked with the same little icon that represents Evaluative metering mode (the left icon in Figure 5-14). The monitor then displays the screen you see in the figure.

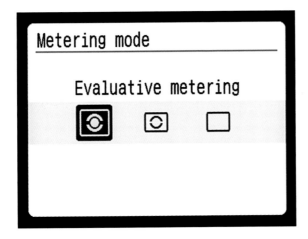

Figure 5-14: Press the left cross key to access your metering mode options.

2. **Press the left or right cross key to highlight your choice.**

   You can also rotate the Main dial to highlight the option.

3. **Press the Set button.**

   Your selected metering mode remains in force until you change it.

In theory, the best practice is to always check the metering mode before you shoot and choose the one that best matches your exposure goals. But in practice, that's a bit of a pain, not just in terms of having to adjust yet one more capture setting but in terms of having to *remember* to adjust one more capture setting.

So here's my advice: Until you're really comfortable with all the other controls on your camera, just stick with the default setting, which is Evaluative metering. That mode produces good results in most situations, and, after all, you can see in the monitor whether you disagree with how the camera metered or exposed the image and simply reshoot after adjusting the exposure settings to your liking. This option, in my mind, makes the whole metering mode issue a lot less critical than it is when you shoot with film.

The one exception to this advice might be when you're shooting a series of images in which a significant contrast in lighting exists between subject and background, as my examples here. Then, switching to Partial or Center-Weighted Average metering may save you the time of having to adjust the exposure for each image.

Setting ISO, f-stop, and Shutter Speed

If you want to control ISO, aperture (f-stop), or shutter speed, you must set the camera to one of the five advanced exposure modes. Formally called Creative Zone modes in Canon nomenclature, these modes include programmed auto (P), shutter-priority autoexposure (Tv), aperture-priority autoexposure (Av), manual exposure (M), and auto depth-of-field (A-DEP).

I explain each of these modes at the start of the chapter, but Table 5-1 offers a quick recap, along with a recommendation of when to use each mode. (In the table, the initials *AE* stand for *autoexposure*.) The next sections provide specifics (finally, you say) on how to adjust ISO, aperture, and shutter speed in all five modes.

Table 5-1	Advanced Exposure Modes (P, Tv, Av, M, A-DEP)	
Mode	*How It Works*	*When to Use It*
P (programmed auto)	The camera selects aperture and shutter speed but enables you to choose which combination of the two you prefer.	You want an easy way to experiment with different aperture/shutter speed combos, or you need more control over all aspects of your picture than provided by full auto mode.
Tv (shutter-priority AE)	You set the shutter speed; the camera selects the appropriate aperture.	Shutter speed is your main concern, as when shooting action or creating motion-blur effects.
Av (aperture-priority AE)	You set the aperture; the camera selects the shutter speed to produce a good exposure.	Your main photographic goal is to control depth of field.
M (manual exposure)	You set both aperture and shutter speed.	You can't get the results you want from any of the other modes, or you simply want to dial in specific aperture and shutter speed settings as quickly as possible.

Mode	How It Works	When to Use It
A-DEP	The camera selects both aperture and shutter speed but gives priority to selecting an aperture that produces the depth of field needed to keep all objects in the frame in sharp focus.	You aren't sure which aperture setting to use to extend the zone of sharp focus to cover all of your subjects.

Controlling ISO

As explained at the start of this chapter, your camera's ISO setting controls how sensitive the image sensor is to light. At higher ISO values, you need less light to expose an image.

Remember the downside to raising ISO however: The higher the ISO, the greater the possibility of noisy images. See Figure 5-8 for a reminder of what that defect looks like.

In the fully automatic exposure modes, the camera selects an ISO of 100, 200, or 400, depending on the available light. You have no control over ISO in those exposure modes. In the advanced exposure modes, you can specify an ISO setting from 100 to 1600.

The current ISO is displayed in the upper-right corner of the Camera Settings display, as shown on the left in Figure 5-15. To adjust the setting, just press the top cross key — the one that sports the label ISO. You then see the screen shown on the right in the figure. Use the cross keys or rotate the Main dial to highlight your choice. Then press the Set button.

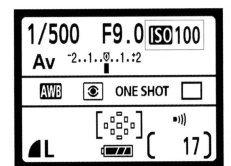 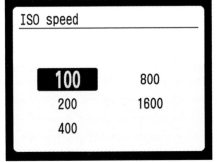

Figure 5-15: Press the top cross key to access the ISO setting.

TIP

Dampening long-exposure image noise

Even if you set your camera to a low ISO value, images may still suffer from noise when you use a very slow shutter speed. The longer the exposure, the greater the chances of this digital defect, which gives your pictures a mottled look.

The Rebel XTi/400D offers an in-camera filter that is designed to help eradicate the type of noise that occurs during long exposures. This feature is provided through a Custom Function, however, which means that you can access it only in the advanced exposure modes. To check it out, visit Setup Menu 2, select Custom Functions, press Set, and then use the cross keys or Main dial to select Custom Function 2, as shown in the figure here. Press Set again to activate the scrolling list of options in the middle of the screen. You can choose from these settings:

✔ *Off:* No noise reduction is applied. This is the default setting.

✔ *Auto:* Noise reduction is applied when you use a shutter speed of 1 second or longer, but

only if the camera detects the type of noise that's caused by long exposures.

✔ *On:* Noise reduction is always applied at exposures of 1 second or longer.

Before you enable noise reduction, be aware that doing so has a couple of disadvantages. First, the filter is applied after you take the picture, as the camera processes the image data and records it to your memory card. The time needed to apply the filter is about the same as the original exposure time, which slows down your shooting speed.

Second, noise-reduction filters work primarily by applying a slight blur to the image. Don't expect this process to totally eliminate noise, and do expect some resulting image softness. You may be able to get better results by using the blur tools or noise-removal filters found in many photo editors because then you can blur just the parts of the image where noise is most noticeable — usually in areas of flat color or little detail, such as skies.

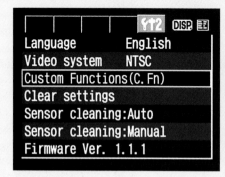

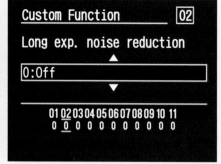

Adjusting aperture and shutter speed

You can adjust aperture and shutter speed only in P, Tv, Av, and M exposure modes. In A-DEP mode, the camera forces you to use its selected exposure settings. (You can, however, tweak the exposure by using the exposure-compensation feature discussed in the next section.)

To see the current exposure settings, start by pressing the shutter button halfway. The following things then take place:

- The camera locks focus, and the exposure meter comes to life.

- The current aperture and shutter speed appear in the viewfinder. (If you take your eye away from the viewfinder, the Camera Settings display appears, and you can view aperture and shutter speed there instead.)

- In Manual mode, the exposure meter also lets you know whether the current settings will expose the image properly. In the other advanced exposure modes — Tv, Av, P, and A-DEP — the camera indicates an exposure problem not with the meter, but by flashing either the shutter speed or f-stop value. (See the section "Monitoring Exposure Settings," earlier in this chapter, for details.)

The technique you use to change the exposure settings depends on the exposure mode, as outlined in the following list:

- **P (programmed auto):** In this mode, the camera initially displays its recommended combination of aperture and shutter speed. To select a different combination, rotate the Main dial.

  - To select a lower f-stop number (larger aperture) and faster shutter speed, rotate the dial to the right.

  - To select a higher f-stop number (smaller aperture) and slower shutter speed, rotate the dial to the left.

- **Tv (shutter-priority autoexposure):** Rotate the Main dial to the right for a faster shutter speed; nudge it to the left for a slower speed. As you change the shutter speed, the camera automatically adjusts the aperture as needed to maintain the proper exposure.

  Remember that as the aperture shifts, so does depth of field — so even though you're working in shutter-priority mode, keep an eye on the f-stop, too, if depth of field is important to your photo. Also note that in extreme lighting conditions, the camera may not be able to adjust the aperture enough to produce a good exposure at your current shutter speed — again, possible aperture settings depend on your lens. So you may need to compromise on shutter speed (or, in dim lighting, raise the ISO).

✔ **Av (aperture-priority autoexposure):** Rotate the Main dial to the right to stop down the aperture to a higher f-stop number. Rotate the dial to the left to open the aperture to a lower f-stop number. As you do, the camera automatically adjusts the shutter speed to maintain the exposure.

If you're handholding the camera, be careful that the shutter speed doesn't drop so low when you stop down the aperture that you run the risk of camera shake. And if your scene contains moving objects, make sure that when you dial in your preferred f-stop, the shutter speed that the camera selects is fast enough to stop action (or slow enough to blur it, if that's your creative goal).

✔ **M (manual exposure):** In this mode, you select both aperture and shutter speed, like so:

   • *To adjust shutter speed:* Rotate the Main dial to the right for a faster shutter speed; rotate left for a slower shutter.

   • *To adjust aperture:* Press and hold the Exposure Compensation button, shown in Figure 5-16, as you rotate the Main dial.

      See the *Av* label under the button? That's your cue as to the aperture-related function of the button — *Av* stands for *aperture value.*

Exposure Compensation button

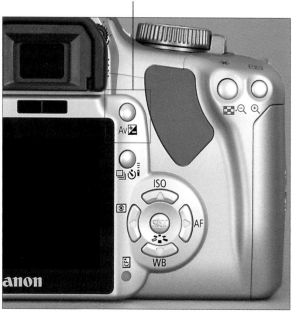

Figure 5-16: To set aperture in M mode, press the Exposure Compensation button as you rotate the Main dial.

Rotate the dial to the right for a higher f-stop (smaller aperture); rotate left to select a lower f-stop. Don't let up on the button as you rotate the Main dial — if you do, you instead adjust the shutter speed.

Keep in mind that when you use P, Tv, Av, and A-DEP modes, the settings that the camera selects are based on what it thinks is the proper exposure. If you don't agree with the camera, you have two options: You can switch to Manual exposure mode and simply dial in the aperture and shutter speed that deliver the exposure you want; or if you want to stay in P, Tv, Av, or A-DEP mode, you can tweak the autoexposure settings by using the feature explained in the very next section.

Overriding Autoexposure Results with Exposure Compensation

When you set your camera to the P, Tv, Av, or A-DEP exposure modes, you can enjoy the benefits of autoexposure support but still retain control over the final, overall exposure. If you think that the image the camera produced is too dark or too light, you can use a feature known as *exposure compensation,* which is sometimes also called *EV compensation.* (The *EV* stands for *exposure value.*)

Whatever you call it, this feature enables you to tell the camera to produce a darker or lighter exposure than what its autoexposure mechanism thinks is appropriate. Best of all, this feature is probably one of the easiest on the whole camera to understand. Here's all there is to it:

- Exposure compensation settings are stated in terms of EV values, as in +2.0 EV. Possible values range from +2.0 EV to –2.0 EV.
- A setting of EV 0.0 results in no exposure adjustment.
- For a brighter image, you raise the EV value. The higher you go, the brighter the image becomes.
- For a darker image, you lower the EV value. The picture becomes progressively darker with each step down the EV scale.

 Each full number on the EV scale represents an exposure shift of one *full stop.* In plain English, that means that if you change the exposure compensation setting from EV 0.0 to EV –1.0, the camera adjusts either the aperture or shutter speed to allow half as much light into the camera as you would get at the current setting. If you instead raise the value to EV +1.0, the settings are adjusted to double the light.

By default, the exposure is adjusted in 1/3 stop increments. In other words, you can shift from EV 0.0 to EV +0.3, +0.7, +1.0, and so on. But you can change the adjustment to 1/2-stop increments if you want to shift the exposure in larger jumps — from EV 0.0 to EV +0.5, +1.0, and so on. To do so, display Setup Menu 2, highlight Custom Functions, and press Set. Then select Custom Function 6, press Set, and press the up or down cross key to change the setting. Press Set again to lock in the new setting. If you make this change, the meter will appear slightly different in the Camera Settings display than you see it in this book. (There will be only one intermediate notch between each number on the meter instead of the usual two.) The viewfinder meter does not change, but the exposure indicator bar appears as a double-line if you set the exposure compensation value to a half-step value (+0.5, +1.5, and so on).

Exposure compensation is especially helpful when your subject and background are significantly different in brightness. As an example, take a look at the first image in Figure 5-17. Because of the very bright sky in the background, the camera chose an exposure that left the palm tree too dark. So I just amped the exposure compensation setting to EV +1.0, which produced the brighter exposure on the right.

EV 0.0   EV +1.0

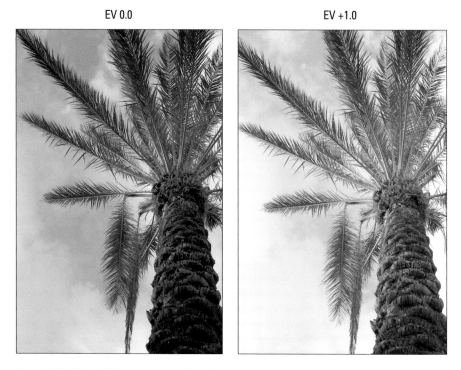

Figure 5-17: For a brighter exposure than the autoexposure mechanism chooses, dial in a positive exposure compensation value.

Another possible way to cope with this kind of background/subject brightness variation is to adjust the exposure metering mode, as discussed earlier in this chapter. I took the images in Figure 5-17 in Evaluative mode, for example, which meters exposure on the entire frame. Switching to Partial or Center-Weighted Average metering might have done the trick, but frankly, I find it easier to use exposure compensation than to fool with metering mode adjustments in most situations.

Some photographers use a slightly lower exposure compensation value — say, minus 0.3 — for all their shots. The thinking is that while this setting may underexpose some images, resulting in a little necessary retouching work later, it helps protect against blown highlights, which are usually not easy to repair.

Whatever your reason for adjusting the exposure compensation setting, you can get the job done as follows:

1. **Hold down the Exposure Compensation button.**

   The button's located near the top-right corner of the camera monitor; you can see the button in the margin here and in Figure 5-16. If the Camera Settings display is active, the exposure meter becomes highlighted, as shown in Figure 5-18. If you're looking through the viewfinder, nothing appears to change, however.

Exposure Compensation setting

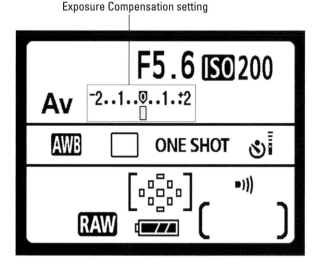

Figure 5-18: In autoexposure modes, the meter indicates the exposure compensation setting.

2. **While keeping the button pressed, rotate the Main dial to change the exposure compensation value.**

   As you rotate the dial, the exposure indicator moves right or left along the exposure meter.

   - Rotate the dial to the left to lower the value and produce a darker exposure.

   - Rotate the dial to the right to raise the value and produce a brighter exposure.

   - To return to no adjustment, rotate the dial until the exposure indicator is back at the center position on the meter.

3. **Release the Exposure Compensation button after you select the value you want to use.**

How the camera arrives at the brighter or darker image you request depends on the exposure mode:

- In Av (aperture-priority) mode, the camera adjusts the shutter speed but leaves your selected f-stop in force. Be sure to check the resulting shutter speed to make sure that it isn't so slow that camera shake or blur from moving objects is problematic.

- In Tv (shutter-priority) mode, the opposite occurs: The camera opens or stops down the aperture, leaving your selected shutter speed alone.

- In P (programmed auto) and A-DEP mode, the camera decides whether to adjust aperture, shutter speed, or both to accommodate the exposure compensation setting.

However, the camera can adjust the aperture only so much, according to the aperture range of your lens. And the range of shutter speeds, too, is limited by the camera itself. So if you reach the ends of those ranges, you either have to compromise on shutter speed or aperture or adjust ISO.

One final, and critical point about exposure compensation: When you power off the camera, it doesn't return you to a neutral setting (EV 0.0). The setting you last used remains in force until you change it.

Using Autoexposure Lock

Occasionally, you may want to use the exact same exposure settings for a series of shots. For example, suppose that you're shooting several images of a large landscape that you want to join together into a panorama in your photo editor. Unless the lighting is even across the entire landscape, the camera may select different exposure settings for each shot, depending on which part of the scene is currently in the frame. That can lead to weird and noticeable breaks in the brightness and contrast of the image when you seam the image together.

 To lock in exposure, you can simply switch to M (manual) exposure mode and use the same settings for each shot. Or, if you prefer to take advantage of auto-exposure, you can press and hold the AE (autoexposure) Lock button, highlighted in Figure 5-19. Exposure remains locked for as long as you press the button, even if you release the shutter button.

You can even go one step further and customize the behavior of the AE Lock button via a Custom Function. You can swap the tasks of the shutter button and AE Lock button, for example, so that pressing the shutter button halfway locks exposure and pressing the AE Lock button locks focus. Chapter 11 offers details. (When working with this book, however, stick with the default arrangement so that my instructions work as they should.)

AE Lock button

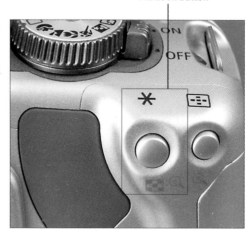

Figure 5-19: You can lock the current autoexposure settings by pressing this button.

Bracketing Exposures Automatically

 One of my favorite exposure features on the Rebel XTi/400D is *automatic exposure bracketing,* or AEB for short. This feature makes it easy to *bracket exposures* — which simply means to take the same shot using several expo-sure settings to up the odds that you come away with a perfectly exposed image.

When you enable AEB, your first shot is recorded at the current exposure set-tings; the second, with settings that produce a darker image; and the third, with settings that produce a brighter image. You can specify how much change in exposure you want between the three images when you turn on the feature.

 You can take advantage of AEB in any of the advanced exposure modes. However, the feature isn't available when you use flash. If you want to bracket exposures when using flash, you have to do it yourself, either by using expo-sure compensation or, in manual exposure mode, by changing the aperture and shutter speed directly.

Speaking of exposure compensation, you can combine that feature with AEB if you want. The camera simply applies the compensation amount when it calculates the exposure for the three bracketed images.

With that preamble out of the way, take these steps to turn on AEB:

1. **Display Setup Menu 2 and highlight AEB, as shown on the left in Figure 5-20.**

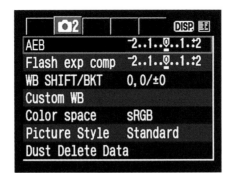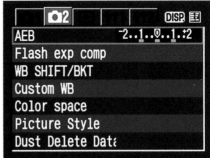

Figure 5-20: Auto exposure bracketing records your image at three exposure settings.

2. **Press Set to activate the little exposure meter, as shown on the right in Figure 5-20.**

3. **Rotate the Main dial to establish the amount of exposure change you want between images.**

   You now see three exposure indicators under the meter. These indicators show you the amount of exposure shift between the three shots the camera will record. As with the Exposure Compensation meter, each whole number represents one full exposure stop.

   For example, if you use the setting shown in Figure 5-20, the camera shoots one image at the actual exposure settings, and then takes the second image using settings that allow half as much light into the camera. The third image is recorded using settings that allow twice as much light.

4. **Press Set.**

   AEB is now enabled. If you press the shutter button halfway, you see the icon labeled in Figure 5-21 in the Camera Settings display, which reminds you that you turned on the feature. In the viewfinder, a flashing asterisk appears instead. In both displays, the exposure meter also displays the three exposure indicators to represent the exposure shift you established in Step 3.

Exposure indicators   AEB icon

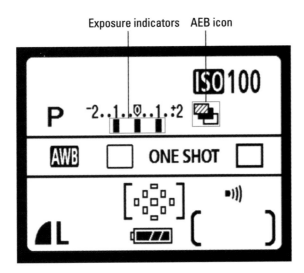

Figure 5-21: These symbols remind you that automatic exposure bracketing is enabled.

 How you actually record your trio of exposures depends on whether the Drive mode is set to Single or Continuous. The Drive mode, which I introduce in Chapter 2, determines whether the camera records a single image or multiple images with each press of the shutter button. (Press the Drive mode button, shown in the margin here, to access the screen that enables you to change this setting.)

✔ **AEB in Single mode:** You take each exposure separately, pressing the shutter button fully three times to record your trio of images.

 If you forget which exposure you're taking, look at the exposure meter. After you press the shutter button halfway to lock focus, the meter shows just a single indicator bar instead of three. If the bar is at 0, you're ready to take the first capture. If it's to the left of 0, you're on capture two, which creates the darker exposure. If it's to the right of 0, you're on capture three, which produces the brightest image.

✔ **AEB in Continuous mode:** The camera records all three exposures with one press of the shutter button. To record another series, release and then press the shutter button again. In other words, when AEB is turned on, the camera doesn't keep recording images until you release the shutter button as it normally does in Continuous mode — you can take only three images with one press of the shutter button.

To turn off auto exposure bracketing, just revisit Setup Menu 2 and change the AEB setting back to 0.

AEB is also turned off when you power down the camera, enable the flash, replace the camera battery, or replace the memory card.

Using Flash in Advanced Exposure Modes

Sometimes, no amount of fiddling with aperture, shutter speed, and ISO produces a bright enough exposure — in which case, you simply have to add more light. The built-in flash on your camera offers the most convenient solution.

To engage the flash, just press the Flash button on the side of the camera, highlighted in Figure 5-22. To turn off the flash, just press down on the flash assembly to close it.

Flash button

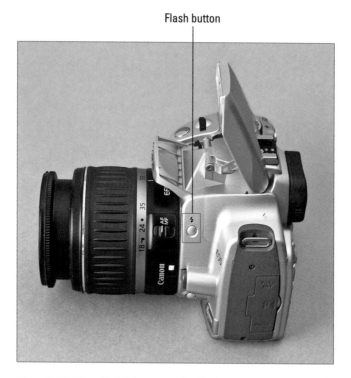

Figure 5-22: Want flash? Just press the Flash button, and you're set to go.

As you can in the fully automatic modes, you also can set the flash to Red-eye Reduction mode. Just display Shooting Menu 1 and turn the Red Eye option on or off. When enabled, the camera emits a brief preflash before the actual flash in an effort to constrict the subject's pupils and thereby lessen the chances of red-eye.

The next section goes into a little background detail about how the camera calculates the flash power that's needed to expose the image. This stuff is a little technical, but it will help you better understand how to get the results you want because the flash performance varies depending on the exposure mode.

Following that discussion, the rest of the chapter covers advanced flash features, including flash exposure compensation and flash exposure lock. You'll find some tips on getting better results in your flash pictures as well. For details on using Red-eye Reduction flash, flip back to Chapter 2, which spells everything out. Be sure to also visit Chapter 7, where you can find additional flash and lighting tips related to specific types of photographs.

Understanding your camera's approach to flash

When you use flash, your camera automatically calculates and adjusts the flash power to match the light on the subject. This process is sometimes referred to as *flash metering.* Your Rebel XTi/400D uses a flash-metering system that Canon calls *E-TTL II.* The *E* stands for *evaluative; TTL,* for *through the lens.* And the II refers to the fact that this system is an update to an earlier version of the system.

It isn't important that you remember what the initials stand for or even the flash system's official name. But what is helpful to keep in mind is how the system is designed to work.

First, you need to know that a flash can be used in two basic ways: as the primary light source or as a *fill flash.* When flash is the primary light source, both the subject and background are lit by the flash. In dim lighting, this typically results in a brightly lit subject and a dark background, as shown on the left in Figure 5-23.

With fill flash, the background is exposed primarily by ambient light, and the flash adds a little extra illumination to the subject. Fill flash typically produces brighter backgrounds and, often, softer lighting of the subject because not as much flash power is needed. The downside is that if the ambient light is dim, as in my nighttime photo, you need a slow shutter speed to properly expose the image, and both the camera and the subject must remain very still to avoid blurring. The shutter speed for my fill-flash image was 1/30 second, for example. Fortunately, I had a tripod, and the deer didn't seem inclined to move.

Flash as primary light source   Fill flash

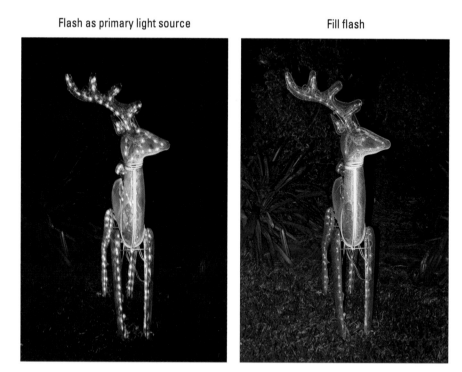

Figure 5-23: Fill flash produces brighter backgrounds.

Neither choice is necessarily right or wrong, by the way: Whether you want a dark background depends on the scene and your artistic interpretation. If you want to diminish the background, you may prefer the darker background you get when you use flash as your primary light source. But if the background is important to the context of the shot, allowing the camera to absorb more ambient light and adding just a small bit of fill flash may be more to your liking.

One more note on flash: Although most people think of flash as a tool for nighttime and low-light photography, most outdoor daytime pictures, especially portraits, also benefit from a little fill flash. As a case in point, Figure 5-24 shows you the same scene, shot at a farmer's market on a sunny morning, captured with and without fill flash.

Using a flash in bright sunlight also produces a slight warming effect, as illustrated in Figure 5-24. This color shift occurs because when you enable the flash, the camera's white balancing mechanism warms color slightly to compensate for the bluish light of a flash. But because your scene is actually lit primarily by sunlight, which is *not* as cool as flash light, the white balance adjustment takes the image colors a step warmer than neutral. If you don't want this warming effect, see Chapter 6 to find out how to make a manual white balance adjustment.

Without flash   With flash

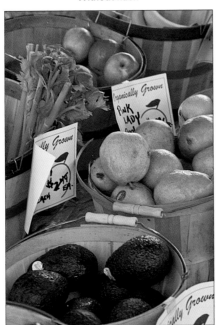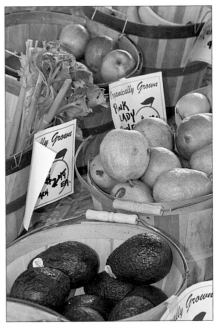

Figure 5-24: Flash often improves daytime pictures outdoors.

So how does this little flash lesson relate to your camera? Well, the exposure mode you use (P, Tv, Av, M, or A-DEP) determines whether the flash operates as a fill flash or as the primary light source. The exposure mode also controls the extent to which the camera adjusts the aperture and shutter speed in response to the ambient light in the scene.

In all modes, the camera analyzes the light both in the background and on the subject. Then it calculates the exposure and flash output as follows:

- **P:** In this mode, the shutter speed is automatically set between 1/60 and 1/200 second. (The bottom end of the range is set to allow handheld shooting without camera shake.) If the ambient light is sufficient, the flash output is geared to providing fill-flash lighting. Otherwise, the flash is determined to be the primary light source, and the output is adjusted accordingly. In the latter event, the image background may be dark, as in the left example in Figure 5-23.

- **Tv:** In this mode, the flash defaults to fill-flash behavior. After you select a shutter speed, the camera determines the proper aperture to expose the background with ambient light. Then it sets the flash power to provide fill-flash lighting to the subject.

You can select a shutter speed between 30 seconds and 1/200 second. If the aperture (f-stop) setting blinks, the camera can't expose the background properly at the shutter speed you selected. You can adjust either the shutter speed or ISO to correct the problem.

✔ **Av:** Again, the flash is designed to serve as fill-flash lighting. After you set the f-stop, the camera selects the shutter speed needed to expose the background using only ambient light. The flash power is then geared to fill in shadows on the subject.

Depending on the ambient light and your selected f-stop, the camera sets the shutter speed at anywhere from 30 seconds to 1/200 second. So be sure to note the shutter speed before you shoot — at anything below about 1/60 second, you may need a tripod to avoid camera shake. Your subject also must stay very still to avoid blurring.

If you want to avoid the possibility of a slow shutter altogether, you can, however. Display Setup Menu 2, select Custom Functions, and press Set. Then select Custom Function 3, as shown in Figure 5-25. At the Auto setting, the camera operates as just described. If you instead select the 1/200 second option, the shutter speed is always set to that value when you use flash. This ensures that you can handhold the camera without blur, but obviously, in dim lighting, it can result in a dark background because the camera doesn't have time to soak up much ambient light.

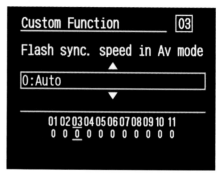

Figure 5-25: You can limit the camera to a fast shutter when using Av mode with flash.

✔ **M:** In this mode, the shutter speed, aperture, and ISO setting you select determine how brightly the background will be exposed. The camera takes care of illuminating the subject with fill flash.

✔ **A-DEP:** You can use flash in this mode, but doing so disables the automatic depth-of-field feature. The flash and exposure systems then operate as described for P mode. However, you can't choose from multiple combinations of aperture and shutter speed as you can in that mode; you're stuck with the combination that the camera selects.

If the flash output in any mode isn't to your liking, you can adjust it by using flash exposure compensation, explained next. Also check out the upcoming section "Locking flash exposure" for another trick you can use to manipulate flash results.

Keep in mind, too, that in any autoexposure mode, you can use exposure compensation, discussed earlier, to tweak the ambient exposure — that is, the brightness of your background. So you have multiple points of control:

exposure compensation to manipulate the background brightness, and flash compensation and flash exposure lock to adjust the flash output.

Adjusting flash power with flash exposure compensation

When you shoot with your built-in flash, the camera attempts to adjust the flash output as needed to produce a good exposure in the current lighting conditions. On some occasions, you may find that you want a little more or less light than the camera thinks is appropriate.

You can adjust the flash output by using a feature called *flash compensation.* This feature works similarly to exposure compensation, discussed earlier in this chapter. But flash compensation affects the output level of the flash unit, whereas exposure compensation affects the brightness of the background in your flash photos. As with exposure compensation, the flash compensation settings are stated in terms of EV *(exposure value)* numbers. A setting of 0.0 indicates no flash adjustment; you can increase the flash power to +2.0 or decrease it to –2.0.

As an example of the benefit of this feature — again, available only when you shoot in the advanced exposure modes — take a look at Figure 5-26. I snapped these tomatoes during bright daylight, but they were shaded by a tent awning. The first image shows you a flash-free shot. Clearly, I needed a little more light, but at normal flash power, the flash was too strong, blowing out the highlights in some areas, as shown in the middle image. By dialing the flash power down to EV –1.3, I got a softer flash that straddled the line perfectly between no flash and too much flash.

No flash   Flash EV 0.0   Flash EV –1.3

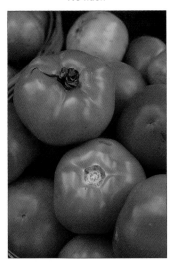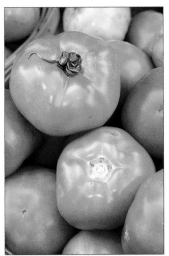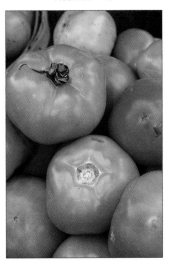

Figure 5-26: When normal flash output is too strong, dial in a lower flash compensation setting.

As for boosting the flash output, well, you may find it necessary on some occasions, but don't expect the built-in flash to work miracles even at a flash compensation of +2.0. Any built-in flash has a limited range, and you simply can't expect the flash light to reach faraway objects. In other words, don't even try taking flash pictures of a darkened recital hall from your seat in the balcony — all you'll wind up doing is annoying everyone.

Whichever direction you want to go with flash power, display Shooting Menu 2 and highlight the Flash Exp Comp option, as shown on the left in Figure 5-27. Press Set to activate the little meter and then rotate the Main dial to specify the amount of flash compensation. A higher value increases flash output; a lower value reduces it.

Flash exposure compensation setting

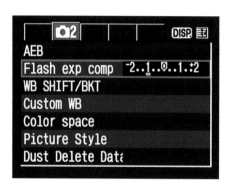 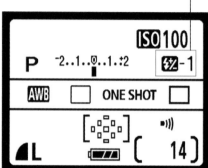

Figure 5-27: Adjust flash power via Shooting Menu 2.

By the way, if you use flash exposure compensation a lot, you can customize the camera so that pressing the Set button displays that control, saving you the trouble of using the menus. Chapter 11 shows you how.

To let you know that flash compensation is in effect, the icon labeled on the right in Figure 5-27 appears in the Camera Settings display when you press the shutter button halfway. You see the same plus/minus flash symbol in the viewfinder, although this time without the actual flash exposure compensation value.

As with exposure compensation, any flash-power adjustment you make remains in force, even if you turn off the camera, until you reset the control. So be sure to check the setting before you next use your flash.

Locking the flash exposure

You might never notice it, but when you press the shutter button to take a picture with flash enabled, the camera emits a very brief *preflash* before the actual flash. This preflash is used to determine the proper flash power needed to expose the image.

On occasion, the information that the camera collects from the preflash can be off-target because of the assumptions the system makes about what area of the frame is likely to contain your subject. To address this problem, your camera has a feature called *flash exposure lock,* or FE Lock. This tool enables you to set the flash power based only on the center of the frame.

Follow these steps to try it out:

1. **Frame your photo so that your subject falls under the center autofocus point.**

   You want your subject smack in the middle of the frame. You can reframe the shot after locking the flash exposure if you want.

2. **Press the shutter button halfway down until autofocus is complete, as indicated by the green confirmation dot in the viewfinder.**

   At this point, focus is set on your subject. You can now lift your finger off the shutter button if you want.

3. **While the subject is still under the center autofocus point, press and release the AE Lock button.**

   You can see the button in the margin here. The camera emits the preflash, and the letters FEL display for a second in the viewfinder. (*FEL* stands for *flash exposure lock.*) You also see the asterisk symbol — the one that appears above the AE Lock button on the camera body — next to the flash icon in the viewfinder.

4. **If needed, press and hold the shutter button halfway to re-establish focus on your subject.**

   You only need to take this step if you released the shutter button after Step 2.

5. **Reframe the image to your desired composition.**

   Keep the shutter button pressed halfway to maintain focus.

6. **Press the shutter button the rest of the way to take the picture.**

   The image is captured using the flash output setting you established in Step 3.

Flash exposure lock is also helpful when you're shooting portraits. The pre-flash sometimes causes people to blink, which means that with normal flash shooting, in which the actual flash and exposure occur immediately after the preflash, their eyes are closed at the exact moment of the exposure. With flash exposure lock, you can fire the preflash and then wait a second or two for the subject's eyes to recover before you take the actual picture.

Better yet, the flash exposure setting remains in force for about 15 seconds, meaning that you can shoot a series of images using the same flash setting without firing another preflash at all.

Exploring flash Custom Functions

Through the Custom Functions options, found on Setup Menu 2, you can customize three aspects of your camera's flash behavior. These options work as follows:

- **Custom Function 3, Flash Sync Speed in Av Mode:** This Custom Function determines what shutter speeds the camera can select when you use flash in the Av (aperture-priority autoexposure) mode. At the default setting, which is Auto, the shutter may be set to any speed between 30 seconds and 1/200 second. But you can also limit the camera to a shutter speed of 1/200 second through Custom Function 3. Doing so eliminates the possibility that a slow shutter speed will result in a blurry image due to camera shake, but it can also result in dark backgrounds. See the earlier section "Understanding your camera's approach to flash" for details about using flash in the various exposure modes.

- **Custom Function 8, E-TTL II:** This option enables you to switch from the default flash metering approach, called Evaluative. In this mode, the camera operates as described in the earlier section, "Understanding your camera's approach to flash." That is, it exposes the background using ambient light when possible and then sets the flash power to serve as fill light on the subject.

  If you set this Custom Function instead to the Average option, the flash is used as the primary light source, meaning that the flash power is set to expose the entire scene without relying on ambient light. Typically, this results in a more powerful (and possibly harsh) flash lighting and dark backgrounds.

- **Custom Function 9, Shutter Curtain Sync:** By default, the flash fires at the beginning of the exposure. This flash timing, known as *first-curtain sync,* is the best choice for most subjects. However, if you use a very slow shutter speed and you're photographing a moving object, first-curtain sync causes the blur that results from the motion to appear in front of the object, which doesn't make much visual sense.

  To solve this problem, Custom Function 9 enables you to change the flash sync timing to *second-curtain sync,* also known as *rear-curtain sync.*

In that flash mode, the motion trails will appear behind the moving object. The flash actually fires twice in this mode: once when you press the shutter button and again at the end of the exposure.

As you can probably discern from these descriptions, these Custom Functions are designed for photographers who are schooled in flash photography and want to mess around with advanced flash options. If you fall into that category, you can access the options by displaying Setup Menu 2, highlighting Custom Functions, and then pressing the Set button. After the Custom Function screen appears, use the right or left cross key to select the function you want to change. For example, in the left image in Figure 5-28, I selected Custom Function 8; in the right image, Custom Function 9.

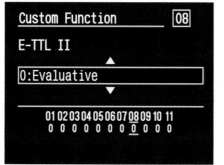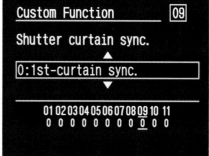

Figure 5-28: Both of these Custom Functions are designed for advanced users.

Press Set to activate the scrolling list of options in the center of the screen, as shown in the figures. Press the up or down cross key to select your choice and then press Set again to lock in that option.

Using an external flash unit

In addition to its built-in flash, your camera has a *hot shoe,* which is photo-geek terminology for a connection that enables you to add an external flash head like the one shown in Figure 5-29. The figure features the Canon Speedlite 580EX II, which currently retails for right around $350.

Although certainly not the cheapest of camera accessories, an external flash may be a worthwhile investment if you do a lot of flash photography, especially portraits. For one thing, an external flash offers greater power, enabling you to illuminate a larger area than you can with a built-in flash. And with flash units like the one in Figure 5-29, you can rotate the flash head so that the flash light bounces off a wall or ceiling instead of hitting your subject directly. This results in softer lighting and can eliminate the harsh shadows often caused by the strong, narrowly focused light of a built-in flash. (Chapter 7 offers an example of the difference this lighting technique can make in portraits.)

Whether the investment in an external flash will be worthwhile depends on the kind of photography you want to do. However, if you simply want a softer, more diffused light than your built-in flash produces, you have another option: You can buy a flash diffuser attachment like the one shown in Figure 5-30. This diffuser, made by LumiQuest (www.lumiquest.com), sells for just $13 and is a heck of a lot lighter and smaller to tuck into your camera bag than a flash head. This is just one of many diffuser designs, so visit your camera store to compare all your options.

If you do decide to purchase an external flash, you may also want to dig into some of the many books that concentrate solely on flash photography. There's a lot more to that game than you may imagine, and you'll no doubt discover some great ideas about lighting your pictures with flash. You can start with Chapter 7, which provides some specific examples of how to get better flash results when you shoot portraits, whether you go with the built-in flash, an external flash, or, my favorite, no flash.

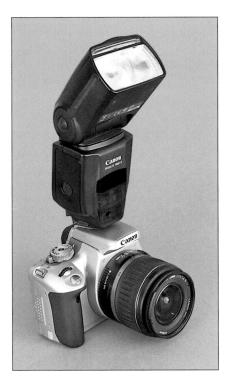

Figure 5-29: An external flash with a rotating head offers greater lighting flexibility.

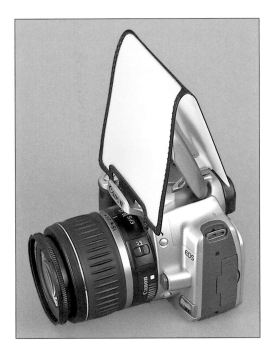

Figure 5-30: If you don't own an external flash head, try using a diffuser to soften the light from your built-in flash.

6

Manipulating Focus and Color

To many people, the word *focus* has just one interpretation when applied to a photograph: Either the subject is in focus or it's blurry. And it's true, this characteristic of your photographs is an important one. There's not much to appreciate about an image that's so blurry that you can't make out whether you're looking at Peru or Peoria.

But an artful photographer knows that there's more to focus than simply getting a sharp image of a subject. You also need to consider *depth of field,* or the distance over which objects remain sharply focused. This chapter explains all the ways to control depth of field and also discusses how to use your Canon's advanced autofocus options.

In addition, this chapter dives into the topic of color, explaining such concepts as *white balancing,* which compensates for the varying color casts created by different light sources, and *color space,* which determines the spectrum of colors your camera can capture. Finally, a section near the end of the chapter introduces you to Picture Styles, which enable you to take even greater control over image sharpness and color.

Reviewing Focus Basics

I touch on various focus issues in Chapters 1, 2, and 5. But just in case you're not reading this book from front to back, here's a recap of the basic process of focusing with your Rebel XTi/400D:

1. **If you haven't already done so, adjust the viewfinder to your eyesight.**

   Look through the viewfinder and pay attention only to the autofocus points, labeled in Figure 6-1. Then nudge the dioptric adjustment knob until the brackets themselves appear sharp — don't worry about the scene in front of the lens. (The knob is located just to the right of the viewfinder; Chapter 1 details this step if you need more help.)

2. **Set the focusing switch on the lens to manual or automatic focusing.**

   If you want to focus manually, set the switch to the MF position. For auto-focusing, set the switch to the AF position, as in Figure 6-2. (These directions are specific to the kit lens sold with the Rebel XTi/D400, shown in the figure. If you use another lens, the switch may look or operate differently, so check the product manual.)

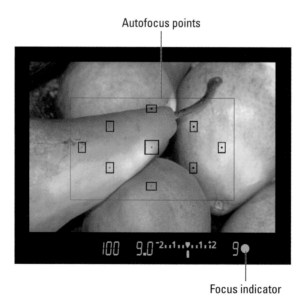

Figure 6-1: The viewfinder offers these focusing aids.

3. **To set focus in autofocus mode, press and hold the shutter button halfway down.**

When focus is established, the focus indicator in the viewfinder lights, and one or more of the autofocus points turns red, as shown in Figure 6-1. Focus is maintained as long as you continue to hold the shutter button down halfway. (Press the button the rest of the way when you're ready to snap the picture.)

A red dot indicates an *active autofocus point,* which the camera will use to establish focus. You can select a specific autofocus point by following the steps laid out in the next section.

AF/MF switch

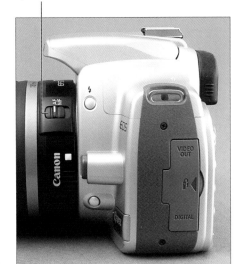

Figure 6-2: Select AF for autofocus or MF for manual focus.

4. **To set focus manually, twist the focusing ring on the lens.**

Note that even in manual mode, you can confirm focus by pressing the shutter button halfway. The autofocus point or points that achieved focus flash for a second or two, and the viewfinder's focus indicator lights up.

Shutter speed and blurry photos

A poorly focused photo isn't always related to the issues discussed in this chapter. Any movement of the camera or subject can also cause blur. Both of these problems are actually related to shutter speed, an exposure control that I cover in Chapter 5. Be sure to also visit Chapter 7, which provides some additional tips for capturing moving objects without blur.

Adjusting Autofocus Performance

You can adjust two aspects of your Rebel XTi/400D's autofocusing system: the active autofocus point and the AF (autofocus) mode. The next two sections explain these features.

Selecting an autofocus point

When you shoot in any of the fully automatic exposure modes (Full Auto, Portrait, Landscape, and so on) as well as in A-DEP mode, all nine of your camera's autofocus points are active. That means that the camera's auto-focusing system looks at all the points when trying to establish focus. Typically, the camera sets focus on the point that falls over the object closest to the lens. If that focusing decision doesn't suit your needs, you have two options:

- ✒ Focus manually.

- ✒ Set the camera to P, Tv, Av, or M exposure mode. In those modes, you can tell the camera to base focus on a specific autofocus point.

Chapter 1 explains how to adjust focus manually. To stay in autofocus mode and specify an autofocus point, take these steps:

1. **Set the Mode dial to P, Tv, Av, or M.**

   Again, you can specify an autofocus point only in these exposure modes.

2. **Press and release the AF Point Selection button, highlighted in Figure 6-3.**

   When you do, you see the AF Point Selection screen on the monitor. The display indicates whether the camera is currently in Automatic AF Point Selection mode or Manual AF Point Selection mode, as follows.

AF Point Selection button

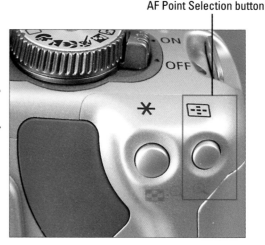

Figure 6-3: Press and hold the AF Point Selection button to select an autofocus point.

- *Automatic AF Point Selection mode:* All the AF points appear yellow in the monitor, as shown in Figure 6-4.

- *Manual AF Point Selection:* Only one of the nine autofocus points is selected and appears yellow, as shown in Figure 6-5.

You can check the current mode by looking through the viewfinder, too. When you press and release the AF Point Selection button, all nine autofocus points turn red if you're in Automatic AF Point Selection mode. A single point turns red if you're in Manual AF Point Selection mode.

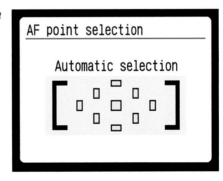

Figure 6-4: In Automatic mode, all nine auto-focus points are active.

3. **Set the camera to Manual AF Point Selection mode if needed.**

   You can do this in two ways:

   - *Rotate the Main dial.* This option is easiest when your eye is up to the viewfinder.

   - *Press the Set button.* Pressing the button toggles you between Automatic AF Point Selection and Manual AF Point Selection with the center point activated.

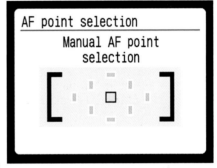

Figure 6-5: You also can base autofocus on a single point.

4. **Specify which AF Point you want to use.**

   Here again, you have two options:

   - *Rotate the Main dial.* Rotating the dial cycles through the nine points and then back to Automatic AF Point Selection mode.

   - *Press the cross keys.* Just press the up, down, left, or right keys to highlight the point you want to use. In this case, cycling through all the options doesn't switch you back to Automatic mode.

That's all there is to it — after you select the autofocus point, just frame your shot so that your subject falls under than point and then press the shutter button halfway to focus.

If you want the benefits of autofocus but find it bothersome to have to worry about selecting an autofocus point, try this approach: Set the camera to Manual AF Point Selection and select the center point as the active point. Remember, you can do this easily by just pressing the Set button in Step 2. Now the camera will always set focus based on whatever is at the center of the frame — a setup that, in my opinion, is the most intuitive way to do things. If you want your subject to appear off-center, you still can: Just frame the picture initially so that the subject is centered, depress the shutter button halfway to establish, and then reframe the image before pressing the shutter button the rest of the way.

Do be careful about exposure if you use this technique, however. If the exposure metering mode is set to either Partial or Center-Weighted Average metering, and you reframe the image so that your subject isn't at the center of the frame, exposure may be off. To compensate, you may need to lock exposure (using the AE Lock button) before you reframe. In Evaluative metering mode, this issue shouldn't be a big problem because exposure is based on the entire frame. Chapter 5 provides details about metering modes, exposure lock, and other exposure issues.

Changing the AF (autofocus) mode

Your camera offers three different autofocusing schemes, which you select through a control called AF mode. The three choices work like so:

- **One-Shot:** In this mode, which is geared to shooting stationary subjects, the camera locks focus when you depress the shutter button halfway. Focus remains locked as long as you hold the shutter button at that halfway position.

- **AI Servo:** In this mode, the camera adjusts focus continually as needed from the time you press the shutter button halfway to the time you take the picture. This mode is designed to make it easier to focus on moving objects.

   For AI Servo to work properly, you must reframe as needed to keep your subject under the active autofocus point if you're working in Manual AF Point Selection mode. If the camera is set to Automatic AF Point Selection, keep the subject within the diamond-shape area covered by the nine autofocus points. (The preceding section explains these two modes.)

   In either case, the green focus dot in the viewfinder blinks rapidly if the camera isn't tracking focus successfully. If all is going well, the focus dot does not light up at all.

- **AI Focus:** This mode automatically switches the camera from One-Shot to AI Servo as needed. When you first press the shutter button halfway, focus is locked on the active autofocus point (or points), as usual in One-Shot mode. But if the subject moves, the camera shifts into AI Servo mode and adjusts focus as it thinks is warranted.

Which of these three modes are available to you, however, depends on the exposure mode, as follows:

- ✔ In P, Tv, Av, and M modes, you can select any of the three Focus mode options.

- ✔ In A-DEP mode as well as in Portrait, Landscape, Night Portrait, and Close Up modes, the camera restricts you to One-Shot mode.

- ✔ Sports mode always uses AI Servo autofocus.

- ✔ Full Auto and No Flash modes always use AI Focus.

So, assuming that you can choose from all three, which mode is best? Well, here's my take: One-Shot mode works best for shooting still subjects, and AI Servo is the right choice for moving subjects. But frankly, AI Focus does a good job in most cases of making that shift for you and saves you the trouble of having to change the mode each time you go from shooting still to moving subjects. So, in my mind, there's no real reason to fiddle with the setting unless you're shooting moving objects and want to be able to lock focus at a specific position — in which case, my recommendation would be to simply switch to manual focusing anyway.

Whatever you decide, you can set the Focus mode as follows:

1. **Press the right cross key (the one labeled AF).**

   The monitor shows the screen you see in Figure 6-6.

2. **Press the left or right cross keys or rotate the Main dial to highlight your choice.**

3. **Press the Set button.**

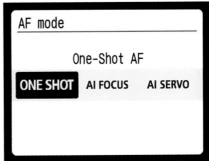

Figure 6-6: Press the right cross key to change the AF mode.

Manipulating Depth of Field

Getting familiar with the concept of *depth of field* is one of the biggest steps you can take to becoming a more artful photographer. I introduce you to depth of field in Chapters 2 and 5, but here's a quick recap just to hammer home the lesson:

- ✔ *Depth of field* refers to the distance over which objects in a photograph appear sharply focused.

✓ With a shallow, or small, depth of field, only your subject and objects very close to it appear sharp. Objects at a distance from the subject appear blurry.

✓ With a large depth of field, the zone of sharp focus extends to include distant objects.

Which arrangement works best depends entirely on your creative vision and your subject. In portraits, for example, a classic technique is to use a short depth of field, as I did for the photo in Figure 6-7. This approach increases emphasis on the subject while diminishing the impact of the background. But for the photo shown in Figure 6-8, I wanted the historical marker, the light-house, and the cottage behind to have equal weight in the scene, so I used settings that produced a large depth of field, keeping them all in sharp focus.

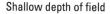

Shallow depth of field

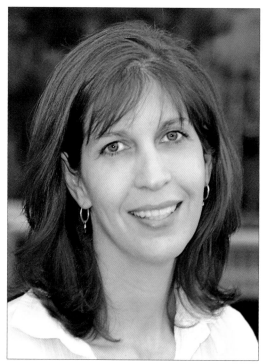

Figure 6-7: A shallow depth of field blurs the background and draws added attention to the subject.

Note, though, that with a short depth of field, you can just as easily throw foreground objects into soft focus as background objects. In the lighthouse scene, for example, if I had used settings that produced a short depth of field, and I set focus on the lighthouse, the historical marker and the cottage both might be outside the zone of sharp focus.

So how do you adjust depth of field? You have three points of control: aperture, focal length, and camera-to-subject distance, as spelled out in the following list:

Large depth of field

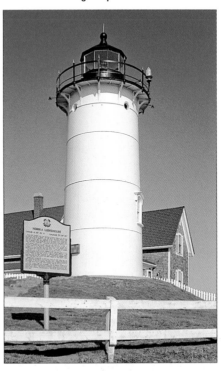

Figure 6-8: A large depth of field keeps both near and far subjects in sharp focus.

- **Aperture setting (f-stop):** The aperture is one of three exposure settings, all explained fully in Chapter 5. Depth of field increases as you stop down the aperture (by choosing a higher f-stop number). For shallow depth of field, open the aperture (by choosing a lower f-stop number).

  Figure 6-9 offers an example. Notice that the trees in the background are much more softly focused in the f/5.6 example than in the f/11 version. I snapped both images using the same focal length and camera-to-subject distance, so aperture is the only depth-of-field variable between the two images.

  Of course, changing the aperture requires adjusting the shutter speed or ISO to maintain the equivalent exposure; for these images, I adjusted shutter speed only.

- **Lens focal length:** In lay terms, *focal length* determines what the lens "sees." As you increase focal length, measured in millimeters, the angle of view narrows, objects appear larger in the frame, and — the important point for this discussion — depth of field decreases. Additionally, the spatial relationship of objects changes as you adjust focal length.

  As an example, Figure 6-10 compares the same scene shot at focal lengths of 138mm and 255mm. I used the same aperture, f/22, for both examples.

f/5.6, 1/1000 second   f/11, 1/200 second

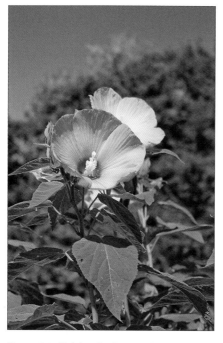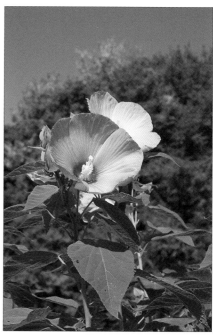

Figure 6-9: Raising the f-stop value increases depth of field.

Whether you have any focal length flexibility depends on your lens: If you have a zoom lens, you can adjust the focal length — just zoom in or out. (The Rebel XTi/400D kit lens, for example, offers a focal range of 18–55mm.) If you don't have a zoom lens, the focal length is fixed, so scratch this means of manipulating depth of field.

For more technical details about focal length and your camera, see the sidebar "Fun facts about focal length."

✔ **Camera-to-subject distance:** As you move the lens closer to your subject, depth of field decreases. This assumes that you don't zoom in or out to reframe the picture, thereby changing the focal length. If you do, depth of field is affected by both the camera position and focal length.

Together, these three factors determine the maximum and minimum depth of field that you can achieve, as illustrated by my clever artwork in Figure 6-11 and summed up in the following list:

✔ **To produce the shallowest depth of field:** Open the aperture as wide as possible (select the lowest f-stop number), zoom in to the maximum focal length of your lens, and get as close as possible to your subject.

✔ **To produce maximum depth of field:** Stop down the aperture to the highest possible f-stop setting, zoom out to the shortest focal length your lens offers, and move farther from your subject.

138mm, f/22
255mm, f/22

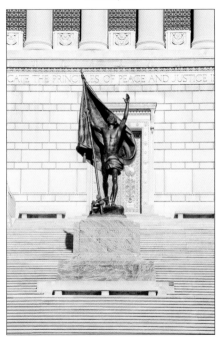 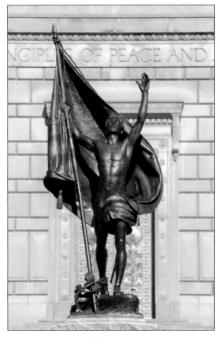

Figure 6-10: Zooming to a longer focal length also reduces depth of field.

Here are a few additional tips and tricks related to depth of field:

✔ When depth of field is a primary concern, try using aperture-priority autoexposure (Av). In this mode, detailed fully in Chapter 5, you set the f-stop, and the camera selects the appropriate shutter speed to produce a good exposure. The range of aperture settings you can access depends on your lens.

✔ Some of the fully automatic scene modes are also designed with depth of field in mind. Portrait and Close-Up modes produce shortened depth of field; Landscape mode produces a greater depth of field. You can't adjust aperture in these modes, however, so you're limited to the setting the camera chooses.

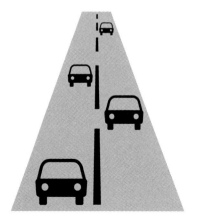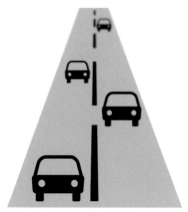

Greater depth of field:
Select higher f-stop
Decrease focal length (zoom out)
Move farther from subject

Shorter depth of field:
Select lower f-stop
Increase focal length (zoom in)
Move closer to subject

Figure 6-11: Aperture, focal length, and your shooting distance determine depth of field.

✔ The Rebel XTi/400D also offers a special autoexposure mode called A-DEP, which stands for *automatic depth of field*. In this mode, the camera selects the aperture setting that it thinks will keep all objects in the frame within the zone of sharp focus. You can read more about this mode in the next section.

✔ Not sure which aperture setting you need to produce the depth of field you want? Good news: You camera offers *depth-of-field preview*, which enables you to see in advance how the aperture affects the focus zone. See the section labeled "Checking depth of field" for details on how to use this feature.

✔ The extent to which background focus shifts as you adjust depth of field also is affected by the distance between the subject and the background. For increased background blurring, move the subject farther in front of the background.

✔ If you adjust aperture to affect depth of field, be sure to always keep an eye on shutter speed as well. To maintain the same exposure, shutter speed must change in tandem with aperture, and you may encounter a situation where the shutter speed is too slow to permit hand-holding of the camera. Lenses that offer optical image stabilization do enable most people to handhold the camera at slower shutter speeds than non-stabilized lenses, but double-check your results just to be sure. (Note that if you use a tripod, most lens manufacturers recommend that you turn off the stabilization feature; check your manual to be sure.)

Using A-DEP mode

In addition to the four advanced exposure modes found on most digital SLR cameras, your Rebel XTi/400D offers a fifth mode called A-DEP, as shown in Figure 6-12. The initials stand for *automatic depth of field.*

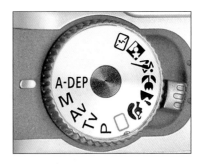

Figure 6-12: A-DEP stands for automatic depth of field.

This mode is designed to assist you in producing photos that have a depth of field sufficient to keep all objects in the frame in sharp focus. The camera accomplishes this by analyzing the lens-to-subject distance for all those objects and then selecting the aperture that results in the appropriate depth of field. After choosing the aperture, the camera then selects the necessary shutter speed to properly expose the image at the selected f-stop.

A-DEP mode isn't a surefire bet, however, and it does have some restrictions that may make it unsuitable for your subject. Here's what you need to know:

✓ In very dim lighting, the shutter speed the camera selects may be too slow to allow you to handhold the camera. So check the shutter speed in the viewfinder after you press the shutter button halfway to meter and focus the image. If the speed is lower than about 1/50 second, use a tripod. (If you're using a long lens, you'll need a tripod even at faster shutter speeds.)

Fun facts about focal length

Every lens can be characterized by its *focal length,* or in the case of a zoom lens, the range of focal lengths it offers. Measured in millimeters, focal length determines the camera's angle of view, the apparent size and distance of objects in the scene, and depth of field. According to photography tradition, a focal length of 50mm is described as a "normal" lens. Most point-and-shoot cameras feature this focal length, which is a medium-range lens that works well for the type of snapshots that users of those kinds of cameras are likely to shoot.

A lens with a focal length under 35mm is characterized as a *wide-angle* lens because at that focal length, the camera has a wide angle of view and produces a long depth of field, making it good for landscape photography. A short focal length also has the effect of making objects seem smaller and farther away. At the other end of the spectrum, a lens with a focal length longer than 80mm is considered a *telephoto* lens and often referred to as a *long lens.* With a long lens, angle of view narrows, depth of field decreases, and faraway subjects appear closer

(continued)

(continued)

and larger, which is ideal for wildlife and sports photographers.

Note, however, that the focal lengths stated here and elsewhere in the book are so-called *35mm equivalent* focal lengths. Here's the deal: For reasons that aren't really important, when you put a standard lens on most digital cameras, including your Rebel XTi/400D, the available frame area is reduced, as if you took a picture on a camera that uses 35mm film negatives (the kind you've probably been using for years) and then cropped it.

This so-called *crop factor*, sometimes also called the *magnification factor,* varies depending on the digital camera, which is why the photo industry adopted the 35mm-equivalent measuring stick as

a standard. With your camera, the cropping factor is roughly 1.6. So the 18–55mm kit lens sold with the Rebel XTi/400D, for example, actually captures the approximate area you would get from a 27–82mm lens on a 35mm film camera. In the figure here, for example, the red outline indicates the image area that results from the 1.6 crop factor.

Note that although the area the lens can capture changes when you move a lens from a 35mm film camera to a digital body, depth of field isn't affected, nor are the spatial relationships between objects in the frame. So when lens shopping, you gauge those two characteristics of the lens by looking at the stated focal length — no digital-to-film conversion math is required.

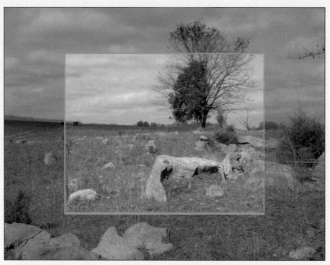

Chuck Pace

 ✓ If the aperture value blinks in the viewfinder, the camera can't set the f-stop so that you get both a good exposure and the depth of field necessary to keep all objects in the frame in sharp focus. In this situation, the camera assumes that your primary goal is a good exposure and so adjusts the aperture as needed based on the available light.

✔ If the shutter speed blinks in the viewfinder, the light is either too bright or too dim for the camera to properly expose the image at any combination of aperture and shutter speed. In bright light, you can lower the ISO, if it isn't already at 100, or reposition or shade your subject. In dim lighting, raise the ISO or add artificial light.

✔ You can use flash with A-DEP mode, but the minute you turn on the flash, the camera no longer does its automatic depth-of-field calculation. Instead, it presents you with a fixed combination of aperture and shutter speed that will properly expose the image. The depth of field may or may not be what you want.

Given these limitations, my personal recommendation is that as soon as you fully understand the impact of aperture on depth of field, you politely decline the option of using A-DEP mode and instead work in aperture-priority autoexposure mode (Av) instead. Then you can simply match the f-stop to the depth of field you have in mind, without giving up the option of using flash.

Checking depth of field

When you look through your viewfinder and press the shutter button halfway, you can get only a partial indication of the depth of field that your current camera settings will produce. You can see the effect of focal length and the camera-to-subject distance, but because the aperture doesn't actually open to your selected f-stop until you take the picture, the viewfinder doesn't show you how that setting will affect depth of field.

By using the depth of field preview button on your camera, however, you can do just that. Almost hidden away on the front of your camera, just below the lens-release button, the Depth-of-Field Preview button is the tiny, unmarked silver button shown in Figure 6-13.

Depth-of-field Preview button

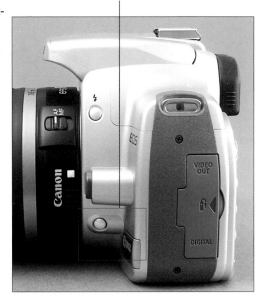

Figure 6-13: Press this button to see how the aperture setting will affect depth of field.

To use this feature, just press and hold the shutter button halfway down and then press and hold the Depth-of-Field Preview button with the other hand. You'll hear a little whirring noise, and the scene in the viewfinder may get either brighter or darker, depending on the f-stop. After the preview engages, you can release the shutter button and then rotate the Main dial to see how changing the f-stop affects the depth of field. (The exception is when the camera is set to A-DEP mode, in which you have no control over aperture.)

Note that the preview doesn't engage in P, Tv, Av, or A-DEP mode if your current aperture and shutter speed aren't adequate to expose the image properly. You have to solve the exposure issue before you can use the preview.

Controlling Color

Compared with understanding some aspects of digital photography — resolution, aperture and shutter speed, depth of field, and so on — making sense of your camera's color options is easy-breezy. First, color problems aren't all that common, and when they are, they're usually simple to fix with a quick shift of your camera's white balance control. And getting a grip on color requires learning only a couple of new terms, an unusual state of affairs for an endeavor that often seems more like high-tech science than art.

The rest of this chapter explains the aforementioned white balance control, plus a couple of menu options that enable you to fine-tune the way your camera renders colors. For information on how to alter colors of existing pictures by using the software that shipped with your camera, see Chapter 10.

Correcting colors with white balance

Every light source emits a particular color cast. The old-fashioned fluorescent lights found in most public restrooms, for example, put out a bluish-greenish light, which is why our reflections in the mirrors in those restrooms always look so sickly. And if you think that your beloved looks especially attractive by candlelight, you aren't imagining things: Candlelight casts a warm, yellow-red glow that is flattering to the skin.

Science-y types measure the color of light, officially known as *color temperature,* on the Kelvin scale, which is named after its creator. You can see the Kelvin scale in Figure 6-14.

When photographers talk about "warm light" and "cool light," though, they aren't referring to the position on the Kelvin scale — or at least not in the way we usually think of temperatures, with a higher number meaning hotter. Instead, the terms describe the visual appearance of the light. Warm light, produced by candles and incandescent lights, falls in the red-yellow spectrum you see at the bottom of the Kelvin scale in Figure 6-14; cool light, in the blue-green spectrum, appears at the top of the scale.

At any rate, most of us don't notice these fluctuating colors of light because our eyes automatically compensate for them. Except in very extreme lighting conditions, a white tablecloth appears white to us no matter whether we view it by candlelight, fluorescent light, or regular houselights.

Similarly, a digital camera compensates for different colors of light through a feature known as *white balancing.* Simply put, white balancing neutralizes light so that whites are always white, which in turn ensures that other colors are rendered accurately. If the camera senses warm light, it shifts colors slightly to the cool side of the color spectrum; in cool light, the camera shifts colors the opposite direction.

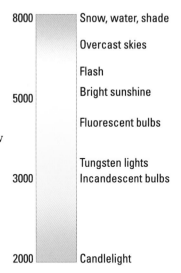

8000	Snow, water, shade
	Overcast skies
	Flash
5000	Bright sunshine
	Fluorescent bulbs
	Tungsten lights
3000	Incandescent bulbs
2000	Candlelight

Figure 6-14: Each light source emits a specific color.

The good news is that, as with your eyes, your camera's automatic white balance setting, which carries the label AWB, tackles this process remarkably well in most situations, which means that you can usually ignore it and concentrate on other aspects of your picture. But if your scene is lit by two or more light sources that cast different colors, the white balance sensor can get confused, producing an unwanted color cast like the one you see in the left image in Figure 6-15.

I shot this product image in my home studio, which I light primarily with a couple of high-powered photo lights that use tungsten bulbs, which produce light with a color temperature similar to regular household incandescent bulbs. The problem is that the windows in that room also permit some pretty strong daylight to filter through. In automatic white balance mode, the camera reacted to that daylight — which has a cool color cast — and applied too much warming, giving my original image a yellow tint. No problem: I just switched the white balance mode from AWB to the Tungsten Light setting. The right image in Figure 6-15 shows the corrected colors.

There's one little problem with white balancing as it's implemented on your Rebel XTi/400D, though. You can't make this kind of manual white balance selection if you shoot in the fully automatic exposure modes. So if you spy color problems in your camera monitor, you need to switch to either P, Tv, Av, M, or A-DEP exposure mode. (Chapter 5 details all five modes).

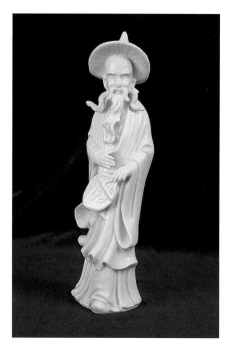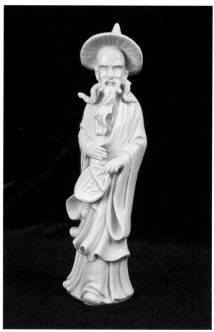

Figure 6-15: Multiple light sources resulted in a yellow color cast in auto white balance mode (left); switching to the Tungsten Light setting solved the problem (right).

The next section explains precisely how to make a simple white balance correction; following that, you can explore some advanced white balance features.

Changing the white balance setting

To switch from automatic to manual white balancing, follow these steps:

1. **Set the camera Mode dial to P, Tv, Av, M, or A-DEP.**

   You can tweak white balance only in these advanced exposure modes.

2. **Press the WB key (the bottom cross key).**

   You see the White Balance screen, shown on the left in Figure 6-16.

3. **Press the right or left cross key or rotate the Main dial to highlight the setting you want to use.**

   As you scroll through the list of options, the name of the selected setting appears above the little icon. For some settings, the camera also displays the approximate Kelvin temperature of the light source that the setting matches. (Refer to Figure 6-14 for a look at the Kelvin scale.)

If the scene is lit by several light sources, choose the setting that corresponds to the strongest source. The Tungsten Light setting is usually best for regular incandescent household bulbs, by the way. And with the Custom option, you can define your own white-balance setting; see the next section for details.

4. Press Set to lock in your choice.

You can confirm the current white balance setting by displaying the Camera Settings screen. The white balance icon appears in the area highlighted in the right image in Figure 6-16. Table 6-1 offers a reminder of what setting each icon represents.

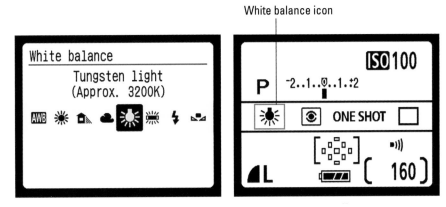

Figure 6-16: Press the bottom cross key (WB) to access white balance options.

Your selected white balance setting remains in force for the P, Tv, Av, M, and A-DEP exposure modes until you change it again. So you may want to get in the habit of resetting the option to AWB (automatic white balance) after you finish shooting whatever subject it was that caused you to switch to manual white balance mode.

Table 6-1	White Balance Settings
Symbol	*Setting*
AWB	Auto
☀	Daylight
🏠	Shade

continued

Table 6-1 *(continued)*

Symbol	Setting
	Cloudy
	Tungsten
	White Fluorescent
	Flash
	Custom

Creating a custom white balance setting

If none of the preset white balance options produces the right amount of color correction, you can create your own custom setting. To use this technique, you need a piece of card stock that's either neutral gray or absolute white — not eggshell white, sand white, or any other close-but-not perfect white. (You can buy reference cards made just for this purpose in many camera stores for under $20.)

Position the reference card so that it receives the same lighting you'll use for your photo. Then take these steps:

1. **Set the camera to the P, Tv, Av, M, or A-DEP exposure mode.**

   You can't create a custom setting in any of the fully automatic modes.

2. **Set the camera to manual focusing and then focus on your reference card.**

   Chapter 1 has details on manual focusing if you need help.

3. **Frame the shot so that your reference card fills the center area of the viewfinder.**

   In other words, make sure that at least the center autofocus point and the six surrounding points fall over the reference card.

4. **Make sure that the exposure settings are correct.**

   Just press the shutter button halfway to check exposure. In M mode, make sure that the exposure indicator is at the midway point of the exposure meter. In other modes, a blinking aperture or shutter speed value indicates an exposure problem. If necessary, adjust ISO, aperture, or shutter speed to fix the problem; Chapter 5 explains how.

5. **Take the picture of your reference card.**

   The camera will use this picture to establish your custom white balance setting.

6. **Display Shooting Menu 2 and highlight Custom WB, as shown on the left in Figure 6-17.**

7. **Press Set.**

   Now you see the screen shown on the right in Figure 6-17. The image you just captured should appear in the display. (If not, press the right or left cross key or rotate the Main dial to scroll to the image.)

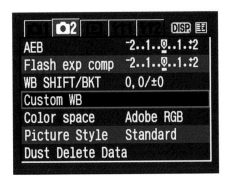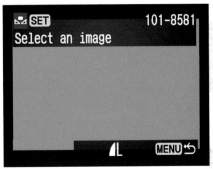

Figure 6-17: You can create a custom white balance setting through Shooting Menu 2.

8. **Press Set.**

   You see the message shown in Figure 6-18. This message tells you that the white balance setting is now stored. The little icon in the message area represents the Custom white balance setting.

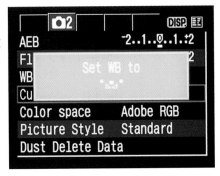

Your custom white balance setting remains stored until the next time you work your way through these steps. So anytime you're shooting in the same lighting conditions and want to apply the same white balance correction, just press the bottom cross key — the one labeled WB — to access the white balance options and then select the Custom option.

Figure 6-18: This message indicates that your white balance setting is stored.

Fine-tuning white balance settings

As yet another alternative for manipulating colors, your Rebel XTi/400D enables you to tweak white balancing in a way that shifts all colors toward a particular part of the color spectrum. The end result is similar to applying a traditional color filter to your lens.

To access this option, called White Balance Correction, take these steps:

1. **Set the Mode dial to P, Tv, Av, M, or A-DEP exposure mode.**

   You can take advantage of White Balance Correction only in these modes.

2. **Display Shooting Menu 2 and highlight WB Shift/Bkt, as shown on the left in Figure 6-19.**

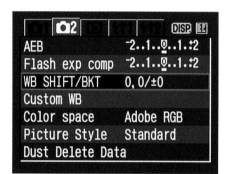
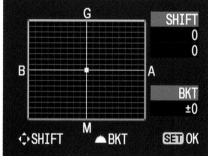

Figure 6-19: White Balance Correction offers one more way to control colors.

3. **Press Set to display the screen you see on the right in Figure 6-19.**

   The screen contains a grid that is oriented around two main color pairs: green and magenta, represented by the G and M labels, and blue and amber, represented by B and A. The little white square indicates the current amount of white balance correction, or shift. When the square is dead center in the grid, as in the figure, no shift is applied.

4. **Use the cross keys to move the square marker in the direction of the shift you want to achieve.**

   As you do, the Shift area of the display tells the amount of color bias that you've selected. For example, in Figure 6-20, I shifted three levels toward amber and one toward magenta.

   If you're familiar with traditional lens filters, you may know that the density of a filter, which determines the degree of color correction it provides, is measured in *mireds* (pronounced *my-redds*). The white balance grid is designed around this system: Moving the marker one level is the equivalent of adding a filter with a density of 5 mireds.

5. **Press Set to apply the change and return to the menu.**

After you apply white balance correction, a little plus or minus sign appears next to the white balance symbol in the Camera Settings display, as shown on the left in Figure 6-21. That's your reminder that white balance shift is being applied. The same symbol appears in the viewfinder. You can see the exact correction values in Shooting Menu 2, as shown on the right in the figure.

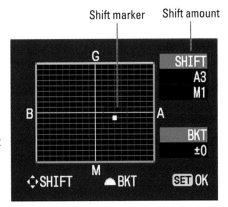

Figure 6-20: Press the cross keys to move the marker and shift white balance.

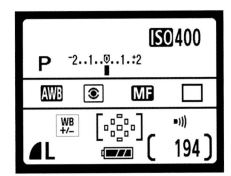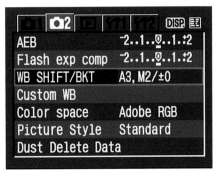

Figure 6-21: The +/- symbol lets you know that white balance shift is being applied.

Your adjustment remains in force for all the advanced exposure modes until you change it. And the correction is applied no matter what white balance setting you choose. So make it a point to check the monitor or viewfinder before your next shoot — otherwise, you may forget to adjust the white balance for the current light.

6. **To cancel white balance correction, repeat these steps and just move the grid marker back to the center position.**

Be sure that values in the Shift area of the display are both set to 0. In other words, your screen should look like what you see on the right in Figure 6-19.

Many film-photography enthusiasts place colored filters on their lenses to either warm or cool their images. Portrait photographers, for example, often add a warming filter to give skin tones a healthy, golden glow. You can mimic the effects of such filters by simply fine-tuning your camera's white balance settings as just described. Experiment with shifting the white balance a tad toward amber and magenta for a warming effect or toward blue and green for a cooling effect.

Bracketing shots with white balance

Chapter 5 introduces you to your camera's automatic exposure bracketing, which enables you to easily record the same image at three different exposure settings. Similarly, you can take advantage of automatic white balance bracketing. With this feature, the camera records the same image three times, using a slightly different white balance setting for each.

This feature is especially helpful when you're shooting in varying light sources — for example, a mix of fluorescent light, daylight, and flash. Bracketing the shots ups the odds that the color renditions of at least one of the shots will be to your liking.

Note a couple of things about this feature:

- ✔ You can't use white balance bracketing if you set the camera's Quality setting to either Raw or Raw+Large/Fine. And frankly, there isn't any need to do so in Raw mode because you can precisely tune colors when you process the Raw files. Chapter 8 has details on Raw processing.

- ✔ Because the camera records three images, white balance bracketing reduces the maximum capture speed that is possible when you use the Continuous shooting mode. See Chapter 2 for more about Continuous mode. Of course, recording three images instead of one also eats up more space on your memory card.

- ✔ The white balance bracketing feature is designed around the same grid used for white balance correction, explained in the preceding section. As a reminder, the grid is based on two color pairs: green/magenta and blue/amber.

- ✔ When white balance bracketing is enabled, the camera always records the first of the three bracketed shots using a neutral white balance setting — or, at least, what it considers to be neutral, given its own measurement of the light. The second and third shots are then recorded using the specified shift along either the green/magenta or blue/amber axis of the color grid.

If all that is as clear as mud, just take a look at Figure 6-22 for an example. I captured these images using a single tungsten studio light and the candle light itself. I set up white balance bracketing to work along the blue/amber color axis. So the camera recorded the first image at neutral, the second with a slightly blue color bias, and the third, with an amber bias.

Neutral +3 Blue bias +3 Amber bias

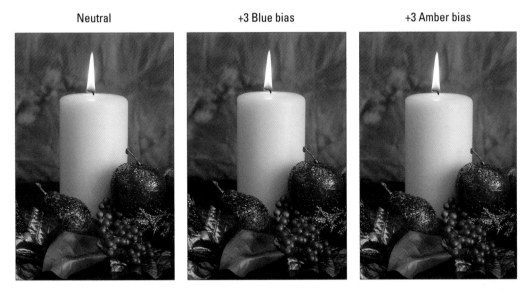

Figure 6-22: I captured one neutral image, one with a blue bias, and one with an amber bias.

To enable white balance bracketing, take these steps:

1. **Make sure the Quality option is not set to record Raw images.**

   You find this setting on Shooting Menu 1. If you select Raw (or Raw+Large/Fine), the camera simply records each image the same way. You then can adjust colors in your Raw processor.

2. **Display Shooting Menu 2 and highlight WB/Shift Bkt.**

3. **Press Set to display the grid shown in Figure 6-23.**

   The screen is the same one you see when you use the White Balance Correction feature, explained in the preceding section.

4. **Use the cross keys and Main dial to set the amount and direction of the bracketing shift.**

   First, press the cross keys to position the white balance marker — that's the little white

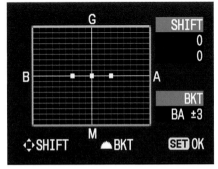

Figure 6-23: I used these settings to capture the bracketed candle images.

square — in the grid. Then rotate the Main dial to specify whether you want the bracketing to be applied across the horizontal axis (blue to amber) or the vertical axis (green to magenta.)

- *Blue to amber bracketing:* Rotate the dial right.

- *Green to magenta bracketing:* Rotate the dial left.

As you rotate the dial, three markers appear on the grid, indicating the amount of shift that will be applied to your trio of bracketed images. You can apply a maximum shift of plus or minus three levels of adjustment.

The BKT area of the screen also indicates the shift; for example, in Figure 6-23, the display shows a bracketing amount of plus and minus three levels on the blue/amber axis. I used the settings shown in Figure 6-23 to record the example images you see in Figure 6-22. As you can see, even at the maximum shift (+/– 3), the difference to the colors is subtle.

5. **Press Set to apply your changes and return to the menu.**

The bracketing symbol shown in Figure 6-24 appears in the Camera Settings display. Your bracketing setting remains in effect until you turn the camera off.

White balance bracketing icon

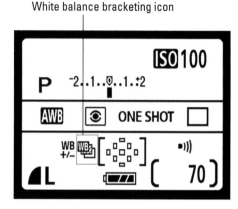

Figure 6-24: This symbol indicates that bracketing is being applied.

Choosing a Color Space: sRGB vs. Adobe RGB

Normally, your camera captures images using the *sRGB color mode,* which simply refers to an industry-standard spectrum of colors. (The *s* is for *standard,* and the RGB is for red-green-blue, which are the primary colors in the digital imaging color world.) This color mode was created to help ensure color consistency as an image moves from camera (or scanner) to monitor and printer; the idea was to create a spectrum of colors that all these devices can reproduce.

However, the sRGB color spectrum leaves out some colors that *can* be reproduced in print and onscreen, at least by some devices. So as an alternative, your camera also enables you to shoot in the Adobe RGB color mode, which includes a larger spectrum (or *gamut)* of colors. Figure 6-25 offers an illustration of the two spectrums.

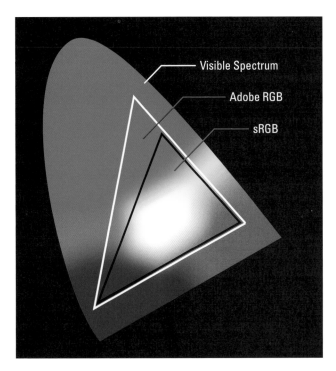

Figure 6-25: Adobe RGB includes some colors not found in the sRGB spectrum.

Some colors in the Adobe RGB spectrum cannot be reproduced in print. Still, I usually shoot in Adobe RGB mode because I see no reason to limit myself to a smaller spectrum from the get-go.

If you want to capture images in Adobe RGB instead of sRGB, visit Shooting Menu 2, highlight the Color Space option, and press Set. Now you see the screen shown in Figure 6-26. Use the up or down cross key to highlight Adobe RGB and press Set again.

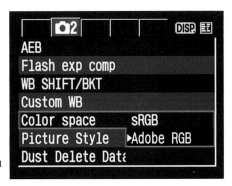

Figure 6-26: Choose Adobe RGB for a broader color spectrum.

Remember that this color mode choice applies only when you shoot in the advanced exposure modes: P, Tv, Av, M, and A-DEP. In all other modes, the camera automatically selects sRGB as the color space.

Exploring Picture Styles

In addition to all the focus and color features already covered in this chapter, your Rebel XTi/400D offers *Picture Styles.* Through Picture Styles, you can further tweak color, saturation, contrast, and image sharpening.

Sharpening, in case you're new to the digital meaning of the term, refers to a software process that adjusts contrast in a way that creates the illusion of slightly sharper focus. I explain sharpening fully in Chapter 10, but the important thing to note for now is that sharpening cannot remedy poor focus, but instead produces a subtle *tweak* to this aspect of your pictures.

In fact, many of the adjustments that Picture Styles apply are pretty subtle, at least to my eye. The impact of any of these settings varies depending on your subject, but on the whole, if you want to make large-scale changes to color, contrast, or sharpening, you're probably going to need to use your computer and photo editing software.

Again, though, your mileage may vary, as they say, as may your opinion of what constitutes the optimum color and sharpening characteristics. So I leave it to you to do your own testing and decide for yourself which of the Picture Style settings you prefer for your photographs. (Inspect your test shots on your computer monitor, where the differences produced by the various Picture Style settings are easier to spot than on the camera monitor or on these pages.)

The next section explains how to apply one of the six prefab Picture Styles your camera provides. Later sections explain how to customize those five Picture Styles and also how to define your very own, custom Picture Styles.

Selecting a Picture Style

When you set the Mode dial to Full Auto or any of the other fully automatic exposure modes, the camera selects a Picture Style for you. In P, Tv, Av, M, and A-DEP modes, however, you can specify which of the Picture Styles you want to use.

You can access Picture Styles through Shooting Menu 2, as shown on the left in Figure 6-27. Just highlight the Picture Styles option and press Set to display the screenful of options you see on the right in the figure. (You can see only five of the Picture Style settings on the first screen; scroll down using the cross keys to view the others.)

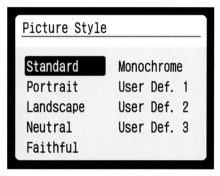

Figure 6-27: You can access Picture Styles options via Shooting Menu 2.

For an even quicker option, though, just press the Set button while no menus are displayed. In that case, you see the screen shown in Figure 6-28. Here, all the available Picture Styles are visible.

Either way, highlight the style you want to use by pressing the cross keys or rotating the Main dial and then press Set again. The selected Picture Style is applied until you change the setting again.

Figure 6-28: Press the Set button with no menus displayed to quickly select a Picture Style.

Here's a description of each Picture Style option:

- **Standard:** The default setting, this option captures the image normally — that is, using the characteristics that Canon offers as suitable for the majority of subjects.

- **Portrait:** This mode reduces sharpening slightly from the amount that's applied in Standard mode, with the goal of keeping skin texture soft. Color saturation, on the other hand, is slightly increased.

  The Canon manual recommends this setting for portraits of women and children — presuming, I guess, that men prefer not to be rendered with slightly soft skin. But I suggest that it's appropriate for portraits regardless of gender or age.

  If you shoot in the Portrait exposure mode, the camera automatically applies this Picture Style for you.

✔ **Landscape:** In a nod to traditions of landscape photography, this Picture Style emphasizes greens and blues and amps up color saturation and sharpness, resulting in bolder images.

The camera automatically applies this Picture Style if you set the Mode dial to the Landscape exposure mode.

✔ **Neutral:** This setting reduces saturation and contrast slightly compared to how the camera renders images when the Standard option is selected.

✔ **Faithful:** The Faithful style is designed to render colors as closely as possible to how your eye perceives them.

✔ **Monochrome:** This setting produces, er, black-and-white photos. Only in the digital world, they're called *grayscale images* because a true black-and-white image contains only black and white, with no shades of gray. Note that when this Picture Style is selected, the initials B/W appear on the Camera Settings display.

If you set the Quality option on Shooting Menu 1 to Raw (or Raw + Large/Fine), the camera displays your image on the monitor in black and white during playback. But during the Raw converter process, you can either choose to go with your grayscale version or view and save a full-color version. Or, even better, you can process and save the image once as a grayscale photo and then process and save it again as a color image.

If you *don't* capture the image in the Raw format, you can't access the original image colors later.

✔ **User Defined 1, 2, and 3:** These options enables you to create and save three of your own Picture Styles. I cover this feature in the last section of the chapter.

Figure 6-29 shows you how the camera rendered the same scene in each of the six preset Picture Styles. As you can see, Landscape has the most noticeable impact. To my taste, in fact, Landscape colors are a little over the top, but that's strictly a personal preference.

If you don't like any of the Picture Styles, you can use the options discussed in the next section to tweak them.

Customizing Picture Styles

You can customize the results that you get from the prefab Picture Styles. For the Standard, Landscape, Portrait, Neutral, and Faithful styles, you can adjust sharpness, contrast, saturation, and color tone.

I'm guessing that the first three effects — sharpness, contrast, and saturation — are self-explanatory. But the color tone option may not be so obvious. This option, which is designed to help you tweak skin colors, enables you to make your colors either a little more red or a little more yellow.

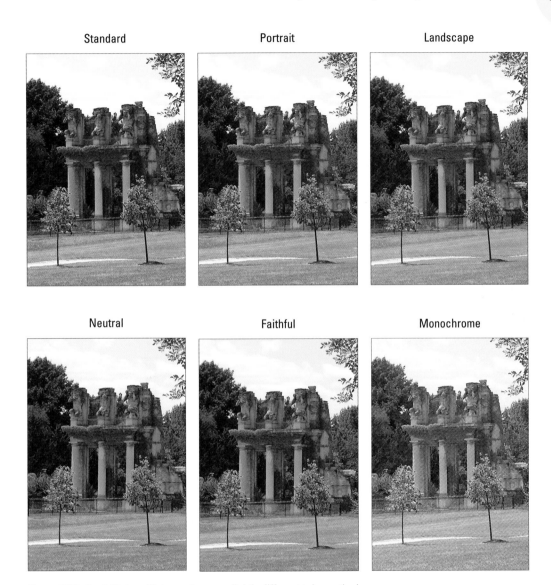

Figure 6-29: Each Picture Style produces a slightly different take on the image.

For the Monochrome Picture Style, saturation and color tone are irrelevant, so they are replaced by two other options, Filter and Toning Effect. The Filter effect options mimic color filters sometimes used by photographers shooting black-and-white film. The color of the filter determines which colors in the original scene become prominent in the black-and-white image. The Toning Effect options enable you to apply a sepia, blue, purple, or green tint to your monochrome image.

To dig into Picture Style customizing, take these steps:

1. **Display Shooting Menu 2, highlight Picture Style, and press Set.**

   You see the screen shown on the left in Figure 6-30.

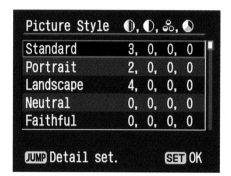 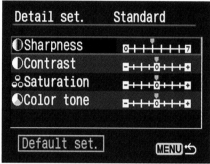

Figure 6-30: You can customize the prefab Picture Styles.

2. **Press the up or down cross key or rotate the Main dial to highlight the Picture Style you want to adjust.**

3. **Press the Jump button.**

   Now you see the screen shown on the right in Figure 6-30, listing the four characteristics that you can adjust for your selected Picture Style. Again, if you selected the Monochrome style (not shown in the figure), you see Filter and Toning Effect options instead of Saturation and Color Tone.

4. **Highlight the characteristic that you want to tweak and press Set.**

   The little scale next to the selection option becomes active.

5. **Press the right or left cross key or rotate the Main dial to adjust the setting.**

   As soon as you adjust the setting, you see two markers: The gray one shows you the default setting; the blue one, your customized setting.

   For contrast, saturation, and sharpness, move the little marker on the scale to the right to increase the effect. For color tone, move the slider toward the minus sign to make colors less yellow and more red; move the slider toward the plus sign to make colors less red and more yellow.

   When you adjust the Filter and Toning Effect options for the Monochrome style, the adjustment scale and slider are replaced by a simple list of options; just highlight the one you want to use.

6. **Press Set to lock in your adjustment.**

7. **Repeat Steps 4 through 6 to adjust the other settings as desired.**

8. Press the Menu button to return to the main Picture Styles screen.

9. Press Set.

If you later want to return to the default settings for the Picture Style, just repeat Steps 1 through 3 and then highlight Default Set (at the bottom of the screen) in Step 4 and press Set.

TIP

Unfortunately, you can't preview how your adjustments will affect your image because the Picture Style attributes are applied to the photo *after* you shoot it, during the time the image is recorded to your memory card. So I'd like to offer another alternative: If you shoot in the Raw format, you don't have to worry about in-camera adjustments to Picture Styles — or even selecting a Picture Style, for that matter — because you can apply the style when you process your Raw images. Just follow the directions laid out in Chapter 8 to use the Raw converter provided in ZoomBrowser EX (Windows) or Image-Browser (Mac). On the Image Quality Adjustment panel, shown in Figure 6-31, you can select a Picture Style and then make the same adjustments to the style as you can in the camera.

The Raw converter method of applying Picture Styles is perhaps most beneficial for creating monochrome images — unless you're schooled in black-and-white photography, it can be difficult to predict which of the Monochrome settings will best translate your colors into a grayscale image. (Note that the Raw processor refers to the Monochrome Picture Style as B/W, as shown in Figure 6-31.)

At the very least, experimenting with Picture Styles in the Raw converter should help you know what adjustments you may want to make to the actual camera settings. And for creating monochrome images, using the Raw converter tools enables you to experiment with all the different Filter and Toning Effects options to find the one you like best.

Creating your own Picture Style

The User Defined option on the Picture Style menu enables you to create and store up to three of your very own Picture Styles. So if you hit upon a combination of customized settings that you really like for a particular type of subject — snow scenes, for example, or pictures of your pooch — you can easily reuse those settings.

Follow these steps to create your custom Picture Style:

1. Display Shooting Menu 2, highlight Picture Style, and press Set.

You see the normal list of Picture Styles, as shown on the left in Figure 6-32.

Picture Style options

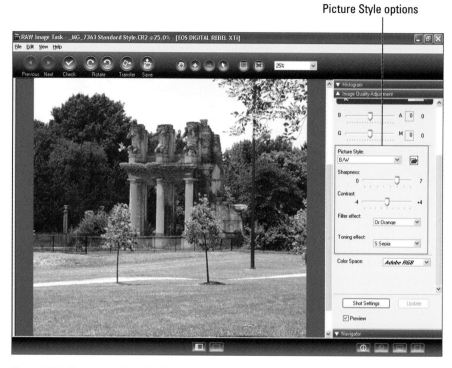

Figure 6-31: You can apply and adjust Picture Style settings in the Raw converter, too.

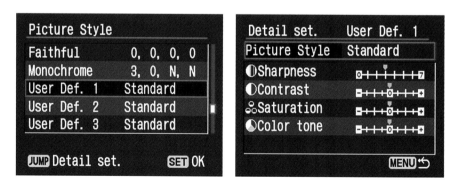

Figure 6-32: You can create up to three of your own Picture Styles.

2. **Highlight one of the three User Def options and press the Jump button.**

   Now you see the screen shown on the right in Figure 6-32.

3. **Highlight the Picture Style option and press Set.**

4. **Select the style on which you want to base your custom style and press Set.**

   If you want to create your own style for portraits, for example, select the Portrait option. Or, if you want to create a special black-and-white style, choose Monochrome. Your new style will be based on the one you select.

5. **Set the rest of the style attributes.**

   The options available are the same as when you customize a style. Highlight the option, press Set to activate the little slider, and then use the cross keys or Main dial to adjust the setting. See the preceding section for details about the options. Press Set again to lock in the adjustment.

6. **Press Menu to store your custom style.**

To use your style, just select it from the Picture Style menu as usual. Note that when you view Picture Styles in Shooting Menu 2, you see the name of the base style you selected in Step 4 along with the User Defined 1, 2, or 3 item.

7

Putting It All Together

*E*arlier chapters of this book break down each and every picture-taking feature on your Rebel XTi/400D, describing in detail how the various controls affect exposure, picture quality, focus, color, and the like. This chapter pulls all that information together to help you set up your camera for specific types of photography.

The first few pages offer a quick summary of critical picture-taking settings that should serve you well no matter what your subject. Following that, I offer my advice on which settings to use for portraits, action shots, landscapes, and close-ups. To wrap things up, the end of the chapter includes some miscellaneous tips for dealing with special shooting situations and subjects.

Keep in mind that although I present specific recommendations here, there are no hard and fast rules as to the "right way" to shoot a portrait, a landscape, or whatever. So don't be afraid to wander off on your own, tweaking this exposure setting or adjusting that focus control, to discover your own creative vision. Experimentation is part of the fun of photography, after all — and thanks to your camera monitor and the Erase button, it's an easy, completely free proposition.

Recapping Basic Picture Settings

Your subject, creative goals, and lighting conditions determine which settings you should use for some picture-taking options, such as aperture and shutter speed. I offer my take on those options throughout this chapter. But for a few basic options, I recommend the same settings for almost every shooting scenario. Table 7-1 lists these options as well as how you access them; Figure 7-1 offers a reminder of the buttons that are referenced in the table.

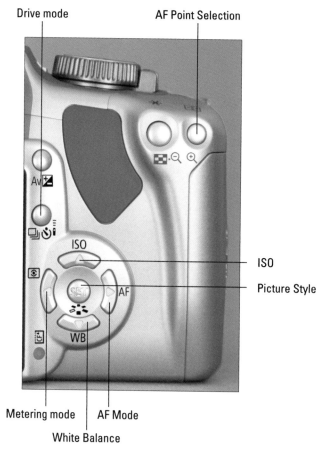

Drive mode   AF Point Selection

ISO

Picture Style

Metering mode   AF Mode

White Balance

Figure 7-1: You can access several critical settings with a press of a single button.

Other chapters detail all these settings, but here's a quick reminder of how each one affects your image:

Table 7-1	All-Purpose Picture-Taking Settings	
Option	*Recommended Setting*	*Access via Menu/Button*
Image Quality	Large/Fine (JPEG), Medium/Fine (JPEG), or Raw (CR2)	Shooting Menu 1
White Balance[1]	Auto	Bottom cross key
ISO[1]	100 or 200	Top cross key
AF mode[2]	AI Focus	Right cross key
Drive mode	Action photos: Continuous; all others: Single	Drive Mode button
AF Point Selection[2]	Auto	AF Point Selection button
Metering[1]	Evaluative	Left cross key
Picture Style[1]	Standard	Shooting Menu 2 or Set button

[1] *Adjustable only in P, Tv, Av, M, and A-DEP exposure modes.*
[2] *Adjustable only in P, Tv, Av, and M exposure modes.*

✔ **Quality:** This setting, introduced in Chapter 3, determines the file format and resolution of picture file the camera creates. For best quality and the largest possible print size, choose Large/Fine or Raw (CR2). Keep in mind that you must process Raw files in a raw converter; Chapter 8 explains that issue. For everyday images that you don't plan to print large or crop, Medium/Fine is also a good choice and creates smaller files than the other two settings.

✔ **White Balance:** White balance compensates for the color casts produced by different light sources. Auto white balance (AWB) mode usually does the trick unless you're dealing with multiple light sources; in that case, you may need to switch to manual white balance control. Chapter 6 tells you how. You can control this setting only in the advanced exposure modes.

✔ **ISO:** This setting determines the light sensitivity of the camera's image sensor. Increasing the ISO value can create noise defects, so stick with the lowest setting possible given the available light. You can't select ISO in the fully automatic exposure modes; the camera sets the value between 100 and 400 for you. Chapter 5 details ISO.

✔ **AF (autofocus) mode:** Chapter 6 details this option, which affects the autofocus system. In the AI Focus mode, the camera chooses the best autofocus mode based on whether it thinks you're shooting a still or moving subject. (The *AI* stands for *artificial intelligence.*) In most cases, this setting works well. You can control this option only in P, Tv, Av, and M exposure modes.

✔ **Drive mode:** This setting enables you to shift from Single mode, in which you record one image each time you press the shutter button, to Continuous mode, in which the camera continues to capture images as long as you hold down the shutter button. The third Drive mode option puts the camera into self-timer or remote-control mode.

Single mode is the best choice in most cases, but Continuous can come in handy for action shots, as covered later in this chapter. Chapter 2 explains all the Drive mode settings. Note that you can select self-timer mode in all exposure modes, but you can select either Continuous or Single only in the advanced exposure modes. In the fully automatic modes, the camera chooses either Single or Continuous for you.

✔ **AF Point Selection:** This control enables you to choose from two auto-focusing setups when you shoot in the P, Tv, Av, or M exposure mode. In Automatic AF Point Selection mode, all nine of the camera's autofocus points are active, and the camera typically locks focus on the point that covers the nearest object or person. In Manual AF Point Selection mode, you can specify which of the nine autofocus points you want the camera to use when establishing focus. The camera always uses the automatic option when you shoot in the fully automatic exposure modes or A-DEP mode.

✔ **Metering mode:** This option determines what part of the frame the camera analyzes when calculating exposure. Evaluative metering takes the whole frame into account, which produces good results for most scenes. See Chapter 5 for the scoop on the other two options, Partial and Center-Weighted Average metering, which are selectable only when you shoot in the advanced exposure modes. All fully automatic modes use Evaluative metering.

✔ **Picture Style:** When you shoot in the advanced exposure modes, you can manipulate color, sharpness, and contrast by selecting from one of six preset Picture Style settings or by defining your own custom style. In the fully automatic modes, the camera selects the Picture Style for you based on which mode you're using. For example, in Portrait exposure mode, the camera selects the Portrait Picture Style setting. See Chapter 6 for a review of all the Picture Style controls.

As indicated in the table, you can adjust only the Quality and Drive mode settings when you shoot in the fully automatic modes. And in the A-DEP mode, you can't adjust the AF Point Selection or AF mode settings. If you want to tweak all these settings, you must set the camera Mode dial to P, Tv, Av, or M.

Setting Up for Specific Scenes

For the most part, the settings detailed in the preceding section fall into the "set 'em and forget 'em" category. That leaves you free to concentrate on a handful of other camera options, such as aperture and shutter speed, that you can manipulate to achieve a specific photographic goal.

The next four sections explain which of these additional options typically produce the best results when you're shooting portraits, action shots, landscapes, and close-ups. I offer a few compositional and creative tips along the way — but again, remember that beauty is in the eye of the beholder, and for every so-called rule, there are plenty of great images that prove the exception.

Shooting still portraits

By "still portrait," I mean that your subject isn't moving. For subjects who aren't keen on sitting still long enough to have their picture taken — children, pets, and even some teenagers I know — skip ahead to the next section and use the techniques given for action photography instead.

Assuming that you do have a subject willing to pose, the classic portraiture approach is to keep the subject sharply focused while throwing the background into soft focus, as shown in the examples in this section. This artistic choice emphasizes the subject and helps diminish the impact of any distracting background objects in cases where you can't control the setting. The following steps show you how to achieve this look:

1. **Set the Mode dial to Av (aperture-priority autoexposure mode) and then select the lowest f-stop value possible.**

   As Chapter 5 explains, a low f-stop setting opens the aperture, which shortens depth of field, or the range of sharp focus. So dialing in a low f-stop value is the first step in softening your portrait background. (The f-stop range available to you depends on your lens.) Also keep in mind that the farther your subject is from the background, the more background blurring you can achieve.

   I recommend aperture-priority autoexposure mode when depth of field is a primary concern because you can control the f-stop while relying on the camera to select the shutter speed that will properly expose the image. Just rotate the Main dial to select your desired f-stop. But if you aren't comfortable with this advanced exposure mode, Portrait mode also results in a more open aperture, although the exact f-stop setting is out of your control. Chapter 2 details Portrait mode.

   Whichever mode you choose, you can monitor the current aperture and shutter speed both in the Camera Settings display, as shown on the left in Figure 7-2, and in the viewfinder display, as shown on the right.

Shutter speed   Aperture

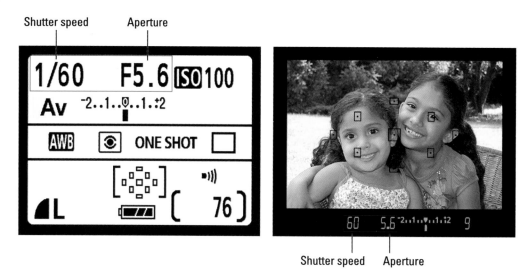

Shutter speed   Aperture

Figure 7-2: You can view exposure settings in the Camera Settings display or viewfinder.

2. To further soften the background, zoom in, get closer, or both.

As covered in Chapter 6, zooming in to a longer focal length also reduces depth of field, as does moving physically closer to your subject.

Avoid using a lens with a short focal length (a wide-angle lens) for portraits. They can cause features to appear distorted — sort of like how people look when you view them through a security peephole in a door.

3. For indoor portraits, shoot flash-free if possible.

Shooting by available light rather than flash produces softer illumination and avoids the problem of red-eye. To get enough light to go flash-free, turn on room lights or, during daylight, pose your subject next to a sunny window.

In the Av exposure mode, simply keeping the built-in flash unit closed disables the flash. In Portrait mode, unfortunately, you can't disable the flash if the camera thinks more light is needed. Your only option is to change the exposure mode to No Flash, in which case the camera may or may not choose an aperture setting that throws the background into soft focus.

If flash is unavoidable, see my list of flash tips at the end of the steps to get better results.

4. For outdoor portraits, use a flash.

Even in bright daylight, a flash adds a beneficial pop of light to subjects' faces, as discussed in Chapter 5 and illustrated here in Figure 7-3.

Unfortunately, the camera doesn't let you use flash in Portrait mode if the light is very bright. In the Av exposure mode, just press the Flash button on the side of the camera to enable the flash.

No flash   With flash

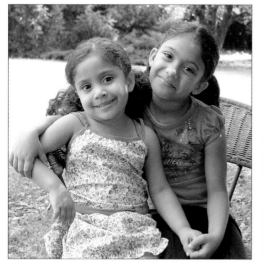 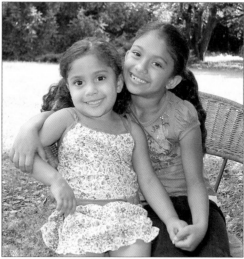

Figure 7-3: To properly illuminate the face in outdoor portraits, use fill flash.

Remember that in dim lighting, the camera may select a shutter speed as slow as 1/30 second when you enable flash in Av mode, so keep an eye on that value and use a tripod if necessary to avoid blurring from camera shake.

5. **Press and hold the shutter button halfway to lock in focus.**

   Make sure that an active autofocus point falls over your subject. (In the viewfinder, active autofocus points turn red.) For best results, try to set focus on your subject's eyes.

   Chapter 6 explains more about using autofocus, but if you have trouble, simply set your lens to manual focus mode and then twist the focusing ring to set focus.

6. **Press the shutter button the rest of the way to capture the image.**

Again, these steps just give you a starting point for taking better portraits. A few other tips can also improve your people pics:

- ✏ **Before pressing the shutter button, do a quick background check.** Scan the entire frame looking for intrusive objects that may distract the eye from the subject. If necessary, reposition the subject against a more flattering backdrop if possible. Inside, a softly textured wall works well; outdoors, trees and shrubs can provide nice backdrops as long as they aren't so ornate or colorful that they diminish the subject (for example, a magnolia tree laden with blooms).

✔ **Frame the subject loosely to allow for later cropping to a variety of frame sizes.** Your Canon produces images that have an aspect ratio of 3:2. That means that your portrait perfectly fits a 4-x-6-inch print size but will require cropping to print at any other proportions, such as 5 x 7 or 8 x 10. Chapter 9 talks more about this issue.

✔ **Pay attention to white balance if your subject is lit by both flash and ambient light.** If you set the white balance setting to automatic (AWB), as I recommend in Table 7-1, enabling flash tells the camera to warm colors to compensate for the cool light of a flash. If your subject is also lit by room lights or daylight, the result may be colors that are slightly warmer than neutral. This warming effect typically looks nice in portraits, giving the skin a subtle glow. But if you aren't happy with the result or want even more warming, see Chapter 6 to find out how to fine-tune white balance. Again, you can make this adjustment only in P, Tv, Av, M, or A-DEP exposure mode.

✔ **When flash is unavoidable, try these tricks to produce better results.** The following techniques can help solve flash-related issues:

  • *Indoors, turn on as many room lights as possible.* With more ambient light, you reduce the flash power that's needed to expose the picture. This step also causes the pupils to constrict, further reducing the chances of red-eye. (Pay heed to my white balance warning, however.)

  • *Try setting the flash to Red-Eye Reduction mode for nighttime and indoor portraits.* Warn your subject to expect both a preflash, which constricts pupils, and the actual flash. See Chapter 2 for details about using this flash mode.

  • *For nighttime pictures, try Night Portrait mode.* In this mode, the camera automatically selects a slower shutter speed than normal. This enables the camera to soak up more ambient light, producing a brighter background and reducing the flash power that's needed to light the subject. A slow shutter, however, means that you need to use a tripod to avoid camera shake, which can blur the photo. You also need to warn your subjects to remain very still during the exposure.

  • *Soften the flash light by attaching a diffuser to the flash head.* This inexpensive tool both softens and spreads the light. You can see a picture of one type of diffuser in Chapter 5. You may need to bump up exposure slightly to compensate for the light filtering that occurs; the camera doesn't know that you attached the diffuser and so doesn't adjust the exposure on its own. In autoexposure mode, you can use exposure compensation to adjust the image brightness. As an alternative, you can increase the flash power slightly. Again, Chapter 5 has details on these exposure features.

  • *For professional results, use an external flash with a rotating flash head.* Then aim the flash head upward so that the flash light bounces off the ceiling and falls softly down onto the subject. An external flash isn't cheap, but the results make the purchase worthwhile if you shoot lots of portraits. Compare the two portraits in Figure 7-4 for an illustration. In the first example, the built-in flash resulted in strong shadowing behind the subject and harsh, concentrated light. To produce the better result on the right, I used the Canon Speedlite 580EX II and bounced the light off the ceiling.

- *To reduce shadowing from the flash, move your subject farther from the background.* I took this extra step for the right image in Figure 7-4. The increased distance not only reduced shadowing but also softened the focus of the wall a bit (because of the short depth of field resulting from my f-stop and focal length).

A good general rule is to position your subjects far enough from the background that they can't touch it. If that isn't possible, though, try going the other direction: If the person's head is smack up against the background, any shadow will be smaller and less noticeable. For example, you get less shadowing when a subject's head is resting against a sofa cushion than if that person is sitting upright, with the head a foot or so away from the cushion.

Direct flash   Bounced flash

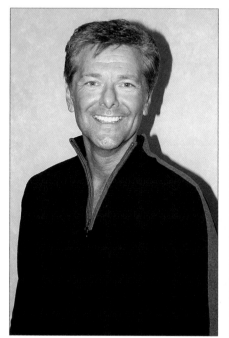 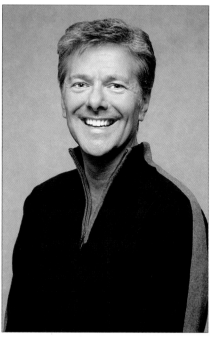

Figure 7-4: To eliminate harsh lighting and strong shadows (left), I used bounce flash and moved the subject farther from the background (right).

- *Study the flash information in Chapter 5, and practice before you need to take important portraits.* How the camera calculates the aperture, shutter speed, and flash power needed to expose your subject and background varies depending on the exposure mode you use. So to fully understand how to get the flash results you want, it pays to experiment with each of the advanced exposure modes, all covered in Chapter 5.

For the maximum control over aperture, shutter speed, and flash power, try working in Manual exposure mode and make friends with the Flash Exposure Compensation and Flash Exposure Lock features.

Capturing action

A fast shutter speed is the key to capturing a blur-free shot of any moving subject, whether it's a spinning Ferris wheel, a butterfly flitting from flower to flower, or in the case of Figures 7-5 and 7-6, a hockey-playing teen. In the first image, a shutter speed of 1/125 second was too slow to catch the subject without blur. For this subject, who was moving at a fairly rapid speed, I needed to bump the shutter speed all the way up to 1/1000 second to freeze the action cleanly, as shown in Figure 7-6.

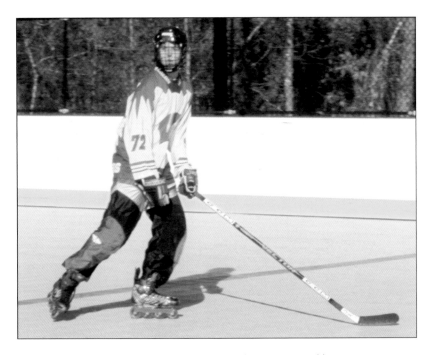

Figure 7-5: A too-slow shutter speed causes the skater to appear blurry.

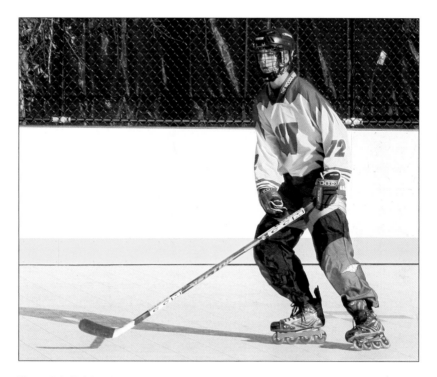

Figure 7-6: Raising the shutter speed to 1/1000 second "froze" the action.

Along with the basic capture settings outlined in Table 7-1, I use the techniques in the following steps to photograph a subject in motion:

1. Set the Mode dial to Tv (shutter-priority autoexposure).

In this mode, you control the shutter speed, and the camera takes care of choosing an aperture setting that will produce a good exposure.

If you aren't ready to step up to this advanced exposure mode, explained in Chapter 5, try using Sports mode, detailed in Chapter 2. But be aware that you have no control over any other aspects of your picture (such as white balance, flash, and so on) in that mode.

2. Rotate the Main dial to select the shutter speed.

Refer to Figure 7-7 to locate shutter speed on the Camera Settings display. After you select the shutter speed, the camera selects an aperture (f-stop) to match.

What shutter speed you need depends on the speed at which your subject is moving, so some experimentation is needed. But generally speaking, 1/500 second should be plenty for all but the fastest subjects — speeding hockey players like my subject, race cars, boats, and so on. For slower subjects, you can even go as low as 1/250 or 1/125 second.

If the aperture value blinks after you set the shutter speed, the camera can't select an f-stop that will properly expose the photo at that shutter speed. See Chapter 5 for more details about how the camera notifies you of potential exposure problems.

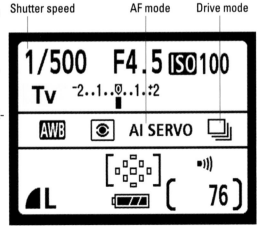

Shutter speed   AF mode   Drive mode

Figure 7-7: Changing the Drive mode to Continuous allows rapid-fire shooting.

3. **Raise the ISO setting or add flash to produce a brighter exposure if needed.**

In dim lighting, you may not be able to get a good exposure at your chosen shutter speed without taking this step. Raising the ISO does increase the possibility of noise, but a noisy shot is better than a blurry shot. The current ISO setting appears in the top-right corner of the Camera Settings display, as shown in Figure 7-7. (Note that in Sports mode, the camera automatically overrides your ISO setting if it deems necessary, but it can go only as high as ISO 400. For more on ISO, see Chapter 5.)

Adding flash is a bit tricky for action shots, unfortunately. First, the flash needs time to recycle between shots, so try to go without if you want to capture images at a fast pace. Second, the built-in flash has limited range — so don't waste your time if your subject isn't close by. And third, remember that the maximum shutter speed decreases when you enable flash; the top speed is 1/200 second. For more on this issue, check out the Chapter 5 sidebar related to flash synch speeds.

If you do decide to use flash, you must bail out of Sports mode, though; it doesn't permit you to use flash.

4. **For rapid-fire shooting, set the Drive mode to Continuous.**

In this mode, you can take as many as three pictures per second. The camera continues to record images as long as the shutter button is pressed. You can switch the Drive mode by pressing the button you see in the margin here; the icon representing the current mode appears in the Camera Settings display, as labeled in Figure 7-7.

If you do enable the flash, the pace at which the camera can record images slows because the flash needs time to recycle between shots. Chapter 2 explains more about all the Drive mode options.

5. **For fastest shooting, switch to manual focusing.**

You then eliminate the time the camera needs to lock focus in autofocus mode. Chapter 1 shows you how to focus manually, if you need help.

If you do use autofocus, try these two autofocus settings for best performance:

- Set the AF Point Selection mode to Automatic. Press the button shown in the margin here to adjust this setting.

- Set the Focus mode to AI Servo (continuous-servo autofocus). Press the right cross key to access this setting.

Chapter 6 details these autofocus options.

6. **Turn off automatic image review to speed up the camera even more.**

You do this via the Review Time option on the Playback menu. Turning the option off can help speed up the time your camera needs to recover between shots.

7. **Compose the subject to allow for movement across the frame.**

You can always crop the photo later to a tighter composition. (I did so for my example images, which originally contained quite a bit more background than you see in the book.) Chapter 10 shows you how to crop pictures.

8. **Lock in autofocus (if used) in advance.**

Press the shutter button halfway to do so. Now when the action occurs, just press the shutter button the rest of the way. Your image-capture time is faster because the camera has already done the work of establishing focus.

Remember that in AI Servo mode, you must keep the subject under the active autofocus point (or points) in order for the camera to maintain focus. Again, Chapter 6 details this feature.

Using these techniques should give you a better chance of capturing any fast-moving subject. But action-shooting strategies also are helpful for shooting candid portraits of kids and pets. Even if they aren't currently running, leaping, or otherwise cavorting, snapping a shot before they do move or change positions is often tough. So if an interaction or scene catches your eye, set your camera into action mode and then just fire off a series of shots as fast as you can.

Capturing scenic vistas

Providing specific capture settings for landscape photography is tricky because there's no single best approach to capturing a beautiful stretch of countryside, a city skyline, or other vast subject. Take depth of field, for example: One person's idea of a super cityscape might be to keep all buildings in the scene sharply focused. But another photographer might prefer to shoot the same scene so that a foreground building is sharply focused while the others are less so, thus drawing the eye to that first building.

That said, I can offer a few tips to help you photograph a landscape the way *you* see it:

✔ **Shoot in aperture-priority autoexposure mode (Av) so that you can control depth of field.** If you want extreme depth of field, so that both near and distant objects are sharply focused, as in Figure 7-8, select a high f-stop value. I used an aperture of f/16 for this shot.

You can also use the Landscape mode to achieve a large depth of field. In this mode, the camera automatically selects a high f-stop number, but you have no control over the exact value (or any other picture-taking settings.) Of course, if the light is dim, the camera may be forced to open the aperture, reducing depth of field, to properly expose the image.

✔ **If the exposure requires a slow shutter, use a tripod to avoid blurring.** The downside to a high f-stop is that you need a slower shutter speed to produce a good exposure. If the shutter speed drops below what you can comfortably hand-hold — for me, that's about 1/50 second — use a tripod to avoid picture-blurring camera shake. No tripod handy? Look for any solid surface on which you can steady the camera. You can always increase the ISO setting to increase light sensitivity, which in turn allows a faster shutter speed, too, but that option brings with it the chances of increased image noise. See Chapter 5 for details.

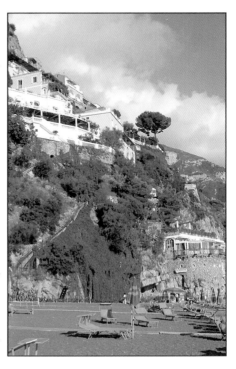

Figure 7-8: Use a high f-stop value (or Landscape mode) to keep foreground and background sharply focused.

✔ **For dramatic waterfall and fountain shots, consider using a slow shutter to create that "misty" look.** The slow shutter blurs the water, giving it a soft, romantic appearance. Figure 7-9 shows you a close-up of this effect. Again, use a tripod to ensure that the rest of the scene doesn't also blur due to camera shake.

✔ **At sunrise or sunset, base exposure on the sky.** The foreground will be dark, but you can usually brighten it in a photo editor if needed. If you base exposure on the foreground, on the other hand, the sky will become so bright that all the color will be washed out — a problem you usually can't fix after the fact.

This tip doesn't apply, of course, if your sunrise or sunset is merely serving as a gorgeous backdrop for a portrait. In that case, you should enable your flash and expose for the subject. (See Figure 7-3, in the preceding section.)

✔ **For cool nighttime city pics, experiment with slow shutter.** Assuming that cars or other vehicles are moving through the scene, the result is neon trails of light like those you see in the foreground of the image in Figure 7-10, taken by my friend Jonathan Conrad. Shutter speed for this image was 8 seconds.

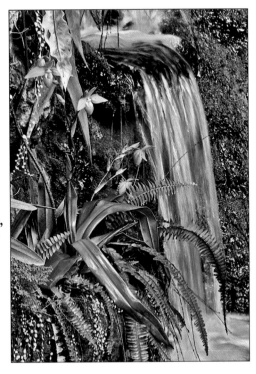

Figure 7-9: For misty waterfalls, use a slow shutter speed (and tripod).

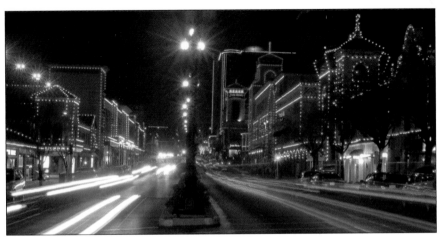

Jonathan Conrad

Figure 7-10: A slow shutter also creates neon light trails in city-street scenes.

Instead of changing the shutter speed manually between each shot, try *bulb* mode. Available only in M (manual) exposure mode, this option records an image for as long as you hold down the shutter button. So just take a series of images, holding the button down for different lengths of time for each shot. In bulb mode, you also can exceed the minimum (slowest) shutter speed of 1/30 second. If you press the DISP button during the exposure, the elapsed capture time appears on the monitor.

Because long exposures can produce image noise, you also may want to enable the Long Exposure Noise Reduction feature. You access this option via the Custom Function option on Setup Menu 2; select Custom Function 2 and change the setting from Off to Auto or On. Chapter 5 discusses this option in more detail.

✔ **For the best lighting, shoot during the "magic hours."** That's the term photographers use for early morning and late afternoon, when the light cast by the sun is soft and warm, giving everything that beautiful, gently warmed look.

Can't wait for the perfect light? Tweak your camera's white balance setting, using the instructions laid out in Chapter 6, to simulate magic-hour light.

✔ **In tricky light, bracket shots.** *Bracketing* simply means to take the same picture at several different exposures to increase the odds that at least one of them will capture the scene the way you envision. Bracketing is especially a good idea in difficult lighting situations such as sunrise and sunset.

Your camera offers automatic exposure bracketing when you shoot in the advanced exposure modes. See Chapter 5 to find out how to take advantage of this feature.

✔ **Worry about wide-angle distortion later.** Shooting with a wide-angle lens can cause vertical structures to appear to tilt either inward or outward, as in Figure 7-11. You can't do anything to avoid this problem, known as *convergence,* unless you buy a very expensive lens designed especially to avoid it.

Fortunately, many photo editing programs enable you to adjust the perspective of your images to straighten things out again. I used the Correct Camera Distortion filter found in Adobe Photoshop Elements to produce the corrected image in Figure 7-12. Note that you do lose some of your original image area in the process, so frame your shot accordingly if you think you will need to correct convergence later.

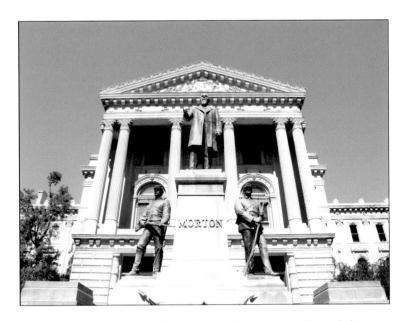

Figure 7-11: Converging verticals are a fact of life with most wide-angle lenses.

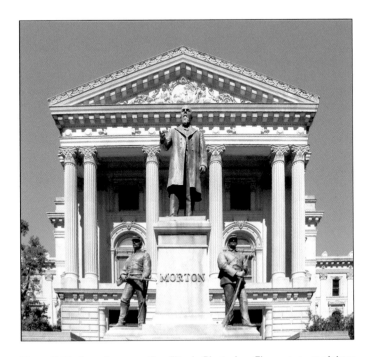

Figure 7-12: I used a correction filter in Photoshop Elements to straighten things out.

Capturing dynamic close-ups

For great close-up shots, start with the basic capture settings outlined in Table 7-1. Then try the following additional settings and techniques:

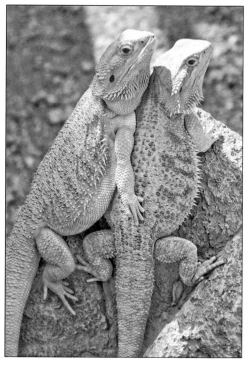

Figure 7-13: Shallow depth of field helps set the subject apart from the similarly colored background.

- ✔ **Check your owner's manual to find out the minimum close-focusing distance of your lens.** How "up close and personal" you can get to your subject depends on your lens, not the camera body itself.

- ✔ **Take control over depth of field by setting the camera mode to Av (aperture-priority autoexposure) mode.** Whether you want a shallow, medium, or extreme depth of field depends on the point of your photo. For the romantic scene shown in Figure 7-13, for example, I wanted to blur the background to help the subjects stand out more, so I set the aperture to f/5.6. But if you want the viewer to be able to clearly see all details throughout the frame — for example, if you're shooting a product shot for your company's sales catalog — you need to go the other direction, stopping down the aperture as far as possible.

Not ready for the advanced exposure modes yet? Try the Close-Up scene mode instead. (It's the one marked with the little flower on your Mode dial.) In this mode, the camera automatically opens the aperture to achieve a short depth of field and bases focus on the center of the frame.

- ✔ **Remember that zooming in and getting close to your subject both decrease depth of field.** So back to that product shot: If you need depth of field beyond what you can achieve with the aperture setting, you may need to back away, zoom out, or both. (You can always crop your image to show just the parts of the subject that you want to feature.)

- ✔ **When shooting flowers and other nature scenes outdoors, pay attention to shutter speed, too.** Even a slight breeze may cause your subject to move, causing blurring at slow shutter speeds.

- ✔ **Use fill flash for better outdoor lighting.** Just as with portraits, a tiny bit of flash typically improves close-ups when the sun is your primary light source. You may need to reduce the flash output slightly, via the camera's Flash Exposure Compensation control. Chapter 5 offers details about using flash.

✔ **When shooting indoors, try not to use flash as your primary light source.** Because you'll be shooting at close range, the light from your flash may be too harsh even at a low Flash Exposure Compensation setting. If flash is inevitable, turn on as many room lights as possible to reduce the flash power that's needed — even a hardware-store shop light can do in a pinch as a lighting source. (Remember that if you have multiple light sources, though, you may need to tweak the white balance setting.)

✔ **To really get close to your subject, invest in a macro lens or a set of diopters.** A true macro lens, which enables you to get really, really close to your subjects, is an expensive proposition; expect to pay around $200 or more. But if you enjoy capturing the tiny details in life, it's worth the investment.

For a less expensive way to go, you can spend about $40 for a set of *diopters,* which are sort of like reading glasses that you screw onto your existing lens. Diopters come in several strengths — +1, +2, + 4, and so on — with a higher number indicating a greater magnifying power. I took this approach to capture the rose in Figure 7-14. The left image shows you the closest I could get to the subject with my regular lens; to produce the right image, I attached a +6 diopter. The downfall of diopters, sadly, is that they typically produce images that are very soft around the edges, as in Figure 7-14 — a problem that doesn't occur with a good macro lens.

No diopter

+6 diopter

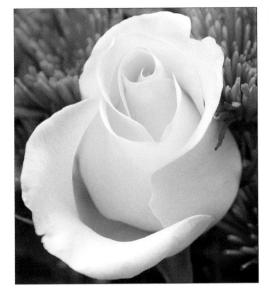 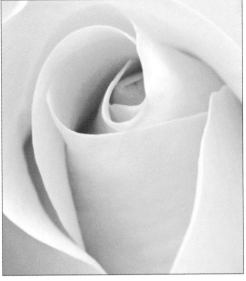

Figure 7-14: To extend your lens' close-focus ability, you can add magnifying diopters.

Coping with Special Situations

A few subjects and shooting situations pose some additional challenges not already covered in earlier sections. So to wrap up this chapter, here's a quick list of ideas for tackling a variety of common "tough-shot" photos:

- **Shooting through glass:** To capture subjects that are behind glass, try putting your lens flat against the glass. Then switch to manual focusing; the glass barrier can give the autofocus mechanism fits. Disable your flash to avoid creating any unwanted reflections, too. I used this technique to capture the image of the turtle sticking his neck out in Figure 7-15.

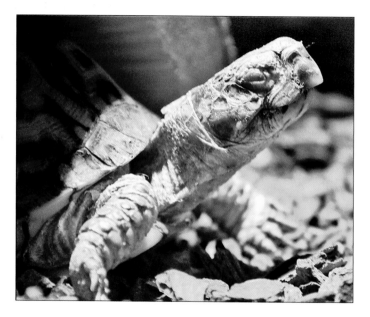

Figure 7-15: To shoot through glass, place your lens flat against the glass.

- **Shooting out a car window:** Set the camera to shutter-priority autoexposure or manual mode and dial in a fast shutter speed to compensate for the movement of the car. Oh, and keep a tight grip on your camera.

- **Shooting in strong backlighting:** When the light behind your subject is very strong and the lighting the subject with flash isn't an option, you have two choices: You can either expose the image with the subject in mind, in which case the background will be overexposed, or you can expose for the background, leaving the subject too dark. By taking the latter route and purposely underexposing the subject, you can create some nice silhouette effects. (In computerland, this is what we call "turning a bug into a feature.") I opted for this technique when capturing the image in Figure 7-16, which shows a young friend standing mesmerized in front of an aquarium. For indoor silhouettes like the one in the figure, disable your flash.

✓ **Shooting fireworks:** First off, use a tripod; fireworks require a long exposure, and trying to handhold your camera simply isn't going to work. If using a zoom lens, zoom out to the shortest focal length. Switch to manual focusing and set focus at infinity (the farthest focus point possible on your lens). Set the exposure mode to manual, choose a relatively high f-stop setting — say, f/16 or so — and start a shutter speed of 1 to 3 seconds. From there, it's simply a matter of experimenting with different shutter speeds.

Be especially gentle when you press the shutter button — with a very slow shutter, you can easily create enough camera movement to blur the image. If you purchased the accessory remote control for your camera, this is a good situation in which to use it.

You also may want to enable your camera's noise-reduction feature because a long exposure also increases the chances of noise defects. See Chapter 5 for details. (Keep the ISO setting low to further dampen noise.)

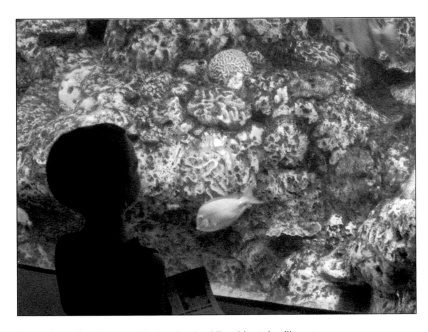

Figure 7-16: Experiment with shooting backlit subjects in silhouette.

✔ **Shooting reflective surfaces:** In outdoor shots taken in bright sun, you can reduce glare from reflective surfaces such as glass and metal by using a *circular polarizing filter,* which you can buy for about $60. A polarizing filter can also help out when you're shooting through glass.

But know that in order for the filter to work, the sun, your subject, and your camera lens must be precisely positioned. Your lens must be at a certain angle from the sun, for example, and the light source must also reflect off the surface at a certain angle and direction. In addition, a polarizing filter also intensifies blue skies in some scenarios, which may or may not be to your liking. In other words, a polarizing filter isn't a surefire cure-all.

A more reliable option for shooting small reflective objects is to invest in a light cube or light tent such as the ones shown in Figure 7-17, from Cloud Dome (www.clouddome.com) and Lastolite (www.lastolite.com), respectively. You place the reflective object inside the tent or cube and then position your lights around the outside. The cube or ten acts as a light diffuser, reducing reflections. Prices range from about $50 to $200, depending on size and features.

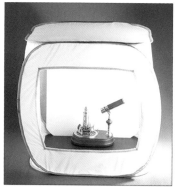 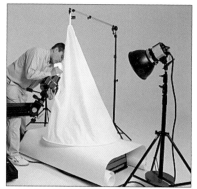

Cloud Dome, Inc. *Lastolite Limited*

Figure 7-17: Investing in a light cube or tent makes photographing reflective objects much easier.

Part III
Working with Picture Files

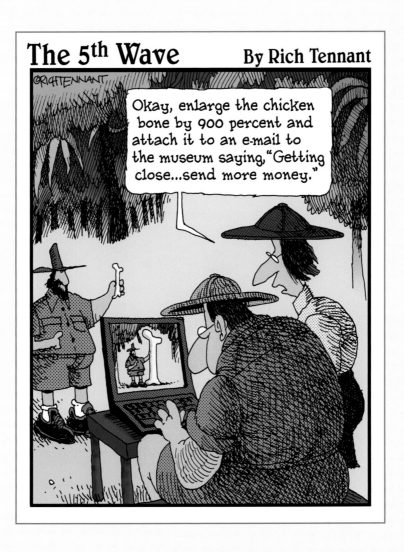

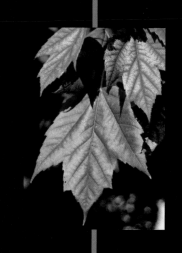

In this part . . .

You've got a memory card full of pictures. Now what? Now you turn to the first chapter in this part, which explains how to get those pictures out of your camera and onto your computer and, just as important, how to safeguard them from future digital destruction. After downloading your files, head for Chapter 9, which offers step-by-step guidance on printing your pictures, sharing them online, and even viewing them on your television.

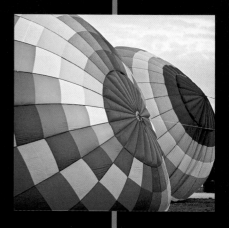

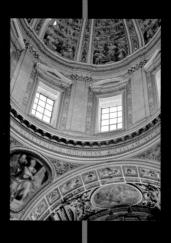

8

Downloading, Organizing, and Archiving Your Photos

In This Chapter

▶ Transferring pictures to your computer

▶ Using the free Canon software to download and organize photos

▶ Looking at other photo-management and editing programs

▶ Processing Raw (CR2) files

▶ Keeping your picture files safe from harm

For many novice digital photographers (and even some experienced ones), the task of moving pictures to the computer and then keeping track of all of those image files is one of the more confusing aspects of the art form. In fact, students in my classes have more questions about this subject than just about anything else.

Frankly, writing about the download and organizing process isn't all that easy, either. (I know, poor me!) The problem is that providing you with detailed instructions is pretty much impossible because the steps you need to take vary widely depending on what software you have installed on your computer and whether you use the Windows or Macintosh operating system.

To give you as much help as possible, however, this chapter shows you how to transfer and organize pictures using the free software that came in your camera box. After exploring these discussions, you should be able to adapt the steps to any other photo program you may prefer.

This chapter also covers a few other aspects of handling your picture files, including converting pictures taken in the Raw format to a standard image format. Finally — and perhaps most important — this chapter explains how to ensure that your digital images stay safe after they leave the camera.

Sending Pictures to the Computer

You can take two approaches to moving pictures from your camera memory card to your computer:

✓ **Connect the camera directly to the computer.** For this option, you need to dig out the USB cable that came in your camera box. Your computer must also have a free USB slot, or *port,* in techie talk. If you aren't sure what these gadgets look like, Figure 8-1 gives you a look.

The little three-pronged icon you see on the plug and between the two ports in Figure 8-1 is the universal symbol for USB. Be sure to check for this symbol because a different type of slot, called a FireWire slot, looks very similar to a USB slot, and your USB cable can even seem to fit (sort of) into a FireWire slot.

✓ **Transfer images using a memory card reader.** Many computers now also have built-in memory card readers. If yours has one that accepts a CompactFlash card, you can simply pop the card out of your camera and into the card reader instead of hooking the camera up to the computer.

As another option, you can buy stand-alone card readers such as the SanDisk model shown in Figure 8-2. This particular model accepts a variety of memory cards, including CompactFlash. Check your photo printer, too; many printers now have card readers that accept the most popular types of cards.

USB plug   USB ports

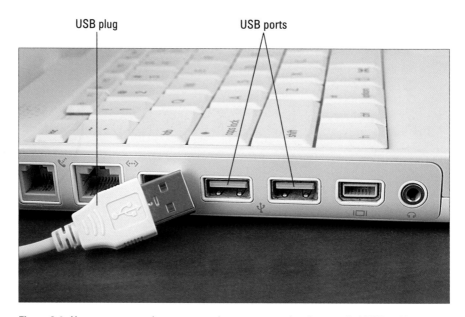

Figure 8-1: You can connect the camera to the computer using the supplied USB cable.

I prefer to use a card reader, for two reasons: First, when you transfer via the camera, the camera must be turned on during the process, wasting battery power. Second, with a card reader, I don't have to keep track of that elusive camera cable. And third, when I copy photos to my desktop system, transferring via the camera requires that I get down on all fours to plug the cable into the computer's USB slot, which is of course located in the least convenient spot possible. The card reader, by contrast, stays perched on my desk, connected to my computer at all times, so there's very little physical activity involved in transferring pictures, which is how I prefer to live my life.

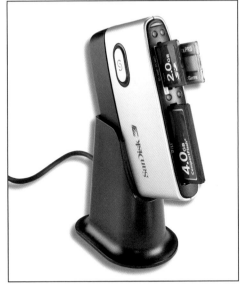

Courtesy SanDisk Corporation

Figure 8-2: A card reader offers a more convenient method of image transfer.

If you want to transfer directly from the camera, however, the next section explains some important steps you need to take to make that option work. If you choose to use a card reader, skip ahead to the section "Starting the transfer process" to get an overview of what happens after you insert the card into the reader.

Connecting camera and computer

You need to follow a specific set of steps when connecting the camera to your computer. Otherwise, you can damage the camera or the memory card.

Also note that in order for your camera to communicate with the computer, the computer must be running one of the following operating systems:

- Windows Vista 32-bit Home Basic, Home Premium, Business, Enterprise, or Ultimate edition
- Windows XP Home or Professional edition
- Windows 2000 Professional
- Windows ME
- Windows 98 Second Edition
- Mac OS X 10.2 and higher

If you use another OS (operating system, for the non-geeks in the crowd), check the support pages on the Canon Web site (www.canon.com) for the latest news about any updates to system compatibility. You can always simply transfer images with a card reader, too.

With that preamble out of the way, the next steps show you how to get your camera to talk to your computer:

1. **Assess the level of the camera battery.**

   Just look at the little battery-status indicator at the bottom of the Camera Settings display. If the battery is low, charge it before continuing. Running out of battery power during the transfer process can cause problems, including lost picture data. Alternatively, if you purchased the optional AC adapter, use that to power the camera during picture transfers.

2. **Turn the computer on and give it time to finish its normal startup routine.**

3. **Turn the camera off.**

4. **Insert the smaller of the two plugs on the USB cable into the USB port on the side of the camera.**

   The slot is hidden under a little rubber door just around the corner from the buttons that flank the left side of the monitor, as shown in Figure 8-3. Gently pry open the little door and insert the cable end into the slot.

5. **Plug the other end of the cable into the computer's USB port.**

   Be sure to plug the cable into a port that is actually built into the computer, as opposed to one that's on your keyboard or part of an external USB hub. Those accessory-type connections can sometimes foul up the transfer process.

6. **Turn the camera on.**

   The Camera Settings screen appears briefly on the camera monitor, displaying a "Busy" message. Then the monitor goes black, and the card

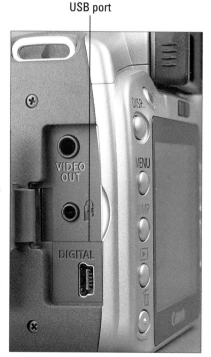

USB port

Figure 8-3: The USB port is hidden under the little rubber door on the left rear side of the camera.

access lamp begins flickering, letting you know that the camera is communicating with the computer. After a few moments (or minutes, depending on the speed of your computer), the Direct Transfer screen appears on the camera monitor, as shown in Figure 8-4, and the Print/Share light, near the upper-left corner of the monitor, glows blue.

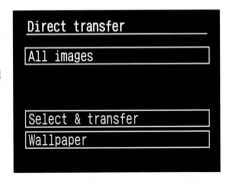

For details about the next step in the downloading routine, move on to the next section.

Figure 8-4: When the camera is ready to download images, the Direct Transfer screen appears.

The options you see on the Direct Transfer screen relate to a method of image downloading that requires you to handle everything through the camera menus. I don't cover this download technique because I think that most people will find the alternative methods I discuss here easier and more user-friendly. Nor do I cover the Transfer Order item on the Playback menu, which is related to the process. However, if you're curious about the Wallpaper option you see in Figure 8-4, turn to Chapter 11, which explains it. Your camera manual also includes specifics about the other download technique as well.

Starting the transfer process

After you connect the camera to the computer (be sure to carefully follow the steps in the preceding section) or insert a memory card into your card reader, your next step depends, again, on the software installed on your computer and the computer operating system.

Here are the most common possibilities and how to move forward:

✔ **On a Windows-based computer, a Windows message box like the one in Figure 8-5 appears.** The box suggests different programs that you can use to download your picture files. Which programs appear depend on what you have installed on your system; if you installed the Canon software, for example, one or more of those programs should appear in the list. The other standard option, Microsoft Camera and Scanner Wizard, enables you to use the operating system's own transfer software. To proceed, just click the transfer program that you want to use and then click OK. (The figure features the Windows XP Home Edition version of the dialog box.)

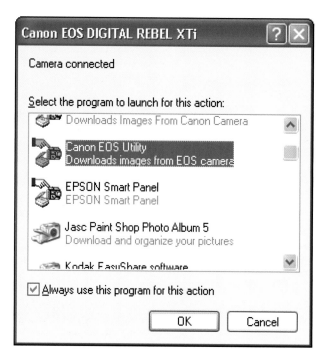

Figure 8-5: Windows may display this initial boxful of transfer options.

If you want to use the same program for all of your transfers, select the Always Use This Program for This Action check box, as I did in Figure 8-5. The next time you connect your camera or insert a memory card, Windows will automatically launch your program of choice instead of displaying the message box.

✔ **An installed photo program automatically displays a photo-download wizard.** For example, if you installed the Canon software, the EOS Utility window or MemoryCard Utility window may leap to the forefront. Or, if you installed some other program, such as Photoshop Elements, its downloader may pop up instead. On the Mac, the built-in iPhoto software may display its auto downloader. (Apple's Web site, www.apple.com, offers excellent video tutorials on using iPhoto, by the way.)

Usually, the downloader that appears is associated with the software that you most recently installed. Each new program that you add to your system tries to wrestle control over your image downloads away from the previous program.

If you don't want a program's auto downloader to launch whenever you insert a memory card or connect your camera, you should be able to turn that feature off. Check the software manual to find out how to disable the auto launch.

✔ **Nothing happens.** Don't panic; assuming that your card reader or camera is properly connected, all is probably well. Someone — maybe even you — simply may have disabled all the automatic downloaders on your system. Just launch your photo software and then transfer your pictures using whatever command starts that process. (I show you how to do it with the Canon software tools later in the chapter; for other programs, consult the software manual.)

As another option, you can use Windows Explorer or the Mac Finder to simply drag and drop files from your memory card to your computer's hard drive. The process is exactly the same as when you move any other file from a CD, DVD, or other storage device onto your hard drive.

As I say in the introduction to this chapter, it's impossible to give step-by-step instructions for using all the various photo downloaders that may be sprinkled over your hard drive. So in the next sections, I cover the basic drag-and-drop process that involves Windows Explorer and the Mac Finder. Following that, I provide details on using Canon software to download and organize your files.

If you use some other software, the concepts are the same, but check your program manual to get the small details. In most programs, you also can find lots of information by simply clicking open the Help menu.

Transferring files using Windows Explorer

Windows Explorer is the basic file-management system built in to the Microsoft Windows operating software. (Don't confuse it with Microsoft Internet Explorer, which is a Web-browsing program.)

You can use this tool to transfer image files just as you do to copy or move any file from a CD, DVD, or other storage device to your hard drive. If you want to try out this method, first close any automated downloaders that may have popped up when you inserted your memory card or attached your camera to the computer.

Many people have not yet upgraded to the latest Microsoft operating system, Vista, so the following steps show you how to transfer files using the version of Explorer found in Microsoft Windows XP. If you're a Vista user, the process is virtually the same, although the design and layout of the dialog boxes you encounter may be different than what you see in the figures.

1. **Click the Windows Start button and then choose All Programs⇨ Accessories⇨Windows Explorer.**

   Or, for faster results, locate the My Computer icon on your Windows desktop. Then right-click the icon and choose Explore.

   Either way, you see a window that lists all the drives and folders on your computer, as shown in Figure 8-6.

Camera icon

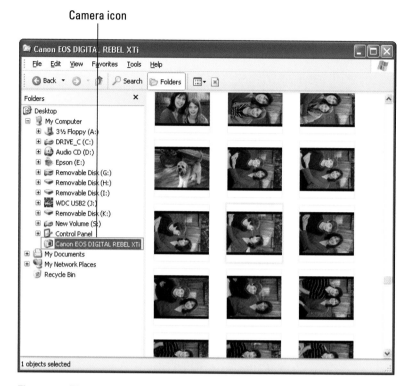

Figure 8-6: The camera shows up as an icon in the list of drives on your computer.

2. **Locate the camera or card reader icon in the list of drives on the left side of the window.**

   The location depends on whether you're transferring from the camera or a card reader:

   - If you're transferring from the camera, you should see an icon named Canon EOS Digital Rebel XTi (or 400D), as in Figure 8-6. When you click the icon, a list of all the files on the camera appears in the right side of the window, as shown in the figure.

   - If you're transferring from a card reader, the drive assigned to the reader should display the name EOS Digital, as in Figure 8-7. Click the plus sign next to the icon to display a folder named DCIM. Then click the plus sign next to *that* folder to display the folder that actually contains your images. (The folder's named 100CANON by default.) Click the 100CANON folder to display your images in the right side of the window.

Memory card drive and folders

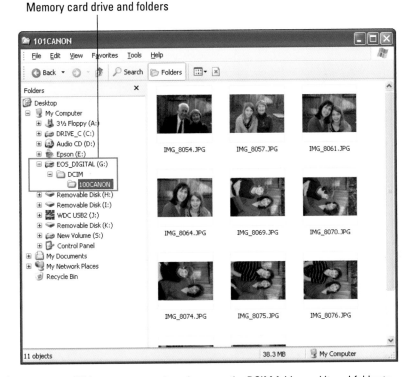

Figure 8-7: With a memory card reader, open the DCIM folder and its subfolder to access image files.

To view thumbnails of your pictures, as shown in Figures 8-6 and 8-7, choose View⇨Thumbnails. Note, though, that Explorer can't display thumbnails for images captured in the Canon Raw format (CR2) until you process them. The section "Processing CR2 (Raw) Files," later in this chapter, explains that bit of business.

3. **Select the files that you want to transfer.**

Click the first file to select it and then hold down the Ctrl key as you click additional files. Or, to select all files, press Ctrl+A.

4. **Drag the files to the folder where you want to store them, as illustrated in Figure 8-8.**

The little plus sign next to your cursor indicates that you're copying files and not moving them off of your memory card.

You can put your files anywhere on your hard drive that you want. But because most photo programs automatically look in the My Pictures or Pictures folder, depending on your version of Windows, placing them in that folder simplifies things down the line. Look for the folder inside the My Documents main folder, as shown in the figure.

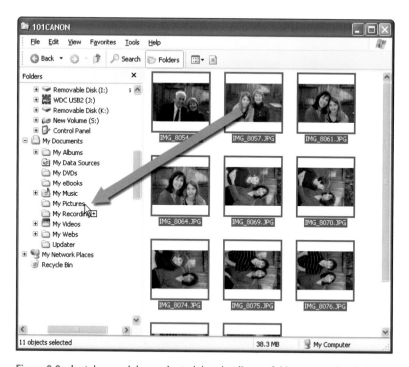

Figure 8-8: Just drag and drop selected thumbnails to a folder on your hard drive.

Transferring files using the Mac Finder

Don't care to install the Canon software on your Mac? You can transfer images through the Finder, just as when you insert a CD or DVD. Insert your memory card into your card reader or connect the camera and computer and then follow these steps:

1. Look for the camera or card icon on the desktop.

The icon should wear the nametag EOS_Digital.

If you did install the Canon software, the camera icon does not appear; instead, the EOS Utility pops to life, and you have to transfer images that way. With a card reader, you should see the card icon but the Canon MemoryCard Utility may appear automatically as well. Just close that utility and move on to Step 2.

2. Double-click the card icon to display its contents in a Finder window.

3. Double-click the DCIM folder.

4. **Double-click the 100CANON folder to display your images.**

   Note that the number of the folder may be higher if you have previously taken and downloaded lots of images.

5. **Select the images that you want to transfer.**

   Click the first image and then ⌘+click additional images to select them. Or press ⌘+A to select all the pictures.

6. **Drag the selected files to the folder where you want to store them.**

   By default, most Mac programs look for image files in the Pictures folder, so putting them in that folder can save you some time hunting down the image files later.

7. **After the transfer is complete, drag the card or camera icon to the Trash to eject the device.**

Downloading images with Canon tools

The software CD that shipped with your Rebel XTi/400D includes several programs for transferring, organizing, and editing your photos. For downloading images, I suggest that you use the tools discussed in the next two sections.

Before you try the download steps, however, you may want to visit the Canon Web site and download the latest versions of the software in the suite. Even if you recently bought your camera, the shipping CD may be a little out of date. Just go to www.canon.com and follow the links to locate the software for your camera. (You can also download updated manuals.)

In this book, the steps relate to Version 2.2 of the EOS Utility and Version 6 for ZoomBrowser EX (Windows) and ImageBrowser (Mac). As I write this, those versions are the most recent available for Windows XP, Windows Vista, and Mac OS 10.3 and higher.

After taking care of the software download and installation chores, see the next two sections for details on how to transfer your images.

Using EOS Utility to transfer images from your camera

Follow these steps to transfer images directly from your camera to the computer using the Canon EOS Utility software:

1. **Connect your camera to the computer.**

   See the first part of this chapter for specifics.

Safeguarding your digital photo files

To make sure that your digital photos enjoy a long, healthy life, follow these storage guidelines:

✔ Don't rely on your computer's hard drive for long-term, archival storage. Hard drives occasionally fail, wiping out all files in the process. This warning applies to both internal and external hard drives.

✔ Camera memory cards, flash memory keys, and other portable storage devices are similarly risky. All are easily damaged if dropped or otherwise mishandled. And being of diminutive stature, these portable storage options also are easily lost.

✔ The best way to store important files is to copy them to nonrewritable CDs. (The label should say CD-R, not CD-RW.) Look for quality, brand-name CDs that have a gold coating, which offer a higher level of security than other coatings.

✔ Recordable DVDs offer the advantage of holding lots more data than a CD. However, as of today, there's still a DVD format war, and until the industry settles on one standard, I'm not quite as comfortable with DVDs as I am with CDs. So I use DVDs only for non-critical images; precious family photos go on CDs.

✔ Online photo-sharing sites such as Shutterfly, Kodak Gallery, and the like aren't designed to be long-term storage tanks for your images. Consider them only a backup to your backup, and read the site terms carefully so that you understand how long the site will hold onto your files if you stop buying prints and other products.

---

2. **Turn the camera on.**

   After a few moments, the EOS Utility window should appear automatically. If it doesn't, just launch the program as you would any other on your system. Figure 8-9 shows the Windows version of the screen; the Mac version looks pretty much the same.

   You can customize the way that the EOS Utility behaves by clicking the Preferences button at the bottom of the window. Doing so opens the dialog box shown in Figure 8-10. Just click through the various panels to discover what aspects of the tool you can tweak to your liking.

3. **In the EOS Utility window (Figure 8-9), click the option named Lets You Select and Download Images.**

   With this option, you can specify which pictures you want to download from the camera. After you click the option, you see a browser window that looks similar to the one in Figure 8-11. The figure shows the Windows version, but the Mac version contains the same basic components.

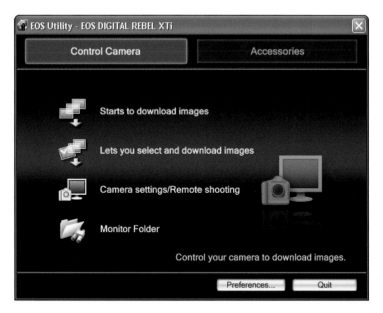

Figure 8-9: EOS Utility is designed for sending pictures from the camera to the computer.

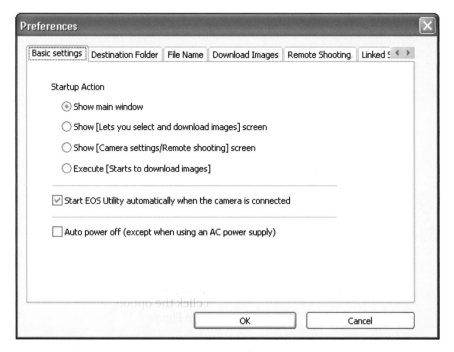

Figure 8-10: Click the Preferences button in the EOS Utility window to customize how the tool behaves.

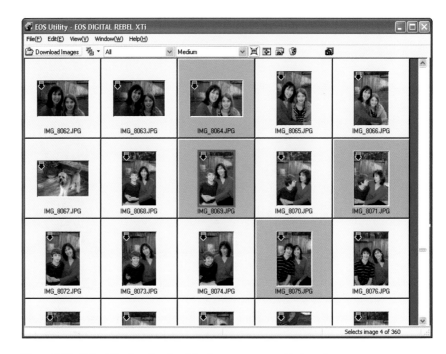

Figure 8-11: Select the thumbnails of the images you want to transfer.

4. Select the images that you want to copy to the computer.

Click the first thumbnail to select it. To select additional images, Ctrl+click (Windows) or ⌘+click (Mac) their thumbnails. Selected thumbnails appear highlighted, as in Figure 8-11.

5. Click the Download Images button near the top of the window.

Now you see a window that resembles the one shown in Figure 8-12. Again, the figure shows you the Windows version, but the Mac version is different only in terms of its color and design.

Either way, the window shows you where the downloader wants to put your files and the name it plans to assign the storage folder. If you want to change this setup, click the Destination Folder button and specify the storage location and folder name you prefer. You also can choose to have the picture files renamed when they're copied; click the File Name button to access the renaming options.

By default, pictures are stored in the My Pictures or Pictures folder in Windows and in the Pictures folder on a Mac. You can put your images anywhere you like; however, most photo editing programs look first for photos in those folders, so sticking with this universally accepted setup makes some sense.

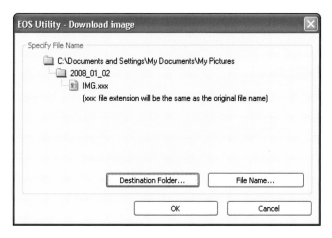

Figure 8-12: You can specify where you want to store the photos.

6. Click OK to begin the download.

A progress window appears, showing you the status of the download. When the transfer is complete, the EOS Utility program closes automatically and either ZoomBrowser EX (Windows) or ImageBrowser (Mac) appears, with your newly downloaded images appearing in the browser window. See the next section, "Using ZoomBrowser EX/ImageBrowser," for details on using that program.

Using MemoryCard Utility for card-to-computer transfers

Transferring images from a memory card reader involves a different Canon tool, MemoryCard Utility. To try it out, put your card in your card reader.

If all the planets are aligned — meaning that the Canon software was the last photo software you installed, and some other program doesn't try to handle the job for you — the MemoryCard Utility window shown in Figure 8-13 appears automatically when you put your memory card into the card reader. The figure shows the Windows version of the window; the Mac version is identical except that the top of the window refers to ImageBrowser, which is the Mac version of ZoomBrowser EX.

If the window doesn't appear, you can access it as follows:

✏ *Windows:* Open the program called ZoomBrowser EX MemoryCard Utility, using the steps you usually take to start a program.

✏ *Mac:* Start the program called Canon Camera Window. The program should detect your memory card and display the MemoryCard Utility window.

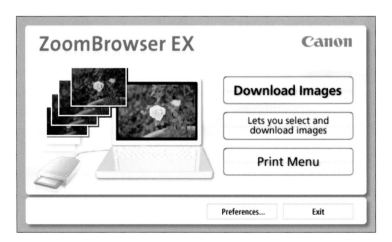

Figure 8-13: The MemoryCard Utility enables you to transfer pictures using a card reader.

From here on in, everything works just as it does when you download using the EOS Utility. So just follow the same steps outlined in the preceding section, starting with Step 3.

Using ZoomBrowser EX/ImageBrowser

In addition to the aforementioned software tools, your Canon CD contains two additional programs: ZoomBrowser EX (Windows) or ImageBrowser (Mac), plus Digital Photo Professional. In this section, you can find out how to organize your photos using the ZoomBrowser EX/ImageBrowser tool. Although you can view thumbnails of your images in Digital Photo Professional, that tool is designed for advanced users, so I don't cover it in this book.

The next sections give you the most basic of introductions to ZoomBrowser EX/ImageBrowser, which, in the interest of saving type, I may refer to from here on in as just "the browser." If you want more details, the CD that ships with the program offers a very good online manual.

Before you move on, though, I want to clear up one common point of confusion: You can use Canon's software to download and organize your photos and still use any photo editing software you prefer. And to do your editing, you don't need to re-download photos — after you transfer photos to your computer, you can access them from any program, just as you can any file that you put on your system.

Getting acquainted with the program

Figure 8-14 offers a look at the ZoomBrowser EX window; Figure 8-15, the ImageBrowser window. As you can see, the windows contain most of the same basic components, although the Mac version is lacking the row of task buttons found in the upper-left corner of the Windows version. The two versions also offer a different set of image-viewing modes — Preview Mode and List mode on the Mac and Zoom, Scroll, and Preview modes in Windows.

Explore panel   Shooting Information   Information panel

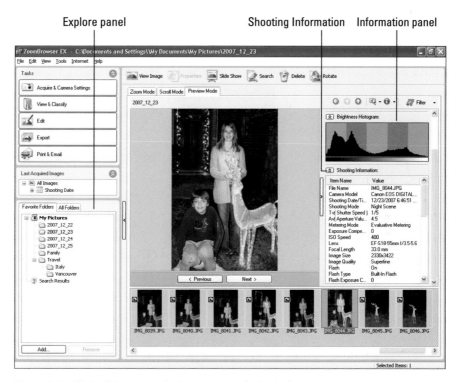

Figure 8-14: Click a folder in the Explore panel to display its images.

Explore panel   Shooting Information   Information panel

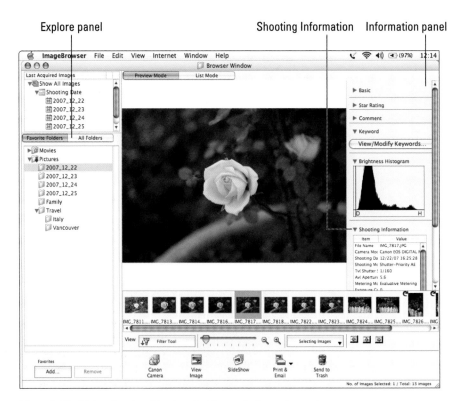

Figure 8-15: Click a thumbnail to view that image in the main preview area.

Whichever version you use, you can customize the window layout via the View menu. The arrangement you see in the figures is the Preview mode setup. I prefer this mode because it provides easy access not just to your images, but also to details about the camera settings you used to shoot the picture. Here's a quick guide to viewing your photos in Preview mode:

✔ **Select the folder you want to view.** Click the folder's icon in the Explore panel, found on the left side of the window and labeled in Figures 8-14 and 8-15. If you click the Favorite Folders tab, you see only the My Pictures or Pictures (Windows) or Pictures folder (Mac) along with any custom Favorites folders that you create, a topic that you can visit in the upcoming section "Organizing your photos." By default, picture files that you transfer from your camera or memory card using the Canon software go into these folders. To view all folders on your computer, click the All Folders button.

✔ **Preview the images in the selected folder.** In Preview mode, the current image appears at a large size in the middle of the window, as shown in the figures, and a "filmstrip" of smaller thumbnails appears beneath.

To view the next image in the filmstrip, click its thumbnail. On a Mac, you then can press the right and left arrow keys on your keyboard to view your photos one by one. In Windows, the same technique works on some keyboards; if not, click the Next and Previous buttons (under the large preview) instead. Drag the scroll bar under the thumbnails to scroll the thumbnail display as needed.

✔ **View an image in full-screen mode.** For a larger view of a photo, double-click its thumbnail. (You must double-click the thumbnail, not the larger preview image.) Doing so opens the image in its own browser window, displaying the image as large as possible to fit the available screen space. This full-screen window is called the Viewer window. The next section explains more about the controls therein. To exit the Viewer window and return to the main browser, just click the window's close button.

TIP

✔ **View shooting information.** Check out the Information panel, located on the right side of the window. If you click the Shooting Information button, you display all the settings that you used to capture the selected image, as shown in Figures 8-14 and 8-15. Reviewing this data — known as *meta-data* — is a great way to better understand what settings work best for different types of pictures, especially when you're just getting up to speed with aperture, shutter speed, white balance, and all the other digital photography basics. (Note that you may need to scroll the Information panel display to access the Shooting Information button, depending on the size of the program window.

Those are the basics of navigating through your images. In the next section, you can find some hints about viewing your photos in full-screen mode, inside the Viewer window. After that, the section "Organizing your folders" explains how to customize the folder setup that the Canon software creates for you.

Viewing photos in full-screen mode

Double-clicking a thumbnail in the main browser window displays the image inside the Viewer window. Figure 8-16 shows the Windows version of the Viewer; Figure 8-17 shows the Mac alternative.

After opening an image in the Viewer window, use these tricks to inspect it more closely:

Previous

Next

Zoom In/Out

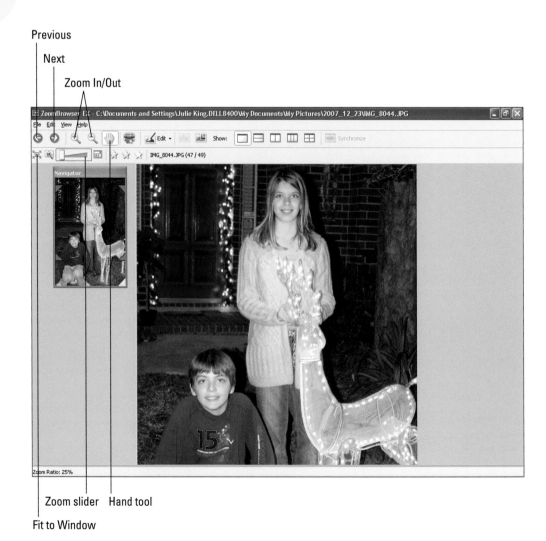

Zoom slider   Hand tool

Fit to Window

Figure 8-16: To display an image in the Viewer window, double-click its thumbnail.

➥ **Magnify the image.** You can zoom in on your image for a closer look by
using these techniques:

- *In ZoomBrowser EX (Windows)*: Drag the Zoom slider or click the
  preview with the Zoom In tool, both labeled in Figure 8-16.

- *In ImageBrowser (Mac)*: Choose a specific magnification level from
  the Display Size drop-down list, labeled in Figure 8-17.

Navigator window

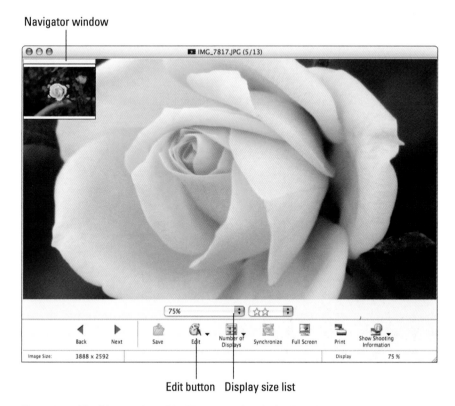

Edit button   Display size list

Figure 8-17: The Mac version of the Viewer window looks like this.

✔ **Scroll a magnified image.** After you magnify the photo, a tiny Navigator window appears in the top-left corner of the screen, as shown in the figures. The little red triangles in the Navigator window indicate the area that you're currently viewing in the main preview. To scroll the display to see another portion of the image, put your cursor in the Navigator window, within the area bounded by those little red triangles, and drag.

In Windows, you also can click the Hand tool, labeled in Figure 8-16, and drag in the preview itself. On a Mac, just drag in the preview; your cursor automatically sets itself to Hand-tool mode as soon as you enlarge the image display.

✔ **Reduce the view size.** In Windows, click the preview with the Zoom Out tool or use the Zoom slider. (See Figure 8-16.) On a Mac, choose a smaller zoom size from the Display Size drop-down list.

To zoom out so that you can see the entire image, click the Fit to Window button in Windows (see Figure 8-16). On a Mac, choose Fit to Window from the Display Size list instead.

✏ **View the next image in the folder.** If you want to inspect more images in the Viewer, just click the Previous and Next buttons, labeled in Figure 8-16, if you use Windows. On a Mac, click the Back or Next button located under the preview.

✏ **Edit the photo.** To use the editing tools provided with the program, click the Edit button, found above the preview in Windows and beneath it on a Mac. Then select the editing task you want to perform. Chapter 10 provides more details about shifting into editing mode and using the available tools.

Keep in mind that the preceding tidbits just give you the basics of using the Viewer window; for additional tips, check out the program manual.

Organizing your photos

By default, the Canon download software puts your picture files into either the My Pictures or Pictures folder in Windows and the Pictures folder on a Mac. Within that folder, the downloading tools organize the images by shooting date, creating a new folder for each date found on the memory card. For example, in Figure 8-18, you see four folders, one for each day from December 22 through 25. Each folder contains only the images shot on that particular day.

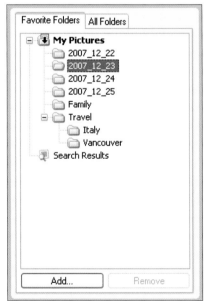

If you don't like this organizational structure, you can change it. For example, you may want to organize images by category — family, travel, work, and so on. I took this approach to my folder collection in Figure 8-18.

To keep things simple, I suggest that you add these custom folders within the My Pictures or Pictures folder (Windows) or Pictures folder (Mac). That way, you'll always know where to look for images on

Figure 8-18: You can create custom folders to organize images by category.

your computer's hard drive. And programs that default to looking to those folders for photos will be able to find them as well. The next mini-sections show you the basics you need to create custom folders and then organize images in them.

Creating custom folders

Take these steps to add a folder to the My Pictures or Pictures (Windows) or Pictures (Mac) list:

1. **Click the Favorite Folders tab of the Explore panel, if it isn't already visible.**

2. **Click My Pictures or Pictures (Windows) or Pictures (Mac).**

   The folder should appear highlighted.

3. **Choose File⇨New Folder.**

   The New Folder dialog box appears.

4. **Type the name of the folder in the text box and click OK.**

   Your folder appears as a subfolder under the My Pictures or Pictures folder.

To create a subfolder within your new folder, follow the same process, but click the new folder in Step 2. For example, I created two subfolders within my Travel folder in Figure 8-18.

Managing your image collection

After you create your folders, you can place images into them in two ways:

- **Move an image from one folder to another.** Display the image thumbnail and then drag it to the desired folder. The program moves the image file to the new folder and removes it from the old one.

- **Download new images directly to your desired folder.** You can specify a custom folder as the download destination when you use the EOS Utility and MemoryCard Utility software to transfer images. See the earlier sections of this chapter for details.

Use these techniques to maintain and further organize your image collection:

- **Delete a folder.** First, click the folder name to select it. Then, in Windows, choose File⇨Delete. On a Mac, choose File⇨Send to Trash. In both cases, the program displays a message asking you to confirm that you want to get rid of the folder; click Yes (Windows) or OK (Mac) to proceed.

  Be careful: This step deletes both the folder and all images inside it!

- **Rename a folder.** Click the folder and choose File⇨Rename. In the dialog box that appears, type the new folder name and then click OK.

✔ **Rename a picture file.** Click the image thumbnail and choose File⇨ Rename. Type the new name in the dialog box that appears and then click OK. *Note:* Do not type the three-letter file extension (.jpg or .CR2) at the end of the new filename. The program adds that data automatically to the filename for you.

✔ **Delete a picture:** Click the image thumbnail to select it. Then, in Windows, choose File⇨Delete; on a Mac, choose File⇨Send to Trash. As with deleting a folder, you're presented with a dialog box asking you whether you really, really want to dump that image. Respond in the affirmative to do so.

Exploring Other Software Options

The Canon browser software is a pretty nifty tool for viewing and organizing your photos. And it does enable you to perform basic retouching: You can crop your image and make some adjustments to color, exposure, and sharpness. Chapter 10 shows you how.

But the program isn't designed for serious photo editing. For one thing, you can't perform *selective editing* — meaning, changing only the part of your image that needs help. And you don't get any tools for removing flaws such as blemishes in portraits and the like.

So my recommendation is that you consider the browser as a good, free tool for organizing your photos and doing simple picture fixes. But if you find yourself doing a lot of photo editing, invest in something more capable. Here are just some of the products to consider:

✔ **Beginning/consumer programs:** Unless you're retouching photos for professional purposes or want to get into photo editing at a serious level for other reasons, a program such as Adobe Photoshop Elements ($100, www.adobe.com) is a good fit. Elements has been the best-selling consumer photo editor for some time, and for good reason. With a full complement of retouching tools, onscreen guidance for novices, a built-in photo organizer, and an assortment of tools and templates for creating artistic photo projects, Elements offers all the features that most consumers need.

Figure 8-19 offers a look at Elements 6 for Windows. At present, Adobe is planning the Mac edition; it may already be on the store shelves by the time you read this. If not, version 4 is the most recent option for the Mac.

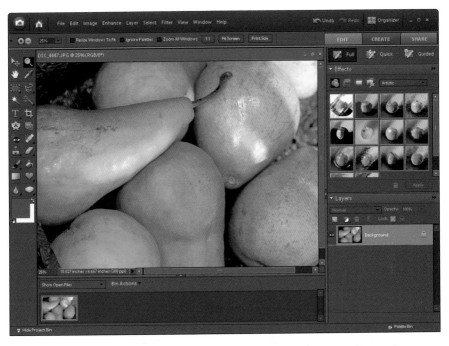

Figure 8-19: Adobe Photoshop Elements offers a good balance of power and ease-of-use.

For other candidates in this category and price range, visit the Web sites of Corel (www.corel.com) and ArcSoft (www.arcsoft.com). Both companies offer multiple programs aimed at the beginner-to-intermediate user.

✔ **Advanced/professional tools:** The best-known option in this category is Adobe Photoshop, shown in Figure 8-20. Photoshop offers professional-grade photo editing tools, a built-in photo organizer, and features needed by people preparing images for commercial printing, Web design, and other high-end uses.

Of course, all that power comes at a price: $650. And expect to spend lots of time getting up to speed with the program, too, because you don't get the friendly interfaces and guidance offered by the beginner-level programs. Nor does Photoshop offer the automated photo-creation features, such as greeting card templates and clip art, that you find in consumer programs.

Other programs aimed at the professional market include Apple Aperture ($300, www.apple.com) and Adobe Lightroom (also $300). These two programs are geared toward users who routinely need to process lots of images but who typically do only light retouching work.

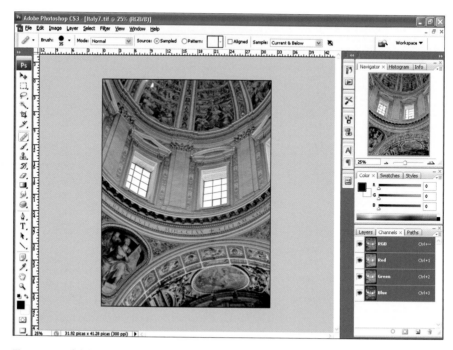

Figure 8-20: Adobe Photoshop is designed for advanced users and imaging professionals.

A few important tips before you buy:

✔ Check the software's system requirements to make sure that your computer can run the program. Some of the products I mention here aren't available for Macintosh computers; Apple Aperture, on the other hand, isn't available for Windows-based systems. Also make sure that your computer offers the system memory (RAM), processor speed, and other components that the software requires.

✔ You also can buy stand-alone photo organizing programs if you aren't interested in serious photo editing but want a more powerful image-management tool than you get with the Canon software. Check out the offerings in this category from ACDSee (www.acdsee.com), ThumbsPlus (www.thumbsplus.com), and Extensis (www.extensis.com).

You may be amused, as I am, to know that the photo industry uses the term *DAM* software — for digital asset management — to refer to the function provided by image-organizing programs. (I dare you to walk into your local computer store and ask where you can find the DAM software. Wait; I double-dare you.)

Using your mouse as a shutter button

Along with providing a convenient way for you to download images, the EOS Utility software enables you to use your computer to actually shoot pictures as well.

While your camera is connected to your computer, clicking the Remote Shooting button in the main EOS Utility window displays a panel containing clickable controls for adjusting the major camera settings, such as aperture, white balance, ISO, and metering mode. After you establish those settings, you click another button to record whatever scene is in front of your camera lens.

What's the point? Well, this feature is great in scenarios that make having a live photographer close to the subject either difficult or dangerous — for example, trying to get a shot of a chemical reaction in a science lab or capture an image of an animal that's shy around humans. Additionally, the software enables easy time-lapse photography, enabling you to set the camera to take pictures automatically at specified intervals over a period of minutes, hours, or even days.

✔ Many software companies enable you to download free trials from their Web sites so that you can actually use the software for a short period to make sure that it fits your needs.

Processing Raw (CR2) Files

Chapter 3 introduces you to the Camera Raw file format, which enables you to capture images as raw data. The advantage of capturing Raw files, which are called CR2 files on your Canon, is that you make the decisions about how to translate the raw data into an actual photograph. You can specify attributes such as color intensity, image sharpening, contrast, and so on — all of which are handled automatically by the camera if you use its other file format, JPEG.

The bad news: You have to specify attributes such as color intensity, image sharpening, contrast, and so on before you can do anything with your pictures. You can't print them, share them online, or edit them in your photo software until you process them using a tool known as a *raw converter*. At the end of the conversion process, you save the finished file in a standard file format, such as JPEG or TIFF.

If you do decide to shoot in the Raw format, you can process them with ZoomBrowserEX (Windows) or ImageBrowser (Mac). Follow these steps:

1. **Click the image thumbnail in the browser window.**

2. **In Windows, choose Tools⇨Processing Raw Images; on a Mac, choose File⇨Processing Raw Image.**

   A message window appears to provide you with general instructions about the conversion. Just click OK to close the window and move on. (If you don't want to be bothered with it each time you want to process a Raw image, select the Don't Show This Message Again check box before you close the window.)

   Now your photo appears inside the Raw Image Task window, shown in Figure 8-21. (The window may appear slightly different, depending on the options you choose from the View menu.)

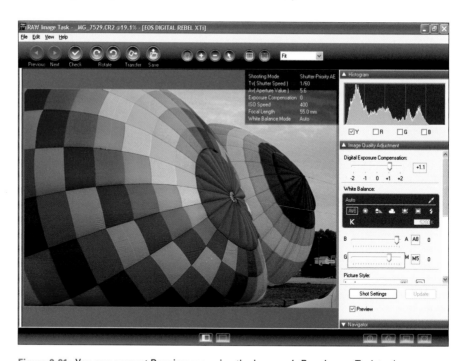

Figure 8-21: You can convert Raw images using the browser's Raw Image Task tool.

3. **Use the controls on the Image Quality adjustment panel to adjust the image as needed.**

   Figure 8-22 gives you a look at the Windows version of the panel; the Mac version contains the same components but is arranged a little differently. Drag the scroll bar on the right side of the panel to scroll the display as needed to access all the controls.

   The panel offers the following controls:

   - *Digital Exposure Compensation:* Drag this slider to adjust image brightness.

   - *White Balance:* These controls, based on the white balance options discussed in Chapter 6, adjust color. You can click one of the white balance icons in the large panel, or you can drag the A/B (amber/blue) and M/G (magenta/green) sliders to tweak the colors. Or click the little white-balance eyedropper, labeled in Figure 8-22, and then click an area of the image that should be white, black, or gray.

   - *Picture Style:* Here, you can actually apply one of the camera's Picture Style options to the photo. Or you can customize the style by dragging the Sharpness, Contrast, Color Saturation, and Color Tone sliders. Chapter 6 talks about Picture Styles.

White balance eyedropper

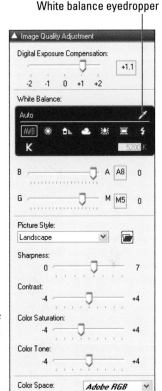

Figure 8-22: Set the characteristics of your photo here.

   - *Color Space:* You can select either sRGB or Adobe RGB as the image color space. As discussed in Chapter 6, the latter offers a broader range of colors, although some of them may be beyond the printable range.

   At any time, you can revert the image to the original settings by clicking the Shot Settings button underneath the Image Adjustment panel. (See Figure 8-21.)

4. **Choose File➪Save Image.**

   You see the Save dialog box shown in Figure 8-23.

5. **Set the Save options.**

Here's the rundown on the options that may be foreign to you:

- *Conversion Target (Windows) or Images to Save (Mac):* These options matter only if you are processing multiple images at a time. If you want to do this, the Help system available in the Raw Image Task window provides how-tos.

- *Image Type:* This one is the critical setting. Choose EXIF-Tiff (8 bits/channel.) This saves your image in the TIFF file format, which preserves all image data. Don't choose the JPEG format; doing so is destructive to the photo because of the lossy compression that is applied. Chapter 3 has details.

- *Resolution:* This option *does not* adjust the pixel count of your image, as you might imagine. It only sets the default output resolution that will be used if you send the photo to a printer. Most photo-editing programs enable you to adjust this value before printing. The Canon software does not, however, so if you plan to print through the browser, I suggest you set this value to 300. Chapter 9 talks more about printing.

- *Save Folder and Rename File:* Use these options to specify a storage folder and filename for your converted image.

6. **Click Save.**

A progress box appears to let you know that the conversion and file-saving is going forward.

7. **Close the Raw Image Task window to return to the browser.**

As you can probably tell from looking at the Raw Task Window in Figure 8-21, these steps give you only a basic overview of the process. If you do regularly shoot in the Raw format, take the time to explore the Raw Task Window Help system so that you can take advantage of its other features.

Also know that this raw processor isn't your only option. Digital Photo Professional, provided in the Canon software suite, offers its own raw conversion tools. Because that program is designed for the more advanced user, the conversion tools are slightly more complex, but they're also a little more powerful in some regards. Additionally, both Adobe Photoshop and Photoshop Elements offer excellent raw converters.

Whichever converter you choose, keep these final pointers in mind:

- Always save your processed files in a nondestructive format, such as TIFF. (If you use Adobe Photoshop Elements or Photoshop, its format, PSD, is also nondestructive.) If you need a JPEG image to share online, Chapter 9 shows you how to create a duplicate of your original, converted image in that format.

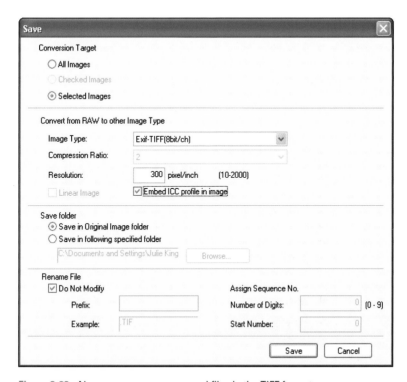

Figure 8-23: Always save your processed files in the TIFF format.

☞ Some raw converters, including the ones in the Canon programs, give you the option of creating a 16-bit image file. (A *bit* is a unit of computer data; the more bits you have, the more colors your image can contain.) Many photo editing programs either can't open 16-bit files or limit you to a few editing tools, so I suggest you stick with the standard, 8-bit image option. Your image will contain more than enough colors, and you'll avoid potential conflicts caused by so-called *high-bit* images.

☞ Resist the temptation to crank up color saturation too much. Doing so can actually destroy image detail. Likewise, be careful about overdoing sharpening, or you can create noticeable image defects. Chapter 10 offers some additional information about sharpening and saturation to help you find the right amounts of each.

9

Printing and Sharing Your Photos

*W*hen my first digital photography book was published, way back in the 1990s, consumer digital cameras didn't offer the resolution needed to produce good prints at anything more than postage-stamp size — and even then, the operative word was "good," not "great." And if you did want a print, it was a pretty much a do-it-yourself proposition unless you paid sky-high prices at a professional imaging lab. In those days, retail photo labs didn't offer digital printing, and online printing services hadn't arrived yet, either.

Well, time and technology march on, and, at least in the case of digital photo printing, to a very good outcome. Your Rebel XTi/400D can produce dynamic prints even at large sizes, and getting those prints made is easy and economical, thanks to an abundance of digital printing services now in stores and online. And for home printing, today's printers are better and cheaper than ever, too.

That said, getting the best output from your camera still requires a little bit of knowledge and prep work on your part. To that end, this chapter tells you exactly how to ensure that your picture files will look as good on paper as they do in your camera monitor.

In addition, this chapter explores ways to share your pictures electronically. First, I show you how to prepare your picture for e-mail — an important step if you don't want to annoy friends and family by cluttering their inboxes with ginormous, too-large-to-view photos. Following that, you can find out how to create a digital slide show, view your pictures on a television, and join online photo-sharing communities.

Avoiding Printing Problems

Although digital printing has come a long way in the past couple of years, a few issues still can cause hiccups in the printing process. So before you print your photos, whether you want to do it on your own printer or send them to a lab, read through the next three sections, which show you how to avoid the most common trouble spots.

Check the pixel count before you print

Resolution, or the number of pixels in your digital image, plays a huge role in how large you can print your photos and still maintain good picture quality. You can get the complete story on resolution in Chapter 3, but here's a quick recap as it relates to printing:

- ✔ On your Rebel XTi/400D, you set picture resolution via the Quality option, found on Shooting Menu 1. You must select this option *before* you capture an image, which means that you need some idea of your ultimate print size before you shoot. And remember that if you crop your image, you eliminate some pixels, so take that factor into account when you do the resolution math.

- ✔ For good print quality, the *minimum* pixel count (in my experience, anyway) is 200 pixels per linear inch, or 200 ppi. That means that if you want a 4-x-6-inch print, you need at least 800 x 1200 pixels.

- ✔ Depending on your printer, you may get even better results at 200+ ppi. Some printers do their best work when fed 300 ppi, and a few (notably those from Epson) request 360 ppi as the optimum resolution. However, going higher than that typically doesn't produce any better prints.

  Unfortunately, because most printer manuals don't bother to tell you what image resolution produces the best results, finding the right resolution is a matter of experimentation. (Don't confuse the manual's statements related to the printer's *dpi* with *ppi.* DPI refers to how many dots of color the printer can lay down per inch; many printers use multiple dots to reproduce one image pixel.)

- ✔ If you're printing your photos at a retail kiosk or at an online site, the printing software that you use to order your prints should determine the resolution of your file and then guide you as to the suggested print size. But if you're printing on a home printer, you need to be the resolution cop.

So what do you do if you find that you don't have enough pixels for the print size you have in mind? You just have to decide what's more important, print size or print quality.

If your print size does exceed your pixel supply, one of two things must happen:

- ✔ The pixel count remains constant, and pixels simply grow in size to fill the requested print size. And if pixels get too large, you get a defect known as *pixelation.* The picture starts to appear jagged, or stairstepped, along curved or digital lines. Or at worst, your eye can actually make out the individual pixels, and your photo begins to look more like a mosaic than, well, a photograph.

✔ The pixel size remains constant, and the printer software adds pixels to fill in the gaps. You can also add pixels, or *resample the image,* in your photo software. Wherever it's done, resampling doesn't solve the low resolution problem. You're asking the software to make up photo information out of thin air, and the result is usually an image that looks worse than it did before resampling. You don't get pixelation, but details turn muddy, giving the image a blurry, poorly rendered appearance.

Just to hammer home the point and remind you one more time of the impact of resolution picture quality, Figures 9-1 and 9-2 show you the same image as it appears at 300 ppi (the resolution required by the publisher of this book), at 50 ppi, and resampled from 50 ppi to 300 ppi. As you can see, there's just no way around the rule: If you want the best quality prints, you need the right pixel count from the get-go.

300 ppi   50 ppi

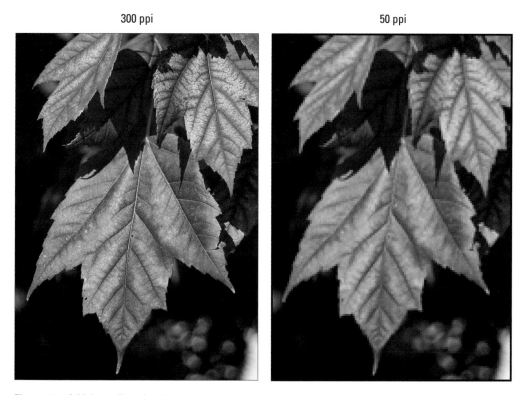

Figure 9-1: A high-quality print depends on a high-resolution original.

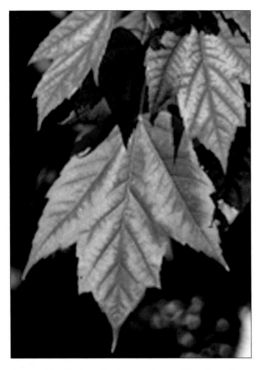

Figure 9-2: Adding pixels in a photo editor doesn't rescue a low-resolution original.

Allow for different print proportions

Unlike many digital cameras, your Canon produces images that have an aspect ratio of 3:2. That is, images are 3 units wide by 2 units tall — just like a 35mm film negative — which means that they translate perfectly to the standard 4-x-6-inch print size. (Most digital cameras produce 4:3 images, which means the pictures must be cropped to fit a 4-x-6-inch piece of paper.)

If you want to print your digital original at other standard sizes — 5 x 7, 8 x 10, 11 x 14, and so on — you need to crop the photo to match those proportions. Alternatively, you can reduce the photo size slightly and leave an empty margin along the edges of the print as needed.

As a point of reference, both images in Figure 9-3 show you an original, 3:2 image. The blue outlines indicate how much of the original can fit within a 5-x-7-inch frame and an 8-x-10-inch frame.

5 x 7 frame area   8 x 10 frame area

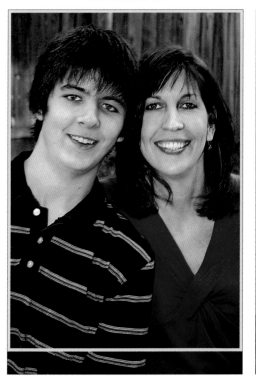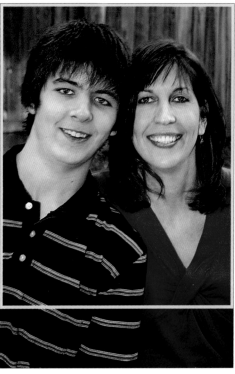

Figure 9-3: Composing your shots with a little head room enables you to crop to different frame sizes.

Chapter 10 shows you how to crop your image using the free Canon software that shipped with your camera. You also can usually crop your photo using the software provided at online printing sites and at retail print kiosks. But if you plan to simply drop off your memory card for printing at a lab, be sure to find out whether the printer automatically crops the image without your input. If so, use your photo software to crop the photo, save the cropped image to your memory card, and deliver that version of the file to the printer.

 To allow yourself printing flexibility, leave at least a little margin of background around your subject when you shoot, as I did for the example in Figure 9-3. Then you don't clip off the edges of the subject no matter what print size you choose. (Some people refer to this margin padding as *head room,* especially when describing portrait composition.)

Get print and monitor colors in synch

Your photo colors look perfect on your computer monitor. But when you print the picture, the image is too red, or too green, or has some other nasty color tint. This problem, which is probably the most prevalent printing issue, can occur because of any or all of the following factors:

✔ **Your monitor needs to be calibrated.** When print colors don't match what you see on your computer monitor, the most likely culprit is actually the monitor, not the printer. If the monitor isn't accurately calibrated, the colors it displays aren't a true reflection of your image colors.

To ensure that your monitor is displaying photos on a neutral canvas, start by running a software-based calibration tool. One better-known tool is Adobe Gamma, shown in Figure 9-4, which ships with the Windows version of Photoshop Elements. If you use a Mac, the operating assistant offers a built-in calibrator called the Display Calibrator Assistant. You also can find free calibration software online; just search for the term *free monitor calibration software.*

Software-based tools, though, depend on your eyes to make decisions during the calibration process. For a more reliable calibration, you may want to invest in a hardware solution, such as the Pantone Huey ($90, www.pantone.com) or the ColorVision Spyder2express ($70, www.data color.com). These products use a device known as a *colorimeter* to accurately measure your display colors.

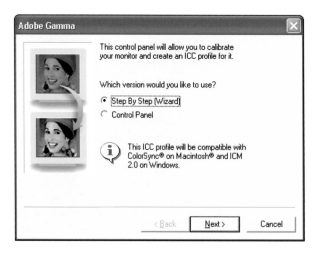

Figure 9-4: Calibration software such as Adobe Gamma helps ensure accurate monitor colors.

Whichever route you go, the calibration process produces a monitor *profile,* which is simply a data file that tells your computer how to adjust the display to compensate for any monitor color casts. Your Windows or Mac operating system loads this file automatically when you start your computer. Your only responsibility is to perform the calibration every month or so, as monitor colors drift over time.

✔ **One of your printer cartridges is empty or clogged.** If your prints look great one day but are way off the next, the number-one suspect is an empty ink cartridge or a clogged print nozzle or head. Check your manual to find out how to perform the necessary maintenance to keep the nozzles or print heads in good shape.

If black-and-white prints have a color tint, you might assume that your black ink cartridge is to blame, if your printer has one. But the problem is usually a color cartridge instead. Most printers use both color and black inks even for black-and-white prints, and if one color is missing, a tint results.

When you buy replacement ink, by the way, keep in mind that third-party brands, while they may save you money, may not deliver the performance you get from the cartridges made by your printer manufacturer. A lot of science goes into getting ink formulas to mesh with the printer's ink-delivery system, and the printer manufacturer obviously knows most about that delivery system.

✔ **You chose the wrong paper setting in your printer software.** When you set up your print job, be sure to select the right setting from the paper-type option — glossy, matte, and so on. This setting affects how the printer lays down ink on the paper.

✔ **Your photo paper is low quality.** Sad but true: The cheap, store-brand photo papers usually don't render colors as well as the higher-priced, name-brand papers. For best results, try papers from your printer manufacturer; again, those papers are engineered to provide top performance with the printer's specific inks and ink-delivery system.

✔ **Your printer and photo software are fighting over color management duties.** Some photo programs offer *color management* tools, which are features that enable the user to control how colors are handled as an image passes from camera to monitor to printer. Most printer software also offers color management features. The problem is, if you enable color management controls both in your photo software and your printer software, you can create conflicts that lead to wacky colors. So check your photo software and printer manuals to find out what color management options are available to you and how to turn them on and off.

Even if all the aforementioned issues are resolved, however, don't expect perfect color matching between printer and monitor. Printers simply can't reproduce the entire spectrum of colors that a monitor can display. In addition, monitor colors always appear brighter because they are, after all, generated with light.

Finally, be sure to evaluate your print colors and monitor colors in the same ambient light — daylight, office light, whatever — because that light source has its own influence on the colors you see.

Printing Online or In-Store

Normally, I'm a do-it-yourself type of gal. I mow my own lawn, check my own tire pressure, hang my own screen doors. I am woman; hear me roar. Unless, that is, I discover that I can have someone *else* do the job in less time and for less money than I can — which just happens to be the case for digital photo printing. Although I occasionally make my own prints for fine-art images that I plan to sell or exhibit, I have everyday snapshots made at my local retail photo lab.

Unless you're already very comfortable with computers and photo printing, I suggest that you do the same. Compare the cost of retail digital printing with the cost of using a home or office photo printer — remember to factor in the required ink, paper, and your precious time — and you'll no doubt come out ahead if you delegate the job.

You can choose from a variety of retail printing options, as follows:

✓ **Drop-off printing services:** Just as you used to leave a roll of film at the photo lab in your corner drug store or camera store, you can drop off your memory card, order prints, and then pick up your prints in as little as an hour.

✓ **Self-serve print kiosks:** Many photo labs, big-box stores, and other retail outlets also offer self-serve print kiosks. You insert your memory card into the appropriate slot, follow the onscreen directions, and wait for your prints to slide out of the print chute.

✓ **Online with mail-order delivery:** You can upload your photo files to online printing sites and have prints mailed directly to your house. Photo-sharing sites such as Shutterfly, Kodak Gallery, and Snapfish are well-known players in this market. But many national retail chains, such as Ritz Cameras, Wal-Mart, and others also offer this service.

✓ **Online with local pickup:** Here's my favorite option. Many national chains enable you to upload your picture files for easy ordering but pick up your prints at a local store.

This service is a great way to share prints with friends and family who don't live nearby. I can upload and order prints from my desk in Indianapolis, for example, and have them printed at a store located a few miles from my parents' home in Texas.

Printing from ZoomBrowser EX/ImageBrowser

If you prefer to print your own pictures on a home or office printer, the process is much the same as printing anything from your computer: You open the picture file in your photo software of choice, choose File⇨Print, and specify the print size, paper size, paper type, and so on, as usual.

The following steps show you how to get the job done using Canon Zoom-Browser EX (Windows) or ImageBrowser (Mac). Chapter 8 introduces you to this free software, so you may want to pop to that chapter to find out how to browse your images using the program if you haven't already done so. Then walk this way:

1. **Click the thumbnail for the image that you want to print.**

2. **Choose File⇨Print⇨Photo Print.**

   Your image then appears inside the Photo Print window, shown in Figure 9-5. The figure shows the Windows XP version of the Photo Print features. If you're a Mac user, your window lacks the gray task panel that appears on the left in Windows, but don't fret: The critical printing settings remain the same, albeit with a slightly different look.

3. **Select a printer.**

   In Windows, choose the printer from the Name drop-down list. On a Mac, select your printer from the Printer drop-down list.

4. **Specify your printer settings.**

   - *Windows:* Click the Properties button.
   - *Mac:* Click the Page Setup button.

   Either way, you're taken to the standard print-setup dialog box for your printer. The options therein depend on your printer, so check your manual for guidance. But be sure to specify the following settings:

   - Paper size
   - Paper type (glossy, plain paper, and so on)
   - Borderless printing on or off (if your printer offers this feature)

   The browser software automatically chooses the print orientation (portrait or landscape) that best fits the image. Even though you can select an orientation option in your printer setup dialog box, the program overrides you later if it deems necessary.

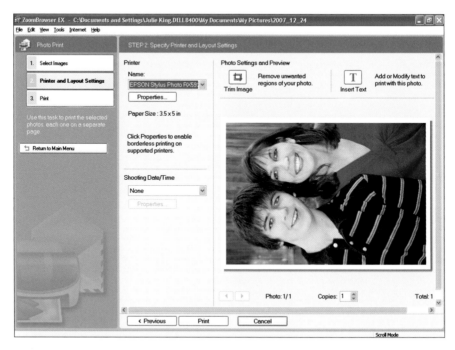

Figure 9-5: Your first step is to select a printer and paper size.

When you finish establishing the printer settings, click OK to return to the Photo Print window.

5. **Adjust the image cropping as necessary.**

By default, the browser automatically enlarges and/or crops your image to fit your chosen paper size if necessary. To see exactly what has been cropped in Windows, click the Trim Image button. On a Mac, click the button labeled Remove Unwanted Regions of Your Photo.

In both cases, your image opens in Trim Image editing window, shown in Figure 9-6, which contains some of the controls that you see when you use the program's editing functions.

Chapter 10 details the Trim Image editing controls, but here's the short story:

- The box with the little white squares around it indicates the crop box. Anything outside the box won't be printed.

- Drag any of those squares to adjust the size of the crop box. You're limited to setting the box to the same proportions as your selected paper size.

Crop box

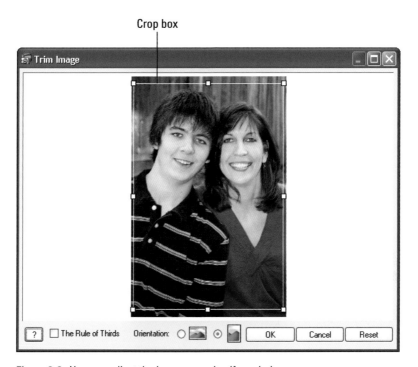

Figure 9-6: You can adjust the image cropping if needed.

- Drag inside the box to move it over a different part of the photo.
- Click the Orientation icons (Windows) or Trimming Frame buttons (Mac) if you want to change the layout of the cropping box (horizontal or vertical).
- Click OK to apply the new cropping and return to the Photo Print window.

If you don't want your photo to be cropped or enlarged at all, you need to exit the printing process and adjust a program preference. See the end of these steps for details.

6. **Add the shooting date/time (optional).**

You can print the date and time that the photo was taken by choosing an option from the Shooting Date/Time drop-down list. The program determines the date and time from data in the image file.

If you do choose to print the date and time, click the Properties button to set the font, size, and placement of the type.

7. **Add a caption to the photo (optional).**

   To add more type to your photo, click the Insert Text button (Windows) or the Add Some Text to Print with This Photo button (Mac). Either way, you're taken to the Insert Text window, which offers most of the same text tools as the regular Insert Text window, which I cover at the end of Chapter 10.

8. **Click the Print button.**

   Your photo file is shipped to the printer.

As I mentioned in Step 5, you can choose to turn off the automatic cropping that occurs by default. First, close the Photo Print window if it's open. Then take these steps:

- *Windows:* Choose Tools⇨Preferences to open the Preferences dialog box. Click the Printing tab and select the Do Not Allow Trimming of the Image option. Click OK to close the dialog box.

- *Mac:* Choose ImageBrowser⇨Preferences. Select Photo Print from the drop-down list at the top of the dialog box that appears. Then select Do Not Trim and click OK.

If you take this step, the Trim function inside the Photo Print dialog box becomes disabled, so you must do any cropping before you print.

Although it's fine for casual printing, Photo Print lacks some features that are typically found in most photo editors and even in the software that ships with most photo printers. You can't print multiple images on the same page, for example, or even multiple copies of the same photo. So if you own other software, you may find it more convenient than using the browser's print functions.

Whatever software you use, be sure to follow the resolution guidelines set out near the beginning of this chapter. And note that the Photo Print window doesn't warn you if your image doesn't contain enough pixels to produce a good print at the size you select. So before you begin printing, check that pixel count by displaying the Shooting Information panel in the main browser window. The Image Size listing, highlighted in Figure 9-7, shows you the pixel count.

Preparing Pictures for E-Mail

How many times have you received an e-mail message that looks like the one in Figure 9-8? Some well-meaning friend or relative has sent you a digital photo that is so large that it's impossible to view the whole thing on your monitor.

Photo resolution

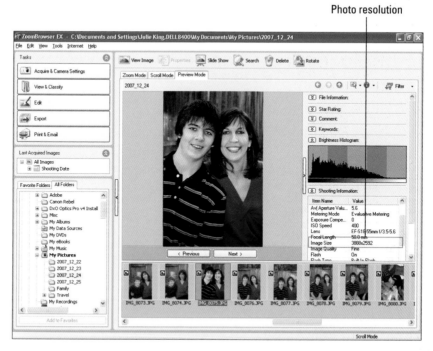

Figure 9-7: Make sure that the pixel count is adequate for the print size.

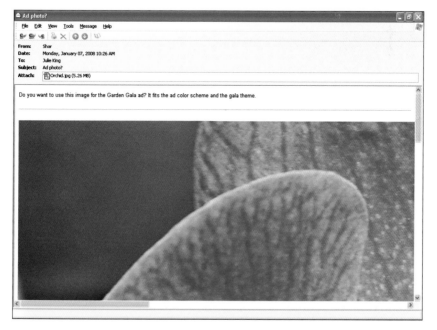

Figure 9-8: The attached image has too many pixels to be viewed without scrolling.

TECHNICAL STUFF

DPOF, PictBridge, and computerless printing

Your Rebel XTi/400D offers two features that enable you to print directly from your camera or memory card — without using the computer as middle-machine — assuming that your printer offers the required options.

The first of these features, called DPOF, stands for Digital Print Order Format. With this option, accessed via your camera's Playback menu, you select the pictures on your memory card that you want to print, and you specify how many copies you want of each image. Then, if your photo printer has a CompactFlash memory card slot and supports DPOF, you just pop the memory card into that slot. The printer reads your "print order" and outputs just the requested copies of your selected images. (You use the printer's own controls to set paper size, print orientation, and other print settings.)

A second direct-printing feature, called *Pict-Bridge*, works a little differently. If you have a PictBridge-enabled photo printer, you can connect the camera to the printer using the USB cable supplied with your camera. A PictBridge interface appears on the camera monitor, and you use the camera controls to select the pictures you want to print. With PictBridge, you specify additional print options, such as page size and whether you want to print a border around the photo, from the camera as well.

Both DPOF and PictBridge are especially useful in scenarios where you need fast printing. For example, if you shoot pictures at a party and want to deliver prints to guests before they go home, DPOF offers a quicker option than firing up your computer, downloading pictures, and so on. And if you invest in one of the tiny portable photo printers on the market today, you can easily make prints away from your home or office — you can take both your portable printer and camera along to your regional sales meeting, for example.

For the record, I prefer DPOF to PictBridge because with PictBridge, you have to deal with cabling the printer and camera together. Also, the camera must be turned on for the whole printing process, wasting battery power. But if you're interested in exploring either printing feature, your camera manual provides complete details.

The problem is that computer monitors can display only a limited number of pixels. The exact number depends on the monitor's resolution setting and the capabilities of the computer's video card, but suffice it to say that the average photo from one of today's digital cameras has a pixel count in excess of what the monitor can handle. Figure 9-8, for example, shows you how much of an image shot at your camera's Medium Quality setting, which produces a 2816-x-1880-pixel photo, is viewable when displayed in a typical e-mail program window.

In general, a good rule is to limit a photo to no more than 450 pixels at its longest dimension. That ensures that people can view your entire picture without scrolling, as in Figure 9-9. This image measures 450 x 300 pixels.

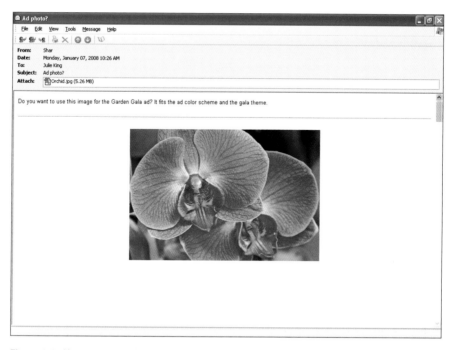

Figure 9-9: Keep e-mail pictures to no larger than 450 pixels wide or tall.

This recommendation means that even if you shoot at your camera's lowest resolution setting (1936 x 1288 pixels), you need to dump pixels from your images before sending them to the cyber post office. You can take care of that task and then send the resized image right from ZoomBrowser EX (Windows) or ImageBrowser (Mac).

As a first step, however, you need to check the file format of the photos you want to share; they must be in the JPEG format. If they are Raw (CR2) or TIFF images, the next section shows you how to create JPEG copies for online sharing. If the pictures are already JPEGs, skip ahead to the section "E-mailing photos from your browser."

Creating Web-friendly copies of Raw and TIFF photos

In Chapter 8, I advise you to save Raw files in the TIFF format after you process them in a raw converter. TIFF is ideal because it is a *nondestructive format* — that is, it retains all your picture data, resulting in the highest image quality. But there's one problem with TIFF files: E-mail programs and Web browsers can't display them. If you want to share your converted raw files online, you need to create a copy of the file in the standard online format, JPEG.

Why not just save your converted raw files as JPEG images at the processing stage? Because JPEG *is* a destructive format, eliminating some image data as a tradeoff for producing smaller file sizes. So the best practice is to save your original raw conversions as TIFF files and then create JPEG copies for online use.

In ZoomBrowser EX (Windows) or ImageBrowser (Mac), you can use the Export command to create a JPEG copy and reduce the pixel count to a resolution suitable for onscreen display at the same time. Follow these steps:

1. **Select the image by clicking its thumbnail in the browser.**

2. **Choose File⇨Export⇨Export Still Images (Windows) or File⇨Export Image (Mac).**

   Export is the geekspeak way of saying "save this file in a different format."

   In Windows, you next see a window that contains the file-saving options, as shown in Figure 9-10. On a Mac, you see the Write a Still Image box instead; click Edit and Save Image and then click the Next button to get to the file-saving options. They're arranged a little differently on the Mac than in Figure 9-10, but the basic controls are the same.

3. **Set the image size.**

   To keep the original pixel count, deselect the Resize Images During Export check box (Windows) or Resize the Image box (Mac). If you do want to resample the image (trim the pixel count), select the box, as shown in the figure. Then click the Long Side option (Windows) or Specify the Length Dimension (Mac) and type a value in the neighboring box. The value you enter determines the number of pixels the image contains along its longest side. When resizing the image, the program will automatically set the pixel count of the shortest side to retain the original image proportions.

   For e-mail images, I suggest setting the long side of the image to 450 pixels or less. This ensures that the recipient can view the entire image without scrolling the e-mail window.

4. **Select the Change Image Type check box.**

5. **Select the JPEG format from the drop-down list under the check box.**

   This sets the file format to JPEG.

6. **Use the Quality slider to set the desired image quality.**

   At the highest Quality setting, the program applies the least amount of *JPEG compression,* which is the process that reduces file sizes by dumping image data. For acceptable image quality, I suggest that you set the slider either to Highest or High. (Your file size is already pretty small because of the reduced pixel count.)

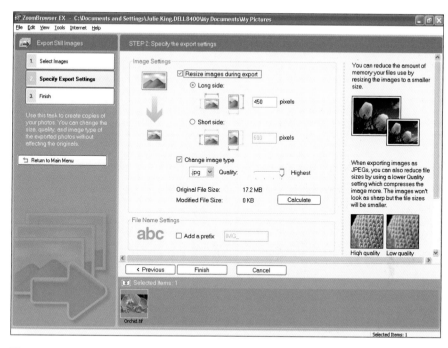

Figure 9-10: Use the Export command to create a JPEG copy of a TIFF photo.

7. **Specify a filename.**

You have two options: If you deselect the Add a Prefix check box (Windows) or the Rename the File box (Mac), the program gives your JPEG copy the same name as the original — for example, IMG_7813.TIF becomes IMG_7813.JPG.

You also can assign a new filename. First, select the Add a Prefix check box (Windows) or the Rename the File box (Mac). Then type the text in the adjacent text box. Note that the program automatically adds the numbers 0001 to the end of whatever text you enter. For example, if you type **Web** in the box, the filename of your JPEG copy will be Web0001.jpg. If you stick with the text that the program enters in the box for you automatically — IMG_ — the filename will be IMG_0001.jpg.

8. **Choose the folder where you want to store the JPEG file.**

In Windows, you do this by using the Save to Folder option. Click Current Folder to put the copy in the same folder as the original. Click My Pictures to put the copy in that folder instead, or click Browse to select another folder.

In Windows, you may need to scroll the window display to access the Save to Folder option, as shown in Figure 9-11.

On a Mac, the current folder destination appears at the bottom of the dialog box; click the Browse button to select a different storage bin.

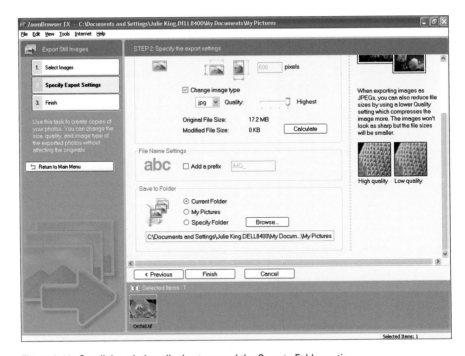

Figure 9-11: Scroll the window display to reveal the Save to Folder option.

 9. Click Finish to save the copy.

After creating your Web-ready image, you can attach it to an e-mail message just as you do any file.

E-mailing photos from the browser

You can resize and e-mail JPEG photos directly from ZoomBrowser EX (Windows) or ImageBrowser (Mac). Follow these steps:

 1. In the browser, select the images that you want to share.

 Click the first image and then either Ctrl+click (Windows) or ⌘+click (Mac) additional images.

 2. Start the e-mail tool.

 How you do it depends on your operating system:

 • *Windows*: Choose Internet➪Send Images by Email.

 • *Mac*: Choose Internet➪Create Images for Email.

 In Windows, you see the dialog box shown in Figure 9-12. The Mac version looks a little different, but contains the same critical controls.

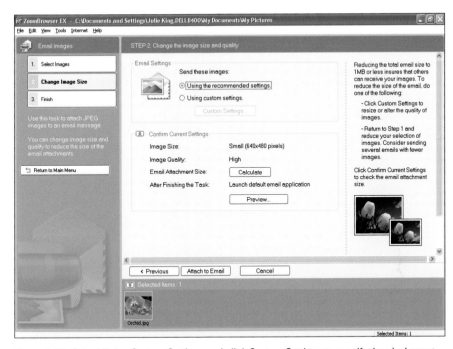

Figure 9-12: Select Using Custom Settings and click Custom Settings to specify the pixel count.

3. Select the Using Custom Settings option button.

Why not use the program's recommended settings? Because if you do, your e-mail image is sized to 640 x 480 pixels. On some computer screens, even that size is too large to be viewed without scrolling.

4. Click the Custom Settings button.

In Windows, you see the dialog box shown in Figure 9-13. The Mac version contains the same basic options, plus a couple additional options related to digital movies, which you can ignore. In both versions, the dialog box enables you to specify the width or height of your

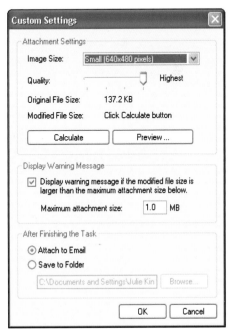

Figure 9-13: You can create a custom setting to apply to all your e-mail photos.

picture and then preview the resulting file size and onscreen display size.

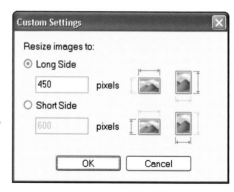

Figure 9-14: Set the pixel count for the picture's longest side.

5. **Open the Image Size drop-down list and click Custom Size.**

Now a second dialog box opens, offering the options shown in Figure 9-14. Here, you can specify the exact pixel count you want the photo to have.

6. **Click the Long Side button and enter a size value in the adjacent box.**

This value determines the maximum height of a vertically oriented picture or the maximum width of a horizontally oriented picture. Again, I recommend a value of 450 pixels, but you make the call.

Whatever value you enter, the program will handle setting the value for the shortest side when it resizes the image.

7. **Click OK to close the dialog box.**

The image size you specified now appears as an option in the drop-down list. So the next time you send an image, you can skip Steps 5 and 6 and simply select that size from the list.

8. **Specify the picture quality by dragging the Quality slider.**

This setting determines how much JPEG compression is applied. As Chapter 3 explains, *JPEG compression* reduces the size of a picture file by getting rid of some image data. The more compression you apply, the smaller the file and the lower the picture quality.

After you drag the slider, click the Calculate button. The program does a quick calculation, and the Modified File Size value then shows you the file size that will result from the chosen Quality setting. And if you click the Preview button, you can view a preview of how the image will look at the selected setting.

Because the new pixel count of your photo already results in a very small file, you can use a high Quality setting without worrying too much about download times. The exception is if you are sending a picture to someone who uses a dial-up connection, in which case I would bump the Quality slider down a notch. You also may want to reduce the Quality slightly if you are attaching multiple pictures to the same e-mail message so that the combined download time isn't excessive.

9. **Tell the program to automatically fire up your e-mail program after it resizes the photo.**

   • *Windows:* Select the Attach to Email option.

   • *Mac*: Select the Start Email Application After Closing option.

10. **Click OK to close the Custom Settings dialog box.**

    You're returned to the main e-mail utility window.

11. **Click the arrow labeled Confirm Current to review the image size settings.**

    If anything is off, click the Custom Settings button to adjust the settings.

12. **Click Attach to Email (Windows) or Finish (Mac).**

    The program creates your e-mail copy, fires up your e-mail program, and creates a new message window. The images are automatically attached to the message, so all you have to do is enter the recipient's e-mail address and any message you want to include. Then just send the message as you normally do.

The software does not save a copy of the resized e-mail image on your computer's hard drive. If you do want to create and save a small copy of the photo, follow Steps 1 through 8 and then proceed like so:

- ✔ *Windows*: Select the Save to Folder button and then click the Browse button to select the folder where you want to store the resized copy of the photo. In Step 12, click the Save to Folder button.

- ✔ *Mac:* Deselect the Attach to Email button in Step 9. Then click the Finish button. You can't specify a different folder location; the copy is automatically placed in the same folder as the original.

Windows or Mac, the program gives the resized image the same name as the original but tags the characters "_1" onto the end of the name so that you don't overwrite the original. Your e-mail program isn't started automatically, but you can take care of that step yourself, creating your message and attaching the picture files just as you do any file that you want to share by e-mail.

Creating an In-Camera Slide Show

Many photo-editing and cataloging programs offer a tool for creating digital slide shows that can be viewed on a computer or, if copied to a DVD, on a DVD player. You can even add music, special transition effects, and the like to jazz up your presentations.

Online photo sharing: Read the fine print

If you want to share more than a couple of photos, consider posting your images at an online photo-album site instead of attaching them to e-mail messages. Photo-sharing sites such as Shutterfly, Kodak Gallery, and Picasa all enable you to create digital photo albums and then invite friends and family to view your pictures and order prints of their favorites.

At most sites, picture-sharing is free, but your albums and images are deleted if you don't order prints or make some other purchase from the site within a specified amount of time. Additionally, many free sites enable you to upload high-resolution files for printing but then don't let you retrieve those files from the site. (In other words, don't think of album sites as archival storage solutions.) And here's another

little bit of fine print to investigate: The membership agreement at some sites states that you agree to let the site use your photos, for free, for any purpose that it sees fit.

If the restrictions of a free site bug you, consider subscribing to a paid site such as Phanfare (www.phanfare.com). For a yearly membership fee — about $50, for Phanfare — you can store and share high-resolution image files with no further purchase obligations. And when you invite others to view your albums, they can not only view your images, but also download those high-res originals if needed, making this a good way to distribute images to clients and colleagues. Paid sites also are usually free of the pop-up advertising that clutters the free sites, giving them a more professional look and feel.

But if you just want a simple slide show — that is, one that just displays all the photos on the camera memory card one by one — you don't need a computer or any photo software. You can create and run the slide show right on your camera. And by connecting your camera to a television, as outlined in the next section, you can present your show to a whole roomful of people.

Follow these steps:

1. **Display the Playback menu and highlight Auto Play, as shown in Figure 9-15.**

2. **Press Set.**

   The images are displayed sequentially on the monitor, with each image appearing for about four seconds. After the last image is displayed, the show automatically begins again.

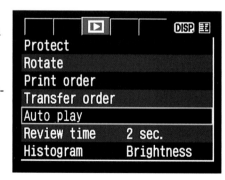

Figure 9-15: Choose Auto Play to set up automatic playback of all pictures on your memory card.

During auto playback, you can control the display as follows:

- ✔ **Pause playback.** Press the Set button. Press the button again to restart playback.

- ✔ **Change the information display style.** Press the DISP button. (See Chapter 4 for details about the available display styles.)

- ✔ **Exit auto playback mode.** Press the Menu button.

Viewing Your Photos on a Television

Your Rebel XTi/400D is equipped with a *video-out port,* which is tucked under the little rubber cover on the left rear side of the camera, as shown in Figure 9-16. That feature means that you can output your pictures for display on a television screen.

To take advantage of this option, dig through your camera box until you find the video cable, which has little yellow plug ends like the one you see on the right in Figure 9-16. Then, making sure that the camera is off, use the cable to connect the camera's video-out port to the video-in port on your television, as shown in the right side of the figure. (The plug end that is long and skinny, with a black ring near its tip, goes into the camera.) You can also insert the plug into the video-in port on a VCR or DVD player that's connected to your TV, as shown in the figure.

Video out port   Video in port

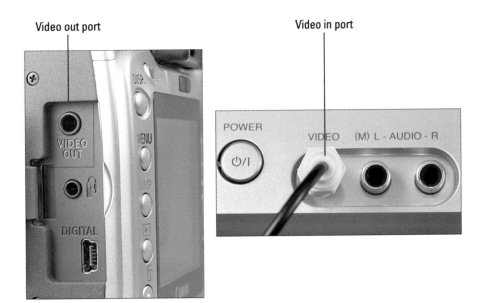

Figure 9-16: You can connect your camera to a television, VCR, or DVD player.

When the two devices are connected, turn the camera and TV (or VCR or DVD) on. At this point, you need to consult your TV/VCR/DVD manual to find out what channel to select for playback of signals from auxiliary input devices like your camera. After you sort that issue out, you can control play-back using the same camera controls as you normally do to view pictures on your camera monitor. (See Chapter 4 for help.) You can also run a slide show by following the steps outlined in the preceding section.

Note that you may need to adjust one camera setting, Video Mode, which is found on Setup Menu 2. You get just two options here: NTSC and PAL. Select the video mode that used by your part of the world. (In the United States, Canada, and Mexico, NTSC is the standard).

Part IV
The Part of Tens

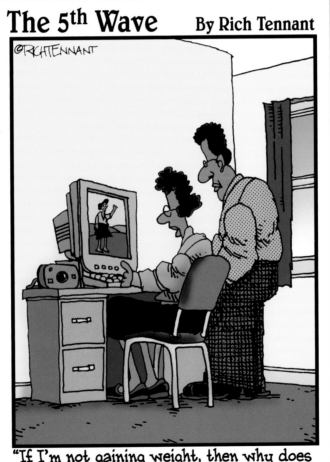

The 5th Wave   By Rich Tennant

"If I'm not gaining weight, then why does this digital image take up 3 MB more memory than a comparable one taken six months ago?"

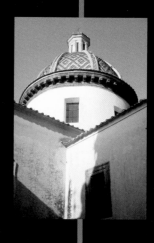

In this part . . .

*I*n time-honored *For Dummies* tradition, this part of the book contains additional tidbits of information presented in the always popular "Top Ten" list format.

Chapter 10 shows you how to do some minor picture touchups, such as cropping and adjusting exposure, by using the free software that shipped with your camera. Following that, Chapter 11 introduces you to ten camera functions that I consider specialty tools — bonus options that, while not at the top of the list of the features I suggest you study, are nonetheless interesting to explore when you have a free moment or two.

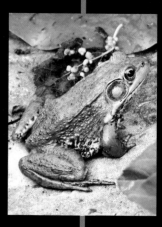

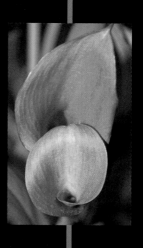

Ten Fast Photo-Editing Tricks

In This Chapter

▶ Using the editing tools in Canon ZoomBrowser and ImageBrowser

▶ Removing red-eye

▶ Cropping your photos

▶ Correcting exposure and color problems

▶ Creating the illusion of sharper focus

▶ Adding text

▶ Saving your edited masterpieces

*E*very photographer produces a clunker image now and then. When it happens to you, don't be too quick to reach for the Erase button on your camera. Many common problems are surprisingly easy to fix using the tools found in most photo editing programs.

In fact, you can perform many common retouching tasks using one of the free programs provided with your camera. Called ZoomBrowser EX in Windows and ImageBrowser on the Mac, this software offers tools for removing red-eye, adjusting exposure, tweaking colors, sharpening focus, and more.

Chapter 8 introduces you to these programs, showing you how to use them to download, view, and organize your pictures. If you aren't already familiar with those basics, you may want to visit that section of the book first. Then return to this chapter, which lays out the step-by-step instructions for using the editing tools to repair and enhance your photos.

A couple of other notes before you start:

✔ If you shot your pictures using the Raw file format, you must process them using the raw-conversion instructions laid out in Chapter 8 before you can edit them.

✔ Although the tools provided in the free software are pretty good, they don't allow selective editing. That is, you can't apply them just to the part of your photo that needs help. You can't brighten someone's face, for example, without also adjusting the rest of the image. For that kind of retouching work, you need a more sophisticated photo editor. Chapter 8 offers some recommendations.

✔ With a couple of exceptions, the figures in this chapter feature the Windows versions of the Canon software. Although the Mac version looks different, the actual steps for getting your retouching work done are the same unless I specifically state otherwise.

✔ For simplicity's sake, I refer to ZoomBrowser EX and ImageBrowser generically in the instructions here as just "the browser."

✔ Finally, Canon occasionally posts updates to its software on its Web site (www.canon.com). So if you've owned your camera for a while, check the Web site to make sure that you're using the most current versions of the available programs. This book features Version 6 of ZoomBrowser EX and ImageBrowser.

Removing Red-Eye

From my experience, red-eye is not a major problem with the Rebel XTi/400D. Typically, the problem occurs only in very dark lighting, which makes sense: When little ambient light is available, the pupils of the subjects' eyes widen, creating more potential for the flash light to cause red-eye reflection.

When red-eye does occur, take these steps to fix the problem:

1. In the main browser window, double-click the image thumbnail.

Again, Chapter 8 shows you how to get your images into the browser and keep track of your picture files.

After you double-click a thumbnail, the picture opens in its own Viewer window. Figure 10-1 offers a look at how the window appears in Windows; Figure 10-2 shows the Mac version.

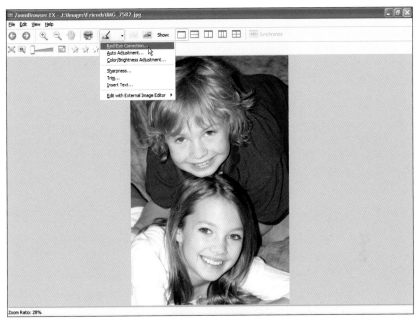

Figure 10-1: In Windows, click the Edit list above the preview to access retouching tools.

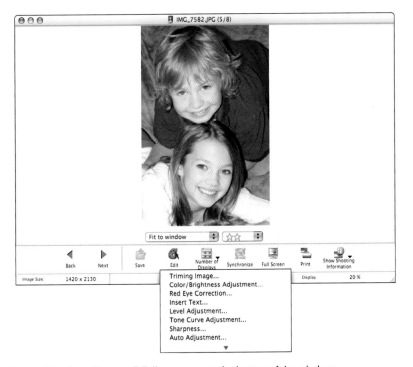

Figure 10-2: On a Mac, the Edit list appears at the bottom of the window.

2. **Open the Edit drop-down list, as shown in Figures 10-1 and 10-2.**

   The list appears above the image preview in Windows and below it on a Mac.

3. **Choose Red Eye Correction from the Edit list.**

   Your photo appears in the Red Eye Correction retouching window. Figure 10-3 shows the Windows version; Figure 10-4, the Mac version.

4. **Zoom in on your photo so that you can get a good view of the eyes.**

   • *In Windows:* Zoom and scroll the display using the controls labeled in Figure 10-3, which work the same way as they do when you view your photo in the initial Viewer window. Chapter 8 details all the controls, but here's a quick reminder: The fastest way to zoom in and out is to drag the Zoom slider; to scroll the display, just drag in the Navigator window, which appears whenever the entire image isn't visible at the current preview size. Or click the Hand tool, labeled in Figure 10-3, and drag in the preview itself.

   • *On a Mac:* Zoom by choosing a magnification level from the Display Size drop-down list, labeled in Figure 10-4, or by clicking the Zoom In and Zoom Out buttons. The Mac version of the retouching window does not sport a Navigator window — instead, you use the scroll bars to scroll the display.

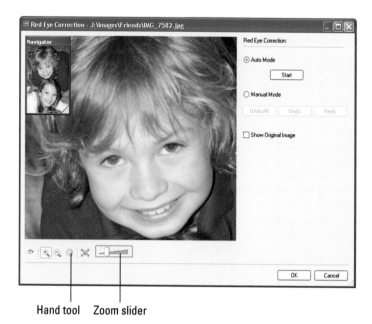

Hand tool   Zoom slider

Figure 10-3: Zoom in for a close look at the eyes.

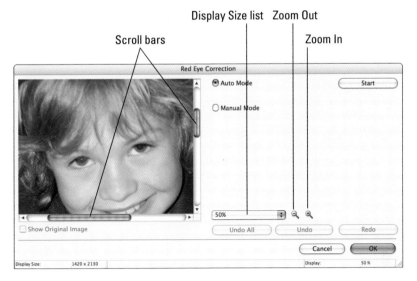

Figure 10-4: On a Mac, use these controls to adjust the preview size.

5. Click the Manual Mode option.

Why not use Auto Mode? Because in that mode, the red-eye correction tool can sometimes trip up, "correcting" red pixels that aren't actually in the eye. You're better off using Manual Mode, which enables you to specify exactly where you want the program to do its retouching work.

6. In Windows, select the Red Eye tool, labeled in Figure 10-5.

The tool is ready to go if it appears highlighted, as in the figure. If not, click the tool icon. Mac users can ignore this step.

7. Position your mouse cursor over one of the red eyes.

If the program detects fixable red pixels, a green circle appears, as shown in Figure 10-5. The circle indicates the area that the tool will try to correct. As you move your cursor around the eye, the circle may change size as the program searches for pixels that meet its red-eye criteria.

8. Click to initiate the repair.

If you like what you see, move on to the next eye. Or click Undo to get rid of the correction and then try again.

9. After you finish all eye repairs, click OK.

The Red Eye Correction window closes, and your repaired photo appears in the Viewer window.

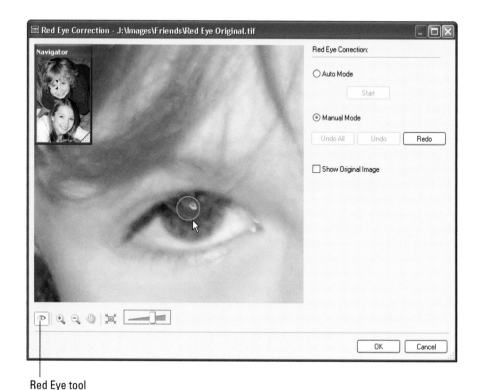

Red Eye tool

Figure 10-5: The little green circle indicates the eye area that will be replaced.

10. Save your picture in the TIFF file format.

The last section of this chapter provides details (and explains why you should use the TIFF format instead of JPEG).

Like most red-eye removal tools, the Canon version can do a good job in the right circumstances. But if the eyes are very bright, the tool may not be able to make the repair. The best solution is to simply paint in the correct eye colors. For that type of retouching, you need a more capable photo editing program; one (relatively) inexpensive yet powerful option is Adobe Photoshop Elements. You can take a look at that program in Chapter 8.

In addition, no red-eye remover works on animal eyes. Red-eye removal tools know how to detect and replace only red-eye pixels, and animal eyes typically turn yellow, white, or green in response to a flash. Again, the only answer is to make the repair with a paint tool.

Cropping Your Photo

To *crop* a photo simply means to trim away some of its perimeter. Removing excess background can often improve an image, as illustrated by my original frog scene, shown on the left in Figure 10-6, and its cropped cousin, shown on the right. In the original image, there's just too much going on — the eye has a hard time figuring out what's important. Eliminating all but a little of the surrounding foliage returned emphasis to the subject and created a stronger composition.

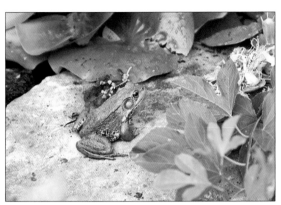
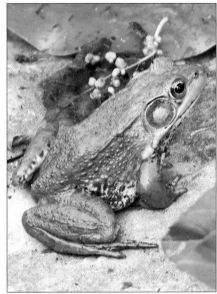

Figure 10-6: Cropping creates a better composition, eliminating background clutter.

You may also want to crop an image so that it fits a specific frame size. As Chapter 8 explains, the original images from your Canon fit perfectly in 4-x-6-inch frames, but if you want a 5 x 7, 8 x 10, or other standard print size, you need to crop your image to those new proportions. (If you don't, the photo printer software or retail print lab will crop for you, and the result may not be the composition that you'd choose.)

Whatever your cropping goal, follow these steps to do it in the Canon browser software:

1. In the main browser window, double-click the image thumbnail.

Your photo appears all by its lonesome in a new Viewer window.

2. **Choose Trim (Windows) or Trimming Image (Mac) from the Edit drop-down list.**

   Refer to Figures 10-3 and 10-4, in the preceding section, if you need help finding the list.

   After you choose the command, your image appears in the Trim Image retouching window. A dotted outline, called a *crop box,* appears around your photo, as shown in Figure 10-7. (The figure shows the Windows version of the screen; the Mac version contains the same cropping controls.)

3. **Click the Advanced Options button to display all the crop-size controls.**

   Figure 10-7 labels the button and shows the controls that appear when you click it. (On a Mac, the control panel pops out of the side of the dialog box instead of appearing within it.)

Handle

Click to display advanced options

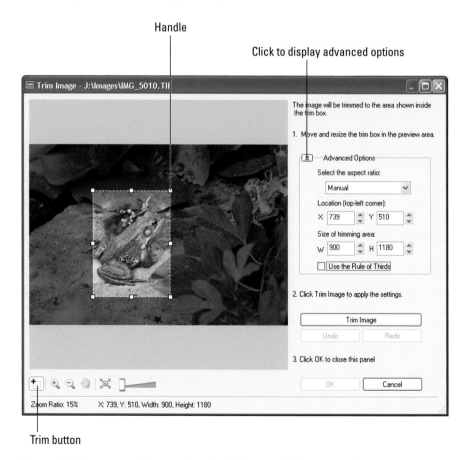

Trim button

Figure 10-7: You can specify a crop size via the Advanced Options controls.

4. **Choose an option from the Aspect Ratio drop-down list.**

Your selection determines the proportions of the cropped image. You can go in three directions:

- *Manual*: This option enables you to crop the image to any proportions. I chose this setting for my frog photo.

- *Maintain Original*: If you choose this option, the program restricts you to cropping to the same proportions as your original. In the case of your Digital Rebel XTi/400D, that's 3:2.

- *Specific Aspect Ratios:* You also can select from six specific aspect ratios: 2:3, 3:2, 3:4, 4:3, 9:16, and 16:9. The first number in the pair indicates the width and the second indicates the height.

5. **In Windows, make sure that the Trim button is selected, as shown in Figure 10-7.**

It should be already selected unless you used the adjacent controls to zoom or scroll the preview. Just click the button to select it if needed. Mac users can skip this step.

6. **Adjust the size and position of the crop box as needed.**

Use these techniques:

- *Move the crop box.* Drag inside the box.

- *Resize the crop box.* Drag any of the *handles* — those little squares around the perimeter of the crop box. I labeled one of the handles in Figure 10-7.

As you drag the handles, the W and H boxes in the Size of Trimming Area portion of the dialog box reflect the new dimensions of the crop box, with the measurement shown in pixels. Keep in mind that pixel count is critical to print quality. Chapters 3 and 9 provide details, but the short story is that you need roughly 200–300 pixels per linear inch of your print. So if you have a finished print size in mind, monitor the W and H values as you adjust the crop box size to make sure that you aren't clipping away too many pixels.

- *Set a specific crop size.* You also can enter specific pixel dimensions in the W and H boxes. The crop box automatically adjusts to the dimensions you enter.

Using the third option is the easiest way to crop your photo to a size that doesn't mesh with any of the specific aspect ratio choices. Say that you want to produce a 5-x-7-inch print from your cropped photo, and you want an image resolution of 300 pixels per inch. Just multiply the print dimensions by the desired resolution and then enter those values into the W and H boxes. For the 5 x 7 at 300 ppi example, the W and H values are 1500 and 2100, respectively. If the resulting crop boundary encompasses too much or too little of your photo, just keep adjusting the W and H values, making sure to always keep the two at the same proportions you originally entered.

7. Turn on the Use the Rule of Thirds gridlines (optional).

A classic composition rule is to imagine that your image is divided into thirds vertically and horizontally and then position the subject at a spot where two dividing lines intersect.

To help you visualize that concept, the Trim box can display those horizontal and vertical grid lines as shown in Figure 10-8. Just click the Use the Rule of Thirds check box to toggle the grid on and off.

8. When you're happy with the crop box, click the Trim Image button.

The cropped photo appears in the preview. If you aren't happy with the results, click the Undo button and try again.

9. Click OK to close the retouching window.

10. Choose File⇨Save As to save your cropped image.

The last section of this chapter has details.

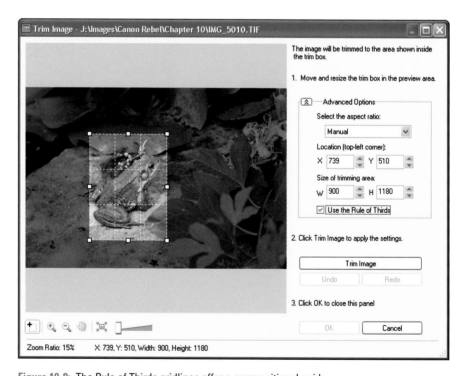

Figure 10-8: The Rule of Thirds gridlines offer a compositional guide.

Adjusting Color Saturation

Saturation refers to the intensity and purity of color. A fully saturated color contains no black, white, or gray. In other words, saturated colors are deep, rich, and bold.

I find that the colors produced by the Rebel XTi/400D are already pretty highly saturated, but on occasion, an image can benefit from a little saturation bump in the digital darkroom. Figure 10-9 offers an example. I was drawn to this scene by the mix of colors, and the original photo, shown on the left in the figure, seemed a little lackluster in that regard. So I increased the saturation ever so slightly to produce the image shown on the right.

Be careful about increasing saturation too much, however. Doing so actually can destroy picture detail as areas that previously contained a range of saturation levels all shift to the fully saturated state. In fact, you can often *reveal* detail by lowering saturation a little in your photo editor. For example, compare the original (left) and desaturated (right) versions of the image in Figure 10-10. Notice that the subtle gradations of color in the flower petals become apparent only in the right, slightly desaturated version.

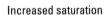

Original   Increased saturation

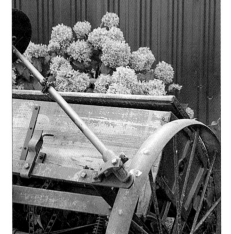
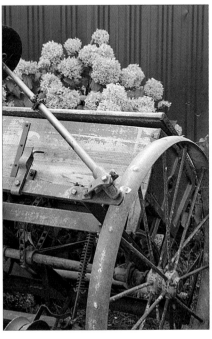

Figure 10-9: I slightly increased saturation to make the colors pop a little more.

Original   Reduced saturation

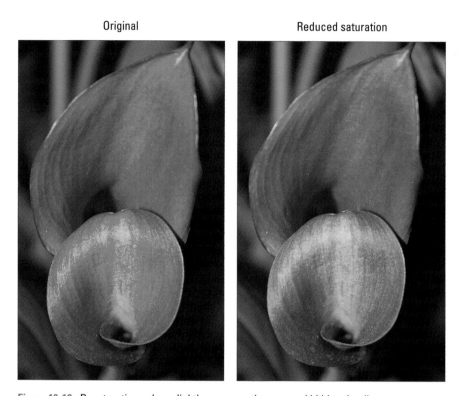

Figure 10-10: Desaturating colors slightly can sometimes reveal hidden details.

Whichever direction you want to go, take these steps to adjust saturation of your image:

1. **In the main browser window, double-click the image thumbnail.**

   Your photo opens inside its own Viewer window.

2. **Click the Edit drop-down list.**

   The list appears above the image preview in Windows; it appears below the preview on a Mac. (Refer to Figures 10-3 and 10-4 for the exact locations.)

3. **Choose Color/Brightness Adjustment from the list.**

   Your image appears in the Color/Brightness Adjustment retouching window. The window contents vary depending whether you're using the Windows or Mac version of the program; Figures 10-11 and 10-12 show you both versions.

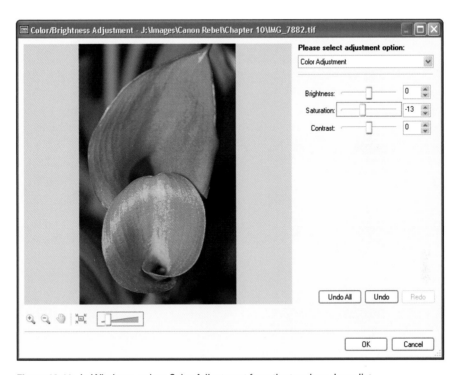

Figure 10-11: In Windows, select Color Adjustment from the top drop-down list.

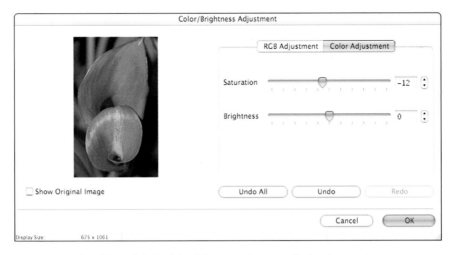

Figure 10-12: On a Mac, click the Color Adjustment button to display these options.

4. **Set the retouching mode to Color Adjustment.**

   - *In Windows*: Select Color Adjustment from the drop-down list at the top of the retouching window, as shown in Figure 10-11. After you do so, the window offers three sliders: Brightness, Saturation, and Contrast.

   - *On a Mac*: Click the Color Adjustment button. The Mac version of the tool offers just a Saturation and Brightness slider. (Don't fret; you don't want to use that Contrast slider anyway, nor its sibling, Brightness. More on that topic a bit later.)

5. **Drag the Saturation slider to adjust the image as desired.**

   Again, I caution you against raising the Saturation value too much; you can easily blow out subtle picture details.

6. **Click OK to apply the change and close the retouching window.**

7. **Save the edited image, following the steps provided at the end of this chapter.**

And now for the promised note about the Brightness and Contrast controls: Despite what their names may lead you to believe, these tools aren't the best options for adjusting image exposure and contrast. You can get much better results by using the Level Adjustment and Tone Curve Adjustment tools, both explained later in this chapter.

Tweaking Color Balance

Chapter 6 explains how to use your camera's white balance and Picture Style controls to manipulate the colors in your pictures. If you can't get the results you want by using those features, you may be able to do the job using the RGB Adjustment filter offered by the Canon browser. In Figure 10-13, for example, I used the filter to tone down the amount of blue in the image and bring out the warm yellow tones of the building instead.

Follow these steps to use the filter:

1. **Open the image in its own Viewer window.**

   You do this by just double-clicking the image thumbnail in the main browser window.

2. **Choose Color/Brightness Adjustment from the Edit drop-down list.**

   Look for the list above the image preview if you're a Windows user; on a Mac, the list is below the preview. After you choose the command, your photo appears in a retouching window. Figure 10-14 shows you both the Windows and Mac versions of the window.

Original   Colors adjusted

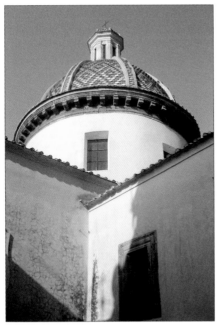 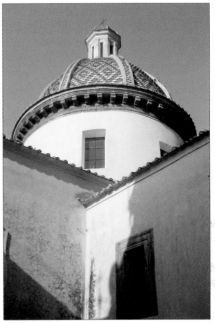

Figure 10-13: I warmed colors to emphasize the buildings rather than the sky.

3. **Select RGB Adjustment as the edit mode.**

   In Windows, select that option from the drop-down list at the top of the window, as shown in the top image in Figure 10-14. On a Mac, just click the RGB Adjustment button, as shown in the lower image.

   Either way, you gain access to three sliders: Red, Green, and Blue.

4. **Drag the sliders to adjust image colors.**

   The filter is based on three color pairs: red-cyan; green-magenta; and blue-yellow. (Those six colors happen to be the primary and secondary colors of the RGB color world, which is the one in which all digital images reside.) As you move the sliders, you affect both the primary color and its secondary opposite, as follows:

   • *Red slider:* As you drag the slider to the right, you increase red and decrease cyan. Drag the slider to the left to diminish reds and embolden cyans.

   • *Green slider:* Drag this slider to the right to add green and reduce magenta. Drag to the left to produce the opposite result.

   • *Blue slider:* Dragging this slider to the right increases the amount of blue and reduces the amount of yellow. Go the other direction to increase yellow and tone down blues.

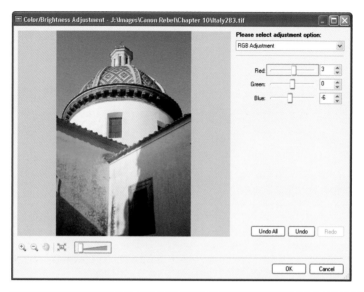

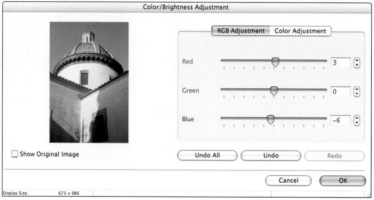

Figure 10-14: Select RGB Adjustment to tweak color balance.

In imaging lingo, tools of this type are known as *color balancing* filters because they shift the balance between the two opposite colors.

I used the slider settings shown in the figure for my example photo.

5. **When you're happy with the image colors, click OK to close the retouching window.**

6. **Save your work according to the steps in the last section of this chapter.**

Adjusting Exposure

Getting exposure just right is one of the trickiest aspects of photography. Fortunately, the Canon browser software gives you three tools for tweaking exposure. The next two sections introduce you to the two most capable of those tools, the Level Adjustment filter and the Tone Curve Adjustment filter. (The latter, by the way, is a professional-grade tool usually found only in expensive programs like Photoshop.)

What about the remaining set of exposure tools — the Brightness and Contrast sliders that appear with the Saturation slider when you choose Adjust Color/ Brightness from the Edit menu? You might naturally assume that those two sliders are meant to do what their names imply. And they do — just not very well.

The problem is that both sliders affect all pixels in your image. You can't brighten just the shadows in your image, for example, without also brightening the midtones (areas of medium brightness) and highlights. Ditto for the contrast adjustment. For that reason, you rarely can get good results. So do yourself a favor and stick with the Level Adjustment or Tone Curve Adjustment tools. They're a little more intimidating at first than using the simple Brightness and Contrast sliders, but they're actually pretty easy to use once you figure out what's what — which is what the next two sections help you do.

Three-point exposure control with the Level Adjustment filter

With a *levels filter,* found in many photo programs, you can adjust your picture's shadows, midtones, and highlights individually. Figure 10-15 shows you the Canon browser's version of this filter.

Now, I know what you're thinking: "Wow, that looks *way* too complicated for me." Trust me, though, that this filter is actually pretty easy to use. First, ignore everything but the graph in the middle of the box, known as a *histogram,* and the three sliders underneath, labeled *Shadows, Midtones,* and *Highlights* in Figure 10-16. See? Easier already.

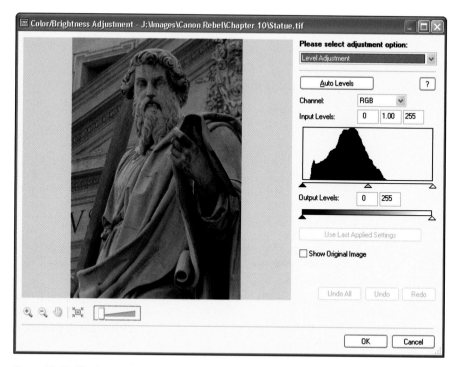

Figure 10-15: The Level Adjustment tool isn't nearly as difficult to use as it appears.

The histogram works just like the one that appears on your camera monitor if you view your images in Shooting Information display mode, which I discuss in Chapter 4. To recap, the horizontal axis of the graph represents the possible brightness values in an image, ranging from black on the left side to white on the right. The vertical axis shows you how many pixels fall at a particular bright-

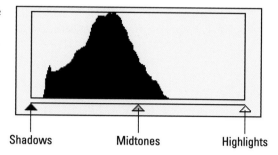

Figure 10-16: All you need to worry about are these three sliders.

ness value. So if you have a tall spike, you have lots of pixels at that brightness value. To adjust exposure, you just drag the three sliders underneath the histogram, depending on whether you want to shift shadows, midtones, or highlights.

Take these steps to try it out:

1. **In the main browser window, double-click the image thumbnail to open it in a new Viewer window.**

2. **Open the Level Adjustment retouching window.**

    • *In Windows:* Choose Color/Brightness Adjustment from the Edit drop-down list, found above the image preview. Then select Level Adjustment from the drop-down list at the top of the retouching window, as shown in Figure 10-15.

    • *On a Mac:* Choose Level Adjustment from the Edit drop-down list, which appears underneath the image preview. (The Mac version of the retouching window looks a little different from the one in Figure 10-15, but the critical controls are the same.)

3. **Set the Channel option to RGB.**

    On a Mac, the option is unlabeled; it's the pop-up list above the histogram.

    RGB should already be selected, but check just to be sure. (The other options enable you to adjust brightness values of the red, green, and blue color components of the image, which is a color-balancing trick used by some advanced photo-editing types.)

4. **Drag the sliders underneath the histogram to adjust exposure.**

    Use the sliders as follows:

    • *To darken shadows:* Drag the Shadows slider to the right.

    • *To adjust midtones:* Drag the middle slider to the right to darken midtones; drag it to the left to brighten them.

    • *To brighten highlights:* Drag the Highlights slider to the left.

    Note that as you drag the Shadows or Highlights slider, the Midtones slider also moves in tandem. So you may need to readjust that slider after you set the other two.

    I dragged the sliders to the positions shown in Figure 10-17 to produce my corrected image.

5. **Click OK to accept the changes and close the dialog box.**

6. **Save your image in the TIFF file format.**

    See the last section of this chapter to find out how.

Gaining more control with the Tone Curve Adjustment filter

Easily the most sophisticated of the browser's retouching tools, the Tone Curve Adjustment filter, often referred to generically as simply a *curves filter,* gives you even greater exposure-adjustment control. Whereas a levels filter offers three control points — you can manipulate shadows, midtones, and highlights — a curves filter enables you to manipulate specific values along the entire brightness spectrum.

Figure 10-18 offers a look at the Windows version of the Tone Curve Adjustment retouching window. The Mac version is slightly different in appearance, but it contains the same main components.

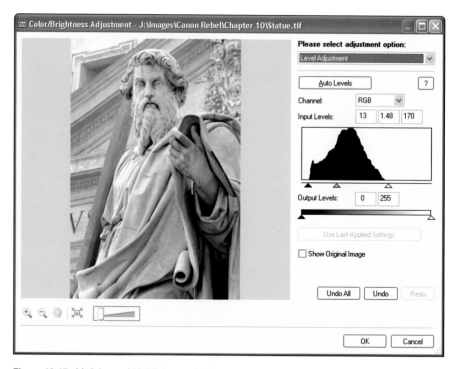

Figure 10-17: I brightened highlights and midtones but darkened shadows slightly.

Again, the controls inside the window seem mighty perplexing at first. But here's all you need to know to take advantage of the filter:

✔ See that line that runs diagonally through the white grid? That's just another representation of the possible brightness values in a digital image. Black falls at the lower end of the line; white, at the top. (The shaded bars that run alongside the left and lower edges of the grid remind you of that orientation.) Medium brightness falls dead center on the line.

✔ To adjust exposure, click and drag at the spot on the line that corresponds to the brightness value you want to change. Drag up to brighten the image; drag down to darken it. For example, in Figure 10-19, I dragged the center of the line up. The resulting curve — *tone curve,* in imaging parlance — produced the exposure change shown in the preview.

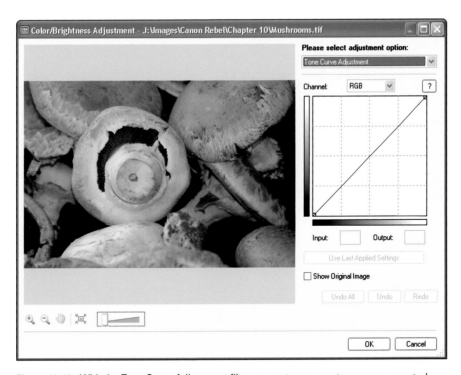

Figure 10-18: With the Tone Curve Adjustment filter, you get even greater exposure control.

Control point   Tone curve

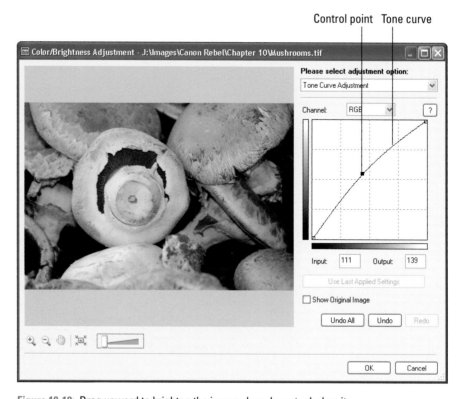

Figure 10-19: Drag upward to brighten the image; drag down to darken it.

✒ After a drag, a control point appears at the spot on the line you dragged to anchor that part of the tone curve, as shown in Figure 10-19.

✒ You can bend the tone curve as much as you want, in any direction you want. Just keep clicking and dragging to add control points. But be careful — extreme curves or curves with tons of points can produce really ugly results and odd breaks in color and brightness. I usually aim for a gentle curve that has no more than six points, including the ones that are provided automatically at the black and white ends of the curve.

✒ To increase contrast, create an s-shaped curve; to decrease contrast, create a reverse-s shape. I used the gentle s-shaped curve shown in Figure 10-20 to produce the finished mushroom photo. The curve resulted in a slight bump in exposure to medium and medium bright pixels and a slight darkening of medium dark and dark pixels. The white and black areas of the image remain unchanged.

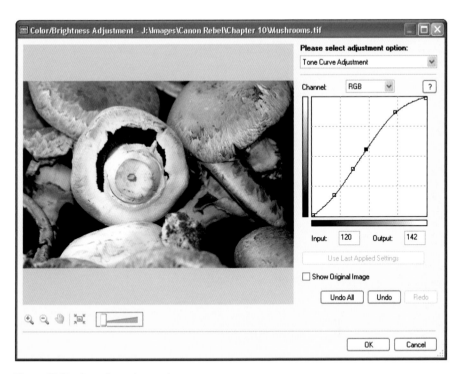

Figure 10-20: An s-shaped curve boosts contrast.

The best way to really understand this filter is to try it for yourself. So take these steps:

1. **Open the image in its own Viewer window.**

   You know the drill: Just double-click the thumbnail in the main browser window. (See Chapter 8 if you need help.)

2. **Open the Tone Curve Adjustment retouching window.**

   - *In Windows*: Click the Edit drop-down list at the top of the browser window and choose Adjust Color/Brightness. When the retouching window appears, select Tone Curve Adjustment from the drop-down list at the top.

   - *On a Mac*: Click the Edit drop-down list underneath the image preview and choose Tone Curve Adjustment to open the retouching window.

3. **Set the Channel option to RGB.**

   On a Mac, the option is the unlabeled pop-up list just above the grid.

As with the Level Adjustment filter, you can also manipulate the brightness values of the red, green, and blue color components of the image independently through this filter. But if you do, you alter the image colors instead of making a pure exposure change. Most people find using a regular color-balancing tool easier; see the earlier section "Tweaking Color Balance" for a look at that option.

4. **Bend the tone curve by adding and dragging control points.**

   See the preceding list for details on this step. If you need to delete a point, click it to select it and then press Delete. (The selected control point appears black.)

5. **Click OK to apply the adjustment and close the retouching window.**

6. **Save your image in the TIFF file format, following the steps at the end of this chapter.**

Sharpening Focus (Sort Of)

Have you ever seen one of those spy-movie thrillers where the good guys capture a photo of the villain's face — only the picture is so blurry that it could just as easily be a picture of pudding? The heroes ask the photo-lab experts to "enhance" the picture, and within seconds, it's transformed into an image so clear you can make out individual hairs in the villain's mustache.

It is with heavy heart that I tell you that this kind of image rescue is pure Hollywood fantasy. You simply can't take a blurry image and turn it into a sharply focused photo, even with the most sophisticated photo software on the market.

There is, however, a digital process called *sharpening* that can *slightly* enhance the apparent focus of pictures that are *slightly* blurry, as illustrated by the before and after images in Figure 10-21. Notice that I say "apparent" focus: Sharpening doesn't really adjust focus but instead creates the *illusion* of sharper focus by increasing contrast in a special way.

Here's how it works: Wherever pixels of different colors come together, the sharpening process boosts contrast along the border between them. The light side of the border gets lighter; the dark side gets darker. Photography experts refer to those light and dark strips as *sharpening halos*. You can get a close-up look at the halos in the right, sharpened example in Figure 10-22, which shows a tiny portion of the pencil image from Figure 10-21. Notice that in the sharpened example, the yellow side of the boundary between the pencils received a light halo, while the blue side received a dark halo.

Original Sharpened

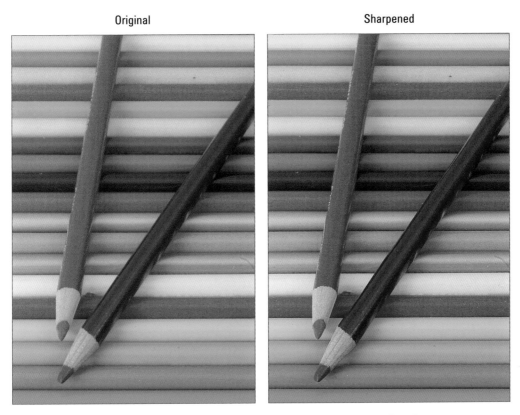

Figure 10-21: A slightly blurry image (left) can benefit from a sharpening filter (right).

Original Sharpened

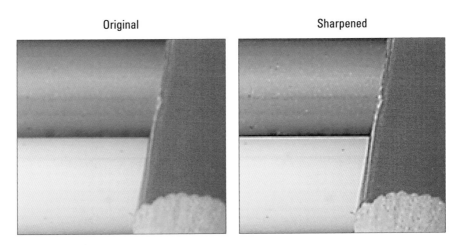

Figure 10-22: Sharpening adds light and dark halos along color boundaries.

A little sharpening can go a long way toward improving a slightly soft image. But too much sharpening does more damage than good. The halos become so strong that they're clearly visible, and the image takes on a sandpaper-like texture. And again, no amount of sharpening can repair a truly out-of-focus image, so all you do when you crank up sharpening is make matters worse.

Both the Windows and Mac versions of the Canon browser software offer a simple Sharpening tool, shown in its Mac incarnation in Figure 10-23. To use this tool, just follow the usual steps: Double-click the image thumbnail to open it in its own Viewer window and then choose Sharpness from the Edit drop-down list. (See Figures 10-3 and 10-4 if you have trouble finding the list.) Drag the slider to the right to add sharpening and then click OK to finish the job.

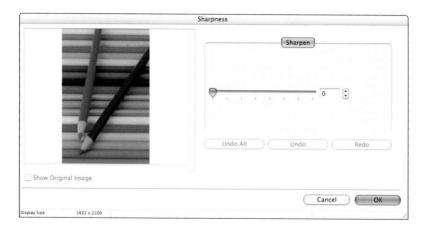

Figure 10-23: The Mac version of the browser offers only a simple sharpening slider.

Windows users, however, have the option of using a more flexible sharpening tool, called an Unsharp Mask filter. To switch to this filter, just click the Unsharp Mask tab at the top of the Sharpness retouching window, as shown in Figure 10-24.

The three sliders provided for the Unsharp Mask filter enable you to control where and how the sharpening halos are applied, as follows:

- **Amount:** This slider adjusts the intensity of the sharpening halos.

- **Radius:** This slider adjusts the width of the halos. Don't go too high, or the sharpening halos will become very noticeable.

- **Threshold:** With this slider, you can limit the sharpening effect just to high-contrast color boundaries. Try raising the value a few notches up from 0 when sharpening portraits to sharpen the image without adding unwanted texture to the skin. I also used this technique to keep the surface of the pencils smooth in my example photo while sharpening the edges between them.

Whichever sharpening filter you use, don't forget to save the altered image in the TIFF file format. The last section of this chapter explains this critical part of the retouching process.

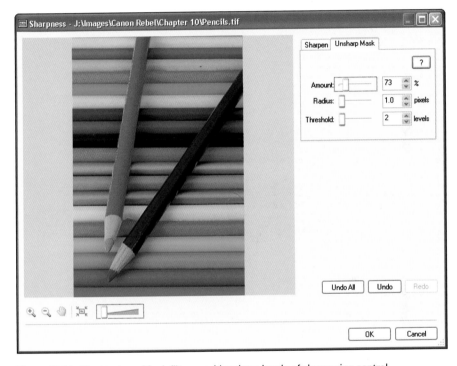

Figure 10-24: The Unsharp Mask filter provides three levels of sharpening control.

Shifting to AutoPilot

You may have noticed as you explored the Edit drop-down list an option called Auto Adjustment. If you select this option, the program opens your image in a retouching window, as usual. Figure 10-25 shows the Windows flavor of the window; the Mac version is virtually identical. After the window opens, you simply click the Auto Adjust Image button and sit back and wait. The program analyzes your image and then makes whatever changes it deems necessary.

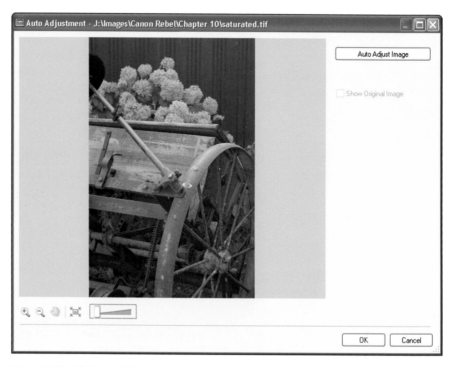

Figure 10-25: Click Auto Adjust Image to see what changes the program thinks are needed.

As a rule, I don't recommend this type of automatic image correction tool because it so often doesn't produce results as good as what you can do by using the manual filter controls. Sometimes, the auto filters even muck up color and exposure more than they "correct" them. And who's to say that the program won't see as a flaw some aspect of the picture that you actually like?

That said, if you aren't working on important images or you just don't have the time or interest in using the more sophisticated tools, go ahead and give that Auto Adjust Image button a click. If you don't like what you see, click the Cancel button and do the job yourself, using the tricks laid out elsewhere in this chapter.

Adding Text

You know that saying, "A picture is worth a thousand words?" Well, you can up that count even more by adding text to your photo. You can do so as follows:

1. **Open your photo in its own Viewer window by double-clicking the image thumbnail in the main browser window.**

2. Choose Insert Text from the Edit drop-down list.

Look for the list at the top of the window if you use the Windows version of the program and at the bottom if you're a Mac user. Either way, you see your photo in the Insert Text retouching window. Figure 10-26 gives you a look at the Windows version of the window. (Again, the Mac version is virtually identical except for sporting different controls for zooming and scrolling the display. See the first section of this chapter for help with those controls.)

3. Click in the preview at the spot you want to add the text.

(In Windows, be sure that the Text tool, next to the Zoom tools, is selected before you click.) A text box appears, as shown in the figure. At any time, you can resize the box as needed by dragging the little boxes that appear around its perimeter. To move the box (and any text inside), just drag inside the box.

4. Type your text.

The text appears both in the image preview and in the Text area on the right side of the window.

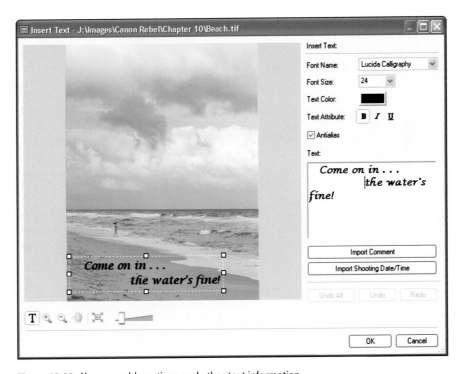

Figure 10-26: You can add captions and other text information.

If you want to add the date and time you shot the picture, don't waste time typing that information. Instead, just click the Import Shooting Date/Time, and the program finds the data in the image file and adds it to the text box for you. Similarly, if you added comment text when organizing your pictures in the main browser, clicking the Import Comment button enters that text for you. (You can add comments via the Comment pane that appears when you browse images in Preview display mode. Chapter 8 explains the basics of browsing images.)

5. **Use the controls at the top of the dialog box to set the type characteristics.**

   You can specify a font (type design), size, and color and add bold, underline, or italic formatting.

The Antialias option smoothes the jagged edges that can occur when letters contain diagonal or curved lines. As a rule, keeping this option enabled is a good idea.

6. **When you finish creating your text, click OK.**

   The retouching window closes.

7. **Save your edited file as outlined in the next section.**

Saving Your Edited Files

Whatever retouching task you do, the last step is to save your edited picture file. After you click OK to close the retouching window and return to the Viewer window, choose the Save As command from the File menu. You then see the standard Windows or Mac file-saving dialog box. Figure 10-27 shows you the Windows XP version of this dialog box.

You need to take two critical steps inside the dialog box:

✔ **Select TIFF as the file type.** TIFF is an image file format that produces the best picture quality for saved images.

Do *not* use JPEG as the file type. Every time you edit and save a picture in the JPEG format, you damage the picture quality slightly because of the *lossy compression* that is applied in that format. Chapter 3 has details on this issue. Should you need a JPEG version of your edited photo for online use, save it first as a TIFF file and then follow the steps provided in Chapter 9 to create a Web-sized copy of the picture in the JPEG format.

✔ **Type a name for the picture in the File Name box (Windows) or the Save As box (Mac).** The filename of the original image appears automatically in the box. You don't have to change the filename — you won't overwrite the original file when you save because you aren't saving it in the JPEG format (and you can't save in the Raw format). But I like to add a tag to the filename that indicates the status of the image — for example, IMG_7582 retouched, or PencilsSharpened, or the like.

After taking care of those two pieces of business, specify where you want to store the file as you usually do. Then click the Save button to save the file and close the dialog box.

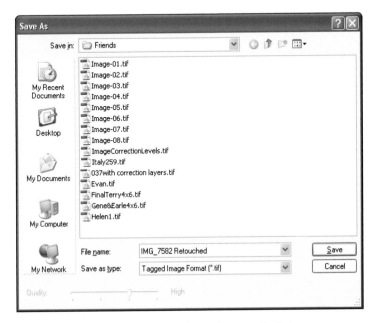

Figure 10-27: Choose TIFF as the file format for any edited photos.

Ten Special-Purpose Features to Explore on a Rainy Day

In This Chapter

▶ Customizing the Set and cross-key functions

▶ Changing the focus and exposure locking controls

▶ Disabling the autofocus-assist beam

▶ Using mirror lockup for shake-free shooting

▶ Recording Dust Delete Data

▶ Viewing magnified images in instant-review mode

▶ Wallpapering your computer monitor with a favorite image

Consider this chapter the literary equivalent of the end of one of those late-night infomercial offers — the part where the host exclaims, "But wait! There's more!"

The ten features covered in these pages fit the category of "interesting bonus." They aren't the sort of features that drive people to choose one camera over another, and they may come in handy only for certain users, on certain occasions. Still, they're included at no extra charge with your Canon purchase, so check 'em out when you have a few spare moments. Who knows; you may discover that one of these bonus features is actually a hidden gem that provides just the solution you need for one of your photography problems.

Changing the Function of the Set Button

When you're using the advanced exposure modes, pressing the Set button while no menu is active displays the Picture Style options, discussed in Chapter 6. If you don't use those options very often, you can change the function of the button so that pressing it displays the Quality options or the Flash Exposure Compensation options. Doing so enables you to access those settings more quickly than by using the menus.

You also can assign the Set button the same function as the Playback button; if you do, you can press either button to set the camera into playback mode. I don't think this option is a terribly useful one, but you be the judge.

To customize the button, take these steps:

1. **Set your camera to one of the advanced exposure modes (P, Tv, Av, M, or A-DEP).**

   You can't adjust the performance of the Set button in the fully automatic modes. Nor does the button perform its menu-bypass function in any of those modes.

2. **Display Setup Menu 2 and highlight Custom Functions, as shown on the left in Figure 11-1.**

   This menu item enables you to customize 11 aspects of the camera's performance.

3. **Press Set to display the Custom Function screen.**

   The screen should look something like the one on the right in Figure 11-1. Here, you choose which of the 11 Custom Functions you want to access.

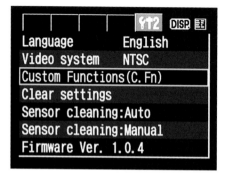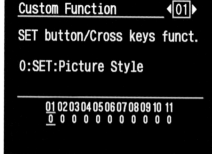

Figure 11-1: The Custom Function menu item provides access to 11 customization options.

4. **If needed, press the right or left cross key to display Custom Function 1, as shown in the figure.**

   You can also rotate the Main dial to cycle through the Custom Functions.

5. **Press the Set button.**

   Now a scrolling list in the center of the screen becomes activated, as shown in Figure 11-2.

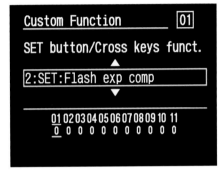

6. **Press the up or down cross keys to select your choice.**

   Only options 0, 1, 2, and 3 relate to the Set button. Option 4 enables you to adjust the performance of the cross keys, as described in the next section. If you do customize the cross keys, you can't also customize the Set button's function.

Figure 11-2: You can use the Set button to access Flash Exposure Compensation settings.

7. **Press the Set button.**

   Now whenever you shoot in the advanced exposure modes and press Set while no menus are displayed, the button takes on the function you just assigned to it. To go back to the default setting, repeat these steps and select option 0 in Step 6.

Using the Cross Keys to Select an Autofocus Point

Through Custom Function 1, introduced in the preceding section, you can assign one of four different functions to the Set button. Or you can instead modify the performance of the cross keys so that you can use them to easily select an autofocus point.

To do so, follow the same steps as outlined in the preceding section but choose option 4 in Step 6. Now the cross keys work as follows:

✔ After you press the shutter button halfway, you can press the cross keys to change the autofocus point. The normal AF Point Selection screen doesn't appear; you just use the autofocus point grid that appears in the Camera Settings display and viewfinder to select the active point. (See Chapter 6 for more about autofocus points and autofocusing.)

✔ You can still use the cross keys for their regular functions — that is, to access the ISO, White Balance, AF Mode, and Metering Mode settings. Just let up on the shutter button and wait until the Camera Settings screen no longer displays both the shutter speed and aperture settings. Then press the cross key for the setting you want to adjust. (Chapter 5 introduces you to shutter speed and aperture.)

Again, this feature works only in the advanced exposure modes. And you can't set the cross keys to work this way and also assign a menu-bypass function to the Set button. So if you do opt to customize the cross keys, pressing the Set button no longer displays the Picture Style menu, for example, as it does by default.

Customizing Exposure and Focus Lock Options

By default, pressing your shutter button halfway establishes and locks focus when you work in autofocus mode. When you shoot in the advanced autoexposure modes, you also can lock in the autoexposure settings the camera selected by pressing and holding the AE (autoexposure) Lock button, labeled in Figure 11-3.

You can customize these locking behaviors via a Custom Functions item on Setup Menu 2. Here's how:

1. **Set the Mode dial to an advanced exposure setting.**

   As with all Custom Functions, you can take advantage of this option only in P, Tv, Av, M, or A-DEP exposure mode. Additionally, the locking setup you specify applies only to those modes.

2. **Display Setup Menu 2 and highlight Custom Functions, as shown on the left in Figure 11-4.**

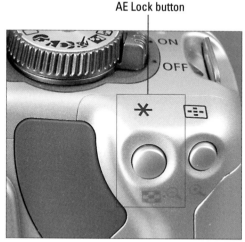

AE Lock button

Figure 11-3: By default, pressing the AE Lock button locks the autoexposure setting.

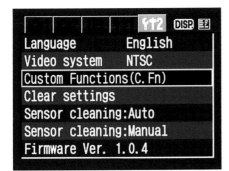 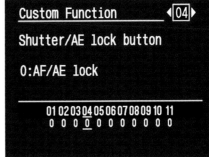

Figure 11-4: Adjust the locking functions via Custom Function 4.

3. **Press the Set button to display the Custom Function screen.**

4. **Select Custom Function 4.**

   Press the right or left cross key or rotate the Main dial until Custom Function 4 appears, as shown on the right in Figure 11-4.

5. **Press the Set button to activate the scrolling list of settings, as shown in Figure 11-5.**

6. **Press the up and down cross keys to select the option you want to use.**

   You have the following four choices. (The first part of the setting name indicates what happens with a half-press of the shutter button; the second part indicates the function of the AE Lock button.)

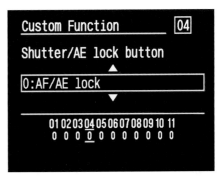

Figure 11-5: Choose 0 to return to the default exposure- and focus-locking setup.

   - *AF/AE Lock:* This is the default setting. Pressing the shutter button halfway establishes and locks autofocus; pressing the AE Lock button locks autoexposure.

   - *AE Lock/AF:* With this option, pressing the shutter button halfway locks autoexposure instead of focus. To focus, you instead press the AE Lock button. In other words, this mode is the exact opposite of the default setup.

- *AF/AF Lock*: This mode is designed to prevent focusing mishaps when you use AI Servo autofocusing, explained in Chapter 6. Here's the deal: In the AI Servo mode, the autofocus motor continually adjusts focus from the time you press the shutter button halfway until the time you actually take the image. This feature helps you keep moving objects sharply focused. But if something happens to move in front of your subject, the camera may mistakenly lock focus on that object.

  To cope with that possibility, this exposure/focus locking option enables you to initiate autofocusing as usual, by pressing the shutter button halfway. But at any time before you take the picture, you can press the AE Lock button to temporarily stop the autofocusing motor from adjusting focus if an intruder does move into the frame. When you release the button, the autofocusing mechanism starts up again.

  If you choose this option, exposure is set when you press the shutter button all the way. You can't lock autoexposure.

- *AE/AF*: Similar to the preceding mode, this one also is designed to help you capture moving subjects in the AI Servo mode. Pressing the shutter button halfway initiates autoexposure metering, which is adjusted continuously as needed until the time you snap the picture. Pressing the AE Lock button starts the autofocusing servo system; releasing the button stops it. You cannot lock autoexposure in this mode.

7. **Press the Set button.**

   Now whenever you shoot in an advanced exposure mode, the camera locks focus and exposure according to the option you selected. In the fully automatic modes, the settings have no effect; a half-press of the shutter button still locks focus, and you can't lock autoexposure.

Disabling the AF-Assist Beam

In dim lighting, your camera emits a brief beam of light from the AF (auto-focus)-assist lamp on the front of the camera when you press the shutter button halfway. This flash of light helps the camera "see" its target better, improving the performance of the autofocusing system.

If you're shooting in a situation where the AF-assist beam may be distracting to your subject or to others in the room, you can disable it. Or, if you attach one of the compatible external flash units to the camera, you can choose to have the flash emit the beam only when necessary.

Take these steps to control this aspect of your camera:

1. **Set the Mode dial to P, Tv, Av, M, or A-DEP.**

   As with the other customization options discussed in preceding sections, this one is available only in these advanced exposure modes.

2. **Display Setup Menu 2, highlight Custom Functions, and press the Set button.**

   You're taken to the main launching pad for adjusting all the Custom Functions.

3. **Press the right or left cross key or rotate the Main dial as needed to select Custom Function 5.**

4. **Press the Set button.**

   Now the scrolling list in the middle of the screen becomes active, as shown in Figure 11-6.

5. **Press the up or down cross key to scroll to your desired setting.**

6. **Press the Set button.**

   Your chosen setting affects all the advanced exposure modes. In fully automatic modes, the auto-focus assist beam continues to light when the camera deems it necessary.

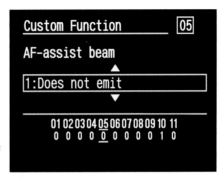

Figure 11-6: You can disable the autofocus-assist beam.

 Without the aid of the assist beam, the camera may have trouble autofocusing in dim lighting. The easiest solution is to simply focus manually; Chapter 1 shows you how.

Enabling Mirror Lockup

One of the components involved in the optical system of an SLR camera is a tiny mirror that moves when you press the shutter button. The small vibration caused by the movement of the mirror can result in slight blurring of the image when you use a very slow shutter speed, shoot with a long telephoto lens, or take extreme close-up shots. To eliminate the possibility, your camera offers a feature called *mirror lockup*. When you enable this feature, the mirror movement is completed well before the shot is recorded, thus preventing any camera shake.

To try out this feature, take these steps:

1. **Set the Mode dial to an advanced exposure mode.**

   Mirror lockup isn't available in the fully automatic exposure modes. So set that dial to P, Tv, Av, M, or A-DEP.

2. **Display Setup Menu 2, highlight Custom Functions, and press the Set button.**

3. **Select Custom Function 7, as shown in Figure 11-7.**

   You can either press the cross keys or rotate the Main dial to scroll through the Custom Functions.

4. **Press the Set button.**

   The scrolling list in the center of the screen becomes highlighted.

5. **Press the up or down cross key to select the Enable option, as shown in the figure.**

6. **Press the Set button.**

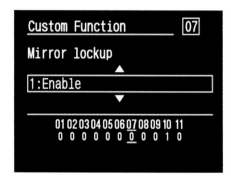

Figure 11-7: Mirror lockup prevents camera shake caused by the movement of the optical system's mirror.

After you enable mirror lockup, you take a slightly different approach to picture-taking than usual. Use this technique:

1. **Frame your shot.**

2. **If using autofocus, press the shutter button halfway to lock focus.**

   Or, if you prefer manual focusing, twist the focusing ring as needed to focus the image.

3. **Press the shutter button all the way down to lock up the mirror.**

   At this point, you can no longer see anything through the viewfinder. Don't panic — that's normal. The mirror's function is to enable you to see in the viewfinder the scene that the lens will capture, and mirror lockup prevents it from serving that purpose.

4. **Press the shutter button all the way again.**

   The camera then takes the picture.

Using a tripod or other support is critical to getting a shake-free shot in situations that call for mirror lockup. For even more protection, set your camera to self-timer mode, introduced in Chapter 2, and take your hands completely off the camera after you press the shutter button in Step 3. The picture is taken about two seconds after the mirror lockup occurs.

Adding Cleaning Instructions to Images

You've no doubt noticed that your camera displays a message that says "Sensor Cleaning" every time you turn the camera off. And when you turn the camera on, a little "cleaning" icon flickers in the lower-right corner of the Camera Settings display. These alerts tell you that the camera is performing a self-maintenance step that is designed to remove from the sensor any dust particles that may have made their way into the camera interior.

If you don't see these alerts, open Setup Menu 2 and be sure that the Sensor Cleaning:Auto option is set to Enabled — there's really no reason to disable this feature, although Canon gives you the choice to do so.

At any rate, the automated sensor cleaning normally is all that's necessary to keep the sensor dust-free. But if you notice that small spots are appearing consistently on your images, you may need to step in and take action on your own.

The best solution, of course, is to take your camera to a good repair shop and have the sensor professionally cleaned. I *do not* recommend that you take on this job yourself; it's a delicate procedure, and you can easily ruin your camera.

Until you can have the camera cleaned, however, you can use a feature on Setup Menu 2 to create a custom dust-removal filter that you can apply in Digital Photo Professional, which is one of the free programs that ships with your camera.

The first step in creating the filter is to record a data file that maps the location of the dust spots on the sensor. To do this, you need a white piece of paper or other white surface and a lens that can achieve a focal length of 55mm or greater. (The kit lens on the Rebel XTi/400D qualifies.) Then take these steps:

1. **Set the lens focal length at 55mm or longer.**

   If you own the kit lens, just zoom in as far as possible, which sets the focal length at 55mm.

2. **Switch the camera to manual focusing.**

   On the kit lens, just move the focus switch on the lens from AF to MF.

3. **Set focus at infinity.**

   Some lenses have a marking that indicates the infinity position — the symbol looks like a number 8 lying on its side. If your lens doesn't have the marking, hold the camera so that the lens is facing you and then turn the lens focusing ring clockwise until it stops.

4. **Set the camera to one of the advanced exposure modes (P, Tv, Av, M, or A-DEP).**

   You can create the dust data file only in these modes.

5. **Display Shooting Menu 2 and highlight Dust Delete Data, as shown on the left in Figure 11-8.**

6. **Press the Set button.**

    Now you see the Dust Delete Data message shown on the right in Figure 11-8.

7. **Use the right or left cross key to highlight OK and then press Set.**

    The camera performs its normal automatic sensor-cleaning ritual, which takes a second or two. Then you see the instruction screen shown on the left in Figure 11-9.

8. **Position the camera so that it's about 8–12 inches from your white card or piece of paper.**

    Your card or paper needs to be large enough to completely fill the view-finder at this distance.

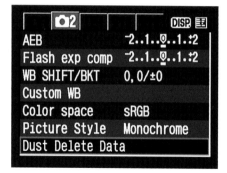 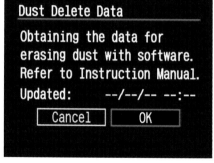

Figure 11-8: You can record dust-removal data that can be read by Digital Photo Professional.

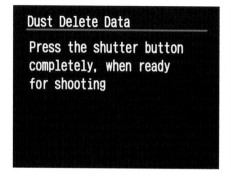 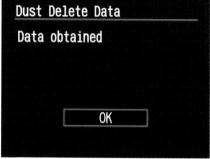

Figure 11-9: The dust delete data is recorded when you press the shutter button all the way.

9. **Press the shutter button all the way to record the dust delete data.**

   No picture is taken; the camera just records the dust-delete data in its internal memory. If the process was successful, you see the congratulatory message shown on the right in Figure 11-9.

   If the camera tells you that it couldn't record the data, the lighting conditions are likely to blame. Make sure that the lighting is even across the entire surface of your white card or paper and that the paper is sufficiently illuminated and then try again.

10. **Highlight OK and press the Set button.**

   The date that you created the dust-delete data now appears on the initial Dust Delete Data screen (shown on the right in Figure 11-8).

After you create your dust-delete data file, the camera attaches the data to every subsequent image, regardless of whether you shoot in the fully automatic or advanced exposure modes.

To clean a photo, open it in Digital Photo Professional and choose Start Stamp Tool from the Tools menu. Your photo then appears in an editing window; click the Apply Dust Delete Data button to start the automated dust-busting feature. The program's manual and Help system offer details about this process; look for the Help entry related to using the Copy Stamp tool.

Magnifying Images During Instant Review

Chapter 4 shows you how to magnify your images when viewing them in playback mode. When you shoot in the advanced exposure modes, you also have the option of zooming in on your images during the instant review period. (See Chapter 1 for information on enabling instant review and changing the length of time that the picture is displayed.)

Follow these steps to activate the feature:

1. **Select one of the advanced exposure modes from the Mode dial.**

   You can choose P, Tv, Av, M, or A-DEP.

2. **Display Setup Menu 2, highlight Custom Functions, and press Set.**

   You're taken to the main Custom Function screen.

3. **Select Custom Function 10 and then press the Set button.**

   Just press the right or left cross key or rotate the Main dial until Custom Function 10 appears. After you press the Set button, the list of options appears activated, as shown in Figure 11-10.

4. Press the up or down cross key to select Image Review and Playback.

At the other setting, which is the default, magnification of images is limited to playback mode.

5. Press the Set button.

After you enable instant-review magnification, just press and hold the Print/Share button during the instant review period. (The button, shown in the margin here, is located near the top-left corner of the monitor.)

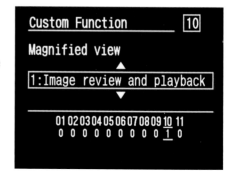

Figure 11-10: Custom Function 10 enables you to magnify images during instant review.

While continuing to hold the button, adjust the magnification of the image by pressing the AE Lock button to zoom in and AF Point Selection button to zoom out. (Those are the two buttons on the upper-right corner of the camera back, marked with the little blue magnifying glass icons.) Use the cross keys to scroll the display. When you're done inspecting the image, release the Print/Share button.

Again, even if you enable instant-review magnification, you can take advantage of it only when you shoot in the advanced exposure modes.

Turning Off the Camera Settings Screen

When you turn on your camera, the monitor automatically turns on and displays the Camera Settings screen. At least, it does if you stick with the default setting selected for Custom Function 11, which bears the lengthy name of LCD Display When Power On.

You can prevent the monitor from displaying the screen every time you power up the camera if you choose. What's the point? Well, the monitor is one of the biggest drains on the camera battery, so limiting it to displaying information only when you need it can extend the time between battery charges.

As with other Custom Functions, this option works only when the camera is set to one of the advanced exposure modes — in other modes, the screen still appears automatically. Still, any battery savings can be helpful when you're running low on juice.

To take advantage of this feature, take these steps:

1. **Set the camera to P, Tv, Av, M, or A-DEP mode.**

   Again, you can access Custom Functions only in these exposure modes.

2. **Display Setup Menu 2, highlight Custom Functions, and press Set.**

   The Custom Function screen appears.

3. **Use the cross keys or Main dial to select Custom Function 11 and then press Set.**

   You see the screen shown in Figure 11-11, with the scrolling list of settings activated.

4. **Press the up or down cross key to select Retain Power Off Status.**

5. **Press Set.**

6. **Press the shutter button halfway to display the Camera Settings screen.**

   You need to take this step before you can complete the process of disabling the automated display.

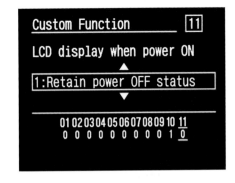

Figure 11-11: You can prevent the monitor from turning on automatically when you power up the camera.

7. **Press the DISP button to shut off the monitor.**

   Now when you turn the camera off and then on again, the monitor will not automatically power up and display the Camera Settings screen — as long as the Mode dial is set to an advanced shooting mode, that is. Nor will the screen appear when you press the shutter button halfway, as it normally does. To view the screen, press the DISP button; press the button again to return to monitor-off status.

Creating Desktop Wallpaper

You can quickly turn an image on your camera memory card into *desktop wallpaper* — a background image that appears on your monitor, behind any icons or program windows. For example, I plastered my Windows desktop with a water lily image, as shown in Figure 11-12.

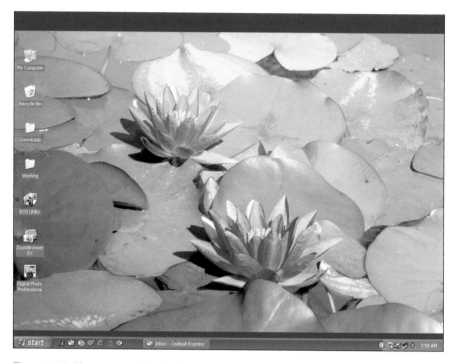

Figure 11-12: You can use a favorite image as your monitor background.

To decorate your monitor, follow these steps:

1. **Connect the camera to the computer, following the instructions in Chapter 8.**

   After a short time, the Direct Transfer screen appears on the camera monitor, as shown in Figure 11-13.

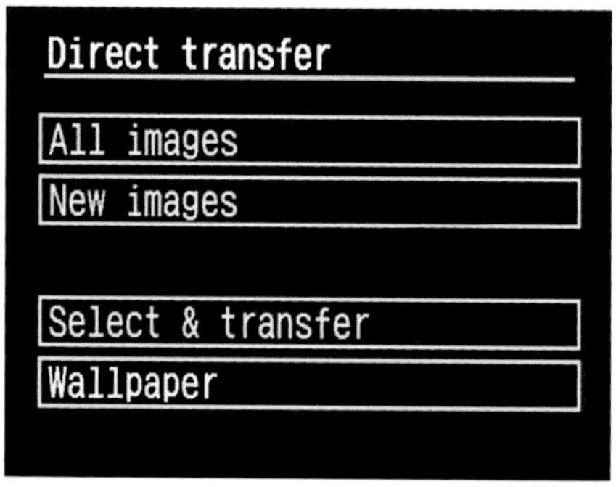

2. **Highlight Wallpaper and then press the Set button.**

   The camera monitor displays your most recent image.

3. **Press the right or left cross key or rotate the Main dial to scroll to the image you want to use as wallpaper.**

Direct transfer

All images

New images

Select & transfer

Wallpaper

Figure 11-13: Highlight Wallpaper and then press Set to select the image.

4. Press the Print/Share button to start the transfer.

The camera, with help from the installed Canon software, downloads the image to your hard drive and then saves a copy of it in the correct format to use for wallpaper. The wallpaper image then appears on the computer desktop, as shown in Figure 11-12.

If you prefer, you also can turn an image that's already on your computer's hard drive into wallpaper by using Canon ZoomBrowser EX (Windows) or ImageBrowser (Mac). See the Help system in those programs for how-tos. Also note that because the images your Canon creates have an aspect ratio of 3:2, they won't fully cover the desktop of most monitors, which typically have an aspect ratio of either 4:3 or 16:9. If you want the image to fully fill the screen, you must edit it to the correct proportions and then use the Windows or Mac display customization tools to turn the edited file into wallpaper. Chapter 10 shows you how to crop to specific proportions.

Getting Free Help and Creative Ideas

Okay, so this last one's a bit of a cheat: It isn't actually found on your camera, but it will help you better understand the features that are. I speak of the Canon Web site, which you can access at www.canon.com.

If you haven't yet visited the site, I encourage you to do so. In the Support section of the site, you can get free technical support for camera problems and even download an electronic copy of your camera manual, should you happen to misplace the one that shipped in the camera box. Most importantly, check periodically to make sure that your camera is running the latest *firmware,* which is the geekspeak term for the camera's internal software. (The appendix of this book provides details on installing a firmware update.)

Be sure to also check out the Learning Center section of the site. There, you can find loads of tutorials and other great instructional offerings not only about your camera but also about the software that ships with it.

Appendix

Firmware Notes and Menu Map

In This Appendix

▷ Checking and updating your camera firmware

▷ Mapping out all your camera's menus

irmware is the internal software that runs your camera. On occasion, the camera manufacturer updates this software, either to fix recently discovered problems or to enable minor new features. You can find out which firmware version your camera is running via Shooting Menu 2, as explained in the next section.

Speaking of menus, the second part of this appendix provides a handy summary of all the commands on each of the five menus on your Rebel XTi/400D. For each menu option, I provide a quick description and, where relevant, a cross-reference to the chapter where you can find any additional details.

Firmware Facts

Keeping your camera's firmware current can help you avoid problems down the road, so periodically visit the Canon Web site to find out whether any updates have been posted. Start from the Canon home page (www.canon.com) and just follow the product support links to the firmware updates. (The actual link names vary depending on which of Canon's international sites you use.)

To check your firmware version, follow these steps:

1. **Set the Mode dial to P, Tv, Av, M, or A-DEP.**

   Otherwise, you can't view the firmware version information.

2. **Display Setup Menu 2.**

   The firmware version is listed at the bottom of the menu. (Refer to Figure A-5, later in the appendix, for a quick look.)

At the time I write this, the current firmware version number is 1.1.1. If your camera has an older version — or a check of the Canon site uncovers an even more recent version than 1.1.1 — follow the instructions on the firmware download site to update your camera. These instructions vary depending on your computer operating system and the firmware release itself, and because the instructions on the Canon site are very detailed, I won't waste space repeating them to you here.

Menu Quick Reference

To help you locate all the features on your Rebel XTi/400D, the following sections list the options found on each of the camera's five menus. Chapter 1 details the process of using menus, if you need help.

The options appearing in the menus here are the default camera settings, which may or may not be the best choice, depending on your subject and other photographic conditions. So visit the chapters referenced in the table for details that will help you lock in the right settings.

Shooting Menu 1

Shown in Figure A-1 and detailed in Table A-1, this menu contains just four options. The most critical is the Quality setting, which determines the pixel count, or resolution of your photos, as well as the file format, which determines whether the camera creates a picture file using the JPEG or Raw format. You can access all menu options regardless of the exposure mode currently selected (Full Auto, Portrait, M, and so on).

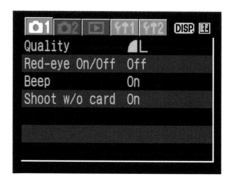

Figure A-1: Be sure to check the Quality option before you shoot.

Table A-1	Shooting Menu 1
Menu Option	*Choose This Option To . . .*
Quality	Set picture resolution (pixel count) and file format (JPEG or Raw). Chapter 3 details this critical setting.
Red-Eye On/Off	Set the flash to Red-eye Reduction mode. See Chapter 2 for details.
Beep	Enable or disable the beep sound that the camera makes after certain operations, including establishing autofocus.
Shoot w/o Card	Specify whether you want to enable or disable the shutter button when no memory card is inserted in the camera. Chapter 1 discusses this option.

Shooting Menu 2

Shown in Figure A-2 and detailed in Table A-2, this menu becomes available only if you set the camera to one of the advanced exposure modes covered in Chapter 5: P, Tv, Av, M, or A-DEP. In the fully automatic modes, the options are either disabled or set for you by the camera.

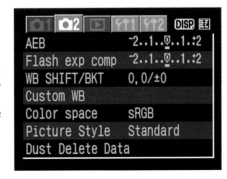

Figure A-2: These options are available only in the advanced exposure modes.

Table A-2	Shooting Menu 2
Menu Option	*Choose This Option To . . .*
AEB	Enable automatic exposure bracketing, which records the same image at three different exposure settings. See Chapter 5 for details.
Flash Exp Comp	Adjust the intensity of the built-in flash. Chapter 5 covers this option, too.
WB Shift/Bkt	Tweak the color correction applied by your camera's white balance control or set up automatic white balance bracketing, which records the image at three slightly different white balance settings. See the end of Chapter 6 for details.
Custom WB	Create a custom white balance setting based on a white or gray reference card. Chapter 6 tells all.
Color Space	Select sRGB or Adobe RGB as the color space, which determines the spectrum of possible colors the camera can record. See Chapter 6 for the lowdown.
Picture Style	Apply one of six preset Picture Styles, each of which adjusts sharpness and color in a slightly different way. You also can customize Picture Styles and record your own Picture Styles through this option. Chapter 6 shows you how.
Dust Delete Data	Record a reference image that can later be used to apply automatic dust removal when you open the image in Digital Photo Professional. Chapter 11 explains the process.

Playback

The Playback menu, as its name implies, contains options related to viewing your pictures on the camera monitor. But the menu (shown in Figure A-3 and detailed in Table A-3) also has features related to transferring images to your computer and to printing directly from the camera, assuming that your printer supports this feature.

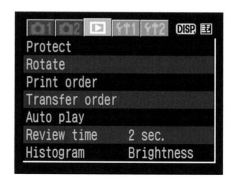

Figure A-3: Playback menu options affect more than image viewing.

Table A-3	The Playback Menu
Menu Option	*Choose This Option To . . .*
Protect	Tag selected images with a bit of data that prevents them from being erased from the memory card during the normal picture-deleting process. See Chapter 4 for details.
Rotate	Display vertically oriented photos in their upright position during playback mode. See Chapter 4.
Print Order	Print directly from a memory card, using a card slot on a photo printer that supports DPOF (Digital Print Order Format). Before removing the card, use this option to select pictures that you want to print and specify the number of copies. Chapter 9 has details.
Transfer Order	Select specific images to download when you transfer picture files to the computer via a USB cable. See Chapter 8 for help with alternative (and easier) options for downloading.
Auto Play	Start automatic playback of all the images on your memory card, one by one, in the camera monitor. Chapter 9 has specifics.
Review Time	Specify how long you want pictures to be displayed on the camera monitor during the instant review period. See Chapter 4 for more information.
Histogram	Choose the style of histogram that appears when you display shooting information along with the image during playback. Chapter 4 details your histogram options.

Setup Menu 1

This menu, featured in Figure A-4, contains options that affect the basic operation of your camera, such as the brightness level of the monitor and the way that new picture files are numbered. Table A-4 offers a review of what each menu option accomplishes.

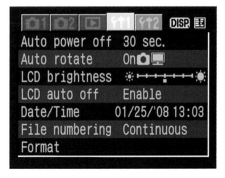

Figure A-4: You can customize basic camera operations here.

Table A-4	Setup Menu 1
Menu Option	*Choose This Option To . . .*
Auto Power Off	Change the length of time that the camera must be idle before it automatically shuts down to conserve battery power. Chapter 1 explains your options.
Auto Rotate	Tell the camera to include information about the original picture orientation (portrait or landscape) along with the image file so that the picture is automatically rotated to the proper position during playback and when viewed in photo programs that can read the data. See Chapter 1 for details.
LCD Brightness	Increase or decrease the monitor brightness; Chapter 1 offers a word of caution on this subject.
LCD Auto Off	Enable or disable the feature that automatically turns off the monitor when you put your eye to the viewfinder. Chapter 1 spells out this option, too.
Date/Time	Set the camera's internal date and time clock, which affects the date and time that's recorded in the picture *metadata* (camera data that you can view in many photo programs). See Chapter 8 for information about viewing metadata.
File Numbering	Determine the numbering scheme the camera uses in picture filenames. Chapter 1 talks about this important setting.
Format	Erase all memory card data and prepare the card for use by the camera. Chapter 4 discusses the difference between formatting the card and simply deleting images.

Setup Menu 2

This second menu of setup options contains many features that are designed for advanced users. For that reason, when the camera is set to Full Auto mode or any of the other fully automatic shooting modes covered in Chapter 2, Setup Menu 2 offers access only to the Language, Video System, and Sensor Cleaning:Auto options. To access the entire list of options, shown in Figure A-5, set the camera's Mode dial to one of the advanced exposure modes (P, Tv, Av, M, or A-DEP). Table A-5 describes the function of each option.

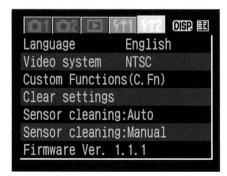

Figure A-5: Set the camera to an advanced exposure mode to access all of these options.

Table A-5	Setup Menu 2
Menu Option	*Choose This Option To . . .*
Language	Select the language used in menus and other text displays.
Video System	Choose the video format (NTSC or PAL) used when you connect the camera to a television or other video device. See Chapter 9 for help.
Custom Functions	Access the 11 Custom Functions, which provide additional control over some advanced exposure and focus features as well as a couple of operational options. Chapter 11 details many of the Custom Functions; also see Chapter 5 for details about the ones related to exposure.
Clear Settings	Restore the camera's default settings.
Sensor Cleaning: Auto	Turn the camera's automatic sensor-cleaning mechanism on or off. Chapter 1 has more information.
Sensor Cleaning: Manual	Prepares the camera for manual sensor cleaning, a job that is best left to the professionals. See Chapter 1 for details and check out Chapter 11 for some other sensor cleaning tips.
Firmware Ver	Displays the current version of the camera's firmware (internal software). See the start of this appendix for details.

Index

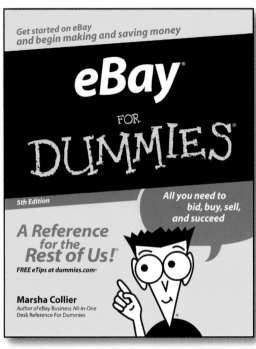
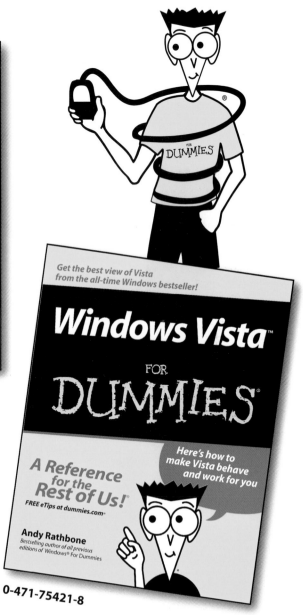

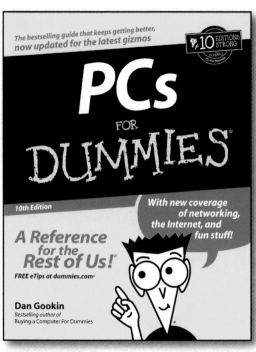
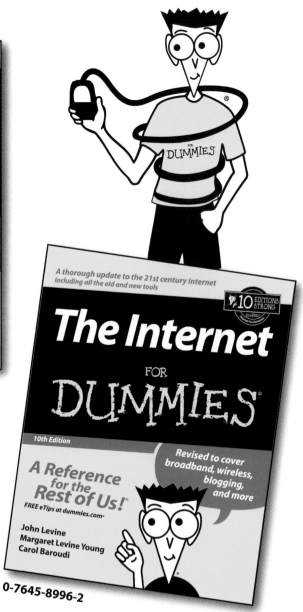

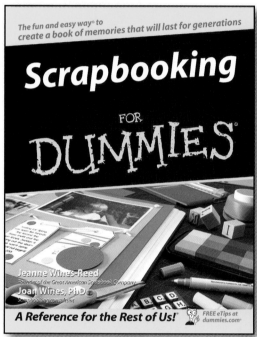
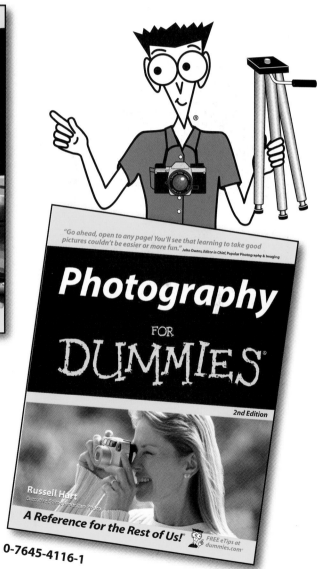

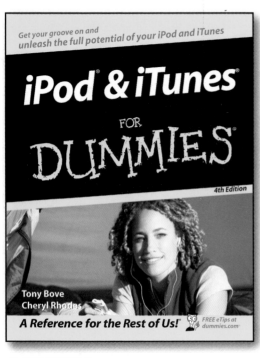
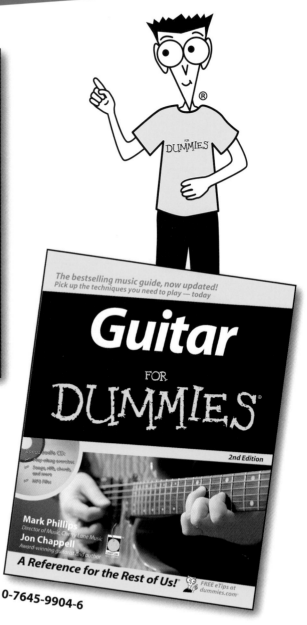